SPARKNOTES™

SAT II Math IIC

2003–2004 Edition

Series Editor Ben Florman

Book Editors Jessica Wang, Sam Yagan

Contributor Kenny Shirley

Production Porter Mason

Technology Tammy Hepps

This edition published by Spark Publishing

Spark Publishing
A Division of SparkNotes LLC
120 Fifth Avenue, 8th Floor
New York, NY 10011

02 03 04 05 SN 9 8 7 6 5 4 3 2 1

Please send all comments and questions or report errors to feedback@sparknotes.com.

Library of Congress information available upon request

Printed and bound in Canada

ISBN 1-58663-429-1

Welcome to SparkNotes™ Test Preparation

S INCE YOU ARE LOOKING AT THIS BOOK, you're probably thinking about taking the SAT II Math IIC. If that's the case, it seems safe to assume that you want to do as well as you can on the test. If we're correct, then you've picked up the right book. Welcome to SparkNotes test preparation: the most helpful, efficient, and honest test preparation books around. This book on the SAT II Math IIC covers:

The precise math topics you'll need to know to do well on the test.
This book won't teach you every mathematical concept; it *will* teach you the math you need to know for the SAT II Math IIC. We won't waste your time with topics you don't need to know. Yet while the math we teach is tailored to the Math IIC test, we won't just present formulas and suggest that you memorize them. Success on the SAT II Math IIC demands flexibility and comprehension, and SparkNotes test preparation helps you achieve them.

Test-taking strategies specific to the SAT II Math IIC. Understanding the fundamentals of math is the most important ingredient for success on the SAT II Math IIC. But only the proper test-taking strategies can make that knowledge sparkle. Spark-Notes explains all of the vital strategies, from the best ways to approach the test to specific methods of dealing with quadratic equations.

Three full-length practice tests, and a study method that will help you transform those practice tests into powerful study tools. Practice tests can and should be an extremely important part of studying for any standardized test. Practice tests help you hone your test-taking skills and become comfortable with the format and time limits of the test; they also gauge the progress you make along the way. In addition, if you follow our methods for studying the practice tests you take, the tests can be a study tool that identifies and helps you eliminate your weaknesses.

General information about SAT II Subject Tests. Beyond teaching you what you need to know to do well on a particular SAT II test, this guide also discusses important information about SAT IIs in general. This first chapter of the book is dedicated to helping you figure out how the SAT II tests are used by colleges, which SAT II tests are right for you, when to take the tests, and how to register for them.

While other test prep companies actually write test preparation books as marketing tools to try to convince you to enroll in expensive courses, SparkNotes' goal is to teach you so well that you don't need those courses. We don't have a hidden agenda; we just want to help you get the best score you can.

Contents

SAT II MATH IIC REVIEW

Math IIC Fundamentals   37

Algebra   71

Plane Geometry   117

Solid Geometry 141

Coordinate Geometry 163

Trigonometry 193

Functions   223

Statistics   249

Miscellaneous Math   263

PRACTICE TESTS

Practice Tests Are Your Best Friends

ORIENTATION

Introduction to the SAT II

THE SAT II SUBJECT TESTS ARE CREATED and administered by the College Board and the Educational Testing Service (ETS), the two organizations responsible for producing the dreaded SAT I (usually referrred to simply as the SAT). The SAT II Subject Tests were created to serve as complements to the SAT. These one-hour tests examine your knowledge about particular subjects, such as Math, Writing, and Biology, whereas the three-hour-long SAT I seeks to test your "critical thinking skills."

In our opinion, the SAT II Subject Tests are better tests than the SAT I because they cover a definitive topic rather than ambiguous, impossible to define "critical thinking skills." However, just because the SAT II Subject Tests do a better job of testing your knowledge about a useful subject, that doesn't mean the tests are necessarily easier or demand less study. A "better" test is not an easier test.

In comparison to the SAT I, there are good and bad things about the SAT II Subject Tests.

The Good

- Because SAT II Subject Tests cover actual topics, you can effectively study for them. If you don't know a topic in mathematics, such as how to interpret the graph of a parabola, you can easily look it up and learn it. For this reason, the SAT II tests are straightforward tests: if you know your stuff, you will do well.

- Often, the classes you've taken in school have already prepared you well for the test. If you've taken two years of algebra, a year of geometry, and a trigonometry or precalculus course, you will have studied most of the topics on the SAT II Math IIC. All you need is some refreshing and refocusing, which this book provides.

- In preparing for the Math, History, or Chemistry SAT II tests, you really are learning Math, History, and Chemistry. In other words, you are gaining valuable, even interesting knowledge. You might actually find the process of studying for an SAT II test to be worthwhile and gratifying. Few can say the same about studying for the SAT I.

The Bad

- Because SAT II Subject Tests quiz you on specific knowledge, it is much harder to "beat" or "outsmart" an SAT II test than it is to outsmart the SAT I. On the SAT I, you can use all sorts of tricks or strategies to figure out an answer. There are far fewer strategies to help you on the SAT II. Don't get us wrong: having test-taking skills will help you on an SAT II, but knowing the subject will help you much more. To do well on the SAT II, you can't just rely on your natural smarts and wits. You need to study.

Colleges and the SAT II Subject Tests

Why would you take an SAT II Subject Test? There's only one reason: colleges want you to, and sometimes require you to.

Colleges care about SAT II Subject Tests for two related reasons. First, the tests demonstrate your interest, knowledge, and skill in specific topics. Second, because SAT II tests are standardized, they show how your skills in math (or biology or writing) measure up to the skills of high school students nationwide. The grades you get in high school don't offer such a measurement to colleges: some high schools are more difficult than others, meaning that students of equal ability might receive different grades. SAT II tests provide colleges with a yardstick against which colleges can measure your, and every other applicant's, knowledge and skills.

When it comes down to it, colleges like the SAT II tests because the tests make the colleges' job easier. The tests are the colleges' tool. But because you know how colleges use the SAT II, you can make the tests your tool as well. SAT II tests allow colleges to easily compare you to other applicants. This means that the SAT II tests provide you with an excellent chance to shine. If you got a 93 in a math class, and some kid in another high school across the country got a 91, colleges won't know how to evaluate the scores. They don't know whose class was harder or whose teacher was a tough grader or whose high school inflates grades. But if you get a 720 on the SAT II Math IIC, and that other kid gets a 650, colleges will recognize the difference in your scores.

The Importance of SAT II Tests in College Applications

Time for some perspective: SAT II tests are *not* the primary tools that colleges use to decide whether to admit an applicant. High school grades, extracurricular activities, and SAT or ACT scores are all more important to colleges than your scores on SAT II tests. If you take AP tests, those scores will also be more important to colleges than your SAT II scores. But because SAT II tests provide colleges with such a convenient measurement tool, they are an important *part* of your application to college. Good SAT II scores can give your application the boost that moves you from the maybe pile into the accepted pile.

College Placement

Occasionally, colleges use SAT II tests to determine placement. For example, if you do very well on the U.S. History SAT II, you might be exempted from a basic history class. Though colleges do not often use SAT II tests for placement purposes, it's worth it to find out whether the colleges to which you are applying do.

Scoring the SAT II Subject Tests

There are three different interpretations of your SAT II Math IIC score. The "raw score" is a simple score of how you did on the test, like the grade you might receive on a normal test in school. The "percentile score" takes your raw score and compares it to the rest of the raw scores in the country for the same test. Percentile scores let you know how you did on the test in comparison to your peers. The "scaled score," which ranges from 200–800, compares your score to the scores received by all students who have ever taken that particular SAT II.

The Raw Score

You will never see your SAT II raw score because the raw score is not included in the SAT II score report. But you should understand how it is calculated, since this knowledge can affect your strategy on the test.

A student's raw score is based entirely on the number of questions that student answered correctly, incorrectly, or left blank. A correct answer earns one point, an incorrect answer results in the loss of a quarter of a point, and no points are given for a question left blank.

Calculating the raw score is easy. Simply add up the number of questions you answered correctly and the number of questions answered incorrectly. Then multiply the number of wrong answers by ¼, and subtract this value from the number of right answers.

$$\text{raw score} = (\text{correct answers}) - \frac{1}{4} (\text{wrong answers})$$

In the chapter called General SAT II Strategies we'll discuss how the rules for calculating a raw score affect strategies for guessing and leaving questions blank.

Percentiles

A student's percentile is based on the percentage of the total test-takers who received a lower raw score than he or she did. Say, for example, you had a friend named Evariste Gaulois who received a score that placed him in the 79th percentile. His percentile score tells him that he scored better on the Math IIC than 78% of the other students who took the same test. It also means that 21% of the students taking that test scored as well or better.

The Scaled Score

The scaled score takes the raw score and uses a formula to place it onto the standard SAT II scale of 200–800. The curve to convert raw scores to scaled scores differs from test to test. For example, a raw score of 33 on the Math IC will scale to a 600 while the same raw score of 33 on the Math IIC will scale to a 700. In fact, the scaled score can even vary on different editions of the *same* test. A raw score of 33 on the February 2002 Math IIC might scale to a 710 while a 33 in June of 2002 might scale to a 690. These differences in scaled scores exist to accommodate for differences in difficultly level and student performance. The difference in the curve for various versions of the same test will not vary by more than 20 points or so.

Which SAT II Subject Tests to Take

There are three types of SAT II tests: those you *must* take, those you *should* take, and those you *shouldn't* take.

- The SAT II tests you must take are those that are required by the colleges you are interested in.

- The SAT II tests you should take are tests that aren't required, but which you'll do well on, thereby impressing the colleges looking at your application.

- You shouldn't take the SAT II tests that aren't required and which cover a subject you don't feel confident about.

Determining Which SAT II Tests are Required

To find out if the colleges to which you are applying require that you take a particular SAT II test, you'll need to do a bit of research. Call the schools you're interested in, look at college web pages, or talk to your guidance counselor. Often, colleges request that you take the following SAT II tests:

- The Writing SAT II test

- One of the two Math SAT II tests (either Math IC or Math IIC)

- Another SAT II in some other subject of your choice

Not all colleges follow these guidelines, however, so you should take the time to research which tests you need to take in order to apply to the colleges that interest you.

Deciding Which Math SAT II to Take

Some students take both Math SAT II tests, but there really isn't a good reason for it. Instead, you should choose to take one test over the other. You should make this choice based on several factors.

1. **Test content.** The two tests cover similar topics, but the Math IIC covers more material than the Math IC does. Level IC covers three years of college-preparatory math: two years of algebra and one year of geometry. Level IIC assumes that in addition to those three years you've also taken a year of trigonometry and/or pre-calculus.

   Math IC

   Algebra

   Plane geometry (lines and angles, triangles, polygons, circles)

   Solid geometry (cubes, cylinders, cones, spheres, etc.)

   Coordinate geometry (in two dimensions)

   Trigonometry (properties and graphs of sine, cosine, and tangent functions, identities)

   Algebraic functions

Math IC (continued)

Statistics and sets (distributions, probability, permutations and combinations, groups and sets)

Miscellaneous topics (logic, series, limits, complex and imaginary numbers)

Math IIC (covers all areas in Math IC with some additional concepts)

Algebra

Plane geometry

Solid geometry

Coordinate geometry (in two and three dimensions, vectors, polar coordinates, parametric equations)

Trigonometry (cosecant, secant, cotangent functions, inverse functions in non-right triangles)

Statistics and Sets

Miscellaneous topics

2. **Question Difficulty.** Not only does the Math IIC cover additional topics, it also covers the basic topics in more difficult ways than the Math IC does.

3. **College Choice.** As you choose between the two tests, keep in mind the specific colleges you're applying to. Colleges with a strong focus on math, such as MIT and Cal Tech, require the Math IIC test. Most other colleges have no such requirement, but some schools may prefer that you take the IIC.

4. **Battle of the Test Curves.** The two tests are scored by very different curves. The Level IIC test is scored on a much more liberal curve: you can miss six or seven questions at the IIC level and still achieve a score of 800. On the IC test, however, you would probably need to answer all the questions correctly to get a perfect score. In another example, if you wanted to get a 600 on either test, you would need around 20 correct answers on the IIC test, and 33 on the IC test. Some students who have a math background that suggests they should take the Math IIC see that the IC is a less difficult test and think that they can get a marvelous score on the IC while their score on the IIC will only be average. But if you get tripped up by just one or two questions on the Math IC, your score will not be the impressive showstopper that you might expect.

All in all, if you have the math background to take the Level IIC test, you should go for it. Some students decide to take the Math IC because it's easier, even though they have taken a pre-calculus course. We don't recommend this plan. True, those students will probably do well on the Math IC test, but colleges will most certainly be more impressed by a student who does pretty well on the Math IIC than one who does very well on the Math IC. Also, the friendly curve on the Math IIC means that students who know enough math to take the IIC might very well get a better score on the IIC than they would on the IC.

If you still can't decide which of the two Math SAT IIs to take, try a practice test of each.

Deciding If You Should Take an SAT II that Isn't Required

To decide whether you should take a test that isn't required, you have to know two things:

1. What a good score on that SAT II test is.

2. Whether you can get that score or higher.

Below, we have included a list of the most commonly taken SAT II tests and the average scaled score on each. If you feel confident that you can get a score that is significantly above the average (50 points is significant) taking the test will probably strengthen your college application. Please note that if you are hoping to attend an elite school, you might have to score significantly more than 50 points higher than the national average. The following list is just a general guideline. It's a good idea to call the schools that interest you, or talk to a guidance counselor, to get a more precise idea of what score you should be shooting for.

Test	Average Score
Writing	590–600
Literature	590–600
American History	580–590
World History	570–580
Math IC	580–590
Math IIC	655–665
Biology E/M	590–600
Chemistry	605–615
Physics	635–645

As you decide which tests to take, be realistic with yourself. Don't just assume you're going to do well without at least taking a practice test and seeing where you stand.

It's a good idea to take three SAT II tests that cover a range of subjects, such as one math SAT II, one humanities SAT II (History or Writing), and one science SAT II. But there's no real reason to take *more* than three SAT II tests. Once you've taken the SAT II tests you need to take, the best way to set yourself apart from other students is to take AP courses and tests. AP tests are harder than the SAT II tests, and as a result they carry quite a bit more distinction. SAT II tests give you the opportunity to show colleges that you can learn and do well when you need to. Taking AP tests shows colleges that you *want* to learn as much as you can.

When to Take an SAT II Subject Test

The best time to take an SAT II Subject Test is right after you've finished a year-long course in that subject. If, for example, you've finished extensive courses on algebra and geometry by the eleventh grade, then you should take the Math IC test near the end of that year when the subject is still fresh in your mind. (This rule does not apply for the writing, literature, and foreign language SAT II tests; it's best to take those after you've had as much study in the area as possible.)

Unless the colleges to which you are applying use the SAT II for placement purposes, there is no point in taking any SAT II tests after November of your senior year, since you won't get your scores back from ETS until after college application deadlines have passed.

ETS usually sets testing dates for SAT II Subject Tests in October, November, December, January, May, and June. However, not every subject test is administered in each of these months. To check when the test you want to take is being offered, visit the College Board website at www.collegeboard.com or do some research in your school's guidance office.

Registering for SAT II Tests

To register for the SAT II test(s) of your choice, you have to fill out some forms and pay a registration fee. We know, we know—it's ridiculous that *you* have to pay for a test that colleges require you to take in order to make *their* jobs easier. But, sadly, there isn't anything we, or you, can do about it. It is acceptable for you to grumble here about the unfairness of the world.

After grumbling, of course, you still have to register. There are two ways to register: online or by mail. To register online, go to www.collegeboard.com. To register by mail, fill out and send in the forms enclosed in the *Registration Bulletin*, which should be available in your high school's guidance office. You can also request a copy of the *Bulletin* by calling the College Board at (609) 771-7600, or writing to:

> College Board SAT Program
> P.O. Box 6200
> Princeton, NJ 08541-6200

You can register to take up to three SAT II tests for any given testing day. Unfortunately, even if you decide to take three tests in one day, you'll still have to pay a separate registration fee for each.

Content and Format of the SAT II Math IIC

I MAGINE TWO PEOPLE TREKKING THROUGH a jungle toward a magical and therapeutic waterfall. Now, who will reach the soothing waters first, the native to the area, who never stumbles because she knows the placement of every tree and all the twists and turns, or the tourist who keeps falling down and losing his way because he doesn't pay any attention to the terrain? The answer is obvious. Even if the tourist is a little faster, the native will still win, because she knows how to navigate the terrain and turn it to her advantage.

There are no waterfalls or gorgeous jungle scenery on the SAT IIs, but this example illustrates an important point. The structure of the SAT II Math IIC is the jungle; taking the test is the challenging trek. Your score is the waterfall.

In this chapter we're going to describe the "terrain" of the Math IIC test. In the next chapter on strategy, we will show you how to navigate and use the terrain to get the best score possible.

Content of the SAT II Math IIC

The Math IIC test covers a variety of mathematical topics. ETS, the company that writes the SAT II Math IIC, provides the following breakdown of the topics covered on the test:

Topic	Percent of Test	Usual Number of Questions
Algebra	18%	9
Plane Geometry	—	—
Solid Geometry	8%	4
Coordinate Geometry	12%	6
Trigonometry	20%	10
Functions	24%	12
Statistics and Sets	6%	3
Miscellaneous	12%	6

While accurate, this breakdown is too broad to really help you direct your studying toward the meaningful areas of the test. We've created the following detailed breakdown based on careful examination of the test:

Topic	Percent of Test	Usual Number of Questions
Algebra	18%	9
Arithmetic	2%	1
Equation solving	5%	2.5
Binomials, polynomials, quadratics	14%	7
Solid Geometry	8%	4
Solids (cubes, cylinders, cones, etc.)	4%	2
Inscribed solids, solids by rotation	1%	0.5
Coordinate Geometry	12%	6
Lines and distance	6%	3
Conic sections (parabolas, circles)	5%	2.5
Coordinate space	2%	1
Graphing	2%	1
Vectors	1%	0.5
Trigonometry	20%	10
Basic functions (sine, cosine, tangent)	12%	6
Trigonometric identities	4%	2
Inverse trigonometric functions	2%	1
Trigonometry in non-right triangles	1%	0.5
Graphing trigonometric functions	1%	0.5

Topic	Percent of Test	Usual Number of Questions
Functions	24%	12
Basic, compound, inverse functions	8%	4
Graphing functions	6%	3
Domain and range of functions	8%	4
Statistics and Sets	6%	3
Mean, median, mode	2%	1
Probability	2%	1
Permutations and combinations	4%	2
Group questions, sets	1%	0.5
Miscellaneous	12%	6
Arithmetic and geometric series	4%	2
Logic	1%	0.5
Limits	1%	0.5
Imaginary numbers	1%	0.5

This book is organized according to the categories in the above breakdown, allowing you to focus on each topic to the degree you feel necessary. In addition, each question in the practice tests at the back of this book has been categorized according to these topics, so that when you study your practice tests you can very precisely identify your weaknesses and then use this book to address them.

General Format of the SAT II Math IIC

The SAT II Math IIC is a one-hour long test made up of 50 multiple-choice questions. The instructions for the test are straightforward. You should memorize them so you don't waste time reading them on the day of the test.

> For each of the following problems, decide which is the BEST of the choices given. If the exact numerical value is not one of the choices, select the choice that best approximates this value. Then fill in the corresponding oval on the answer sheet.

Simple, right? Unfortunately, the instructions don't cover many important aspects about the format and rules of the test:

- The 50 questions progress in order of difficulty, from the easiest to the hardest.

- You can skip to different questions during the test. While you don't want to skip around randomly, the ability to skip the occasional question is helpful, as we will explain in the next chapter.

- All questions are worth the same number of points, regardless of the level of difficulty.

These facts can greatly affect your approach to taking the test, as we will show in the next chapter, on strategy.

The Calculator

Unlike the SAT I, in which a calculator is permitted but not essential to the test, the Math IIC test demands the use of a calculator. In fact, that's what the "C" in IIC signifies. What's more, some questions are specifically designed to test your calculator skills.

It is therefore wise to learn certain calculator essentials before taking the SAT II Math IIC. First off, make sure you have the right type of calculator. Virtually every type of calculator is allowed on the test, including the programmable and graphing kinds. Laptops, minicomputers, or any machine that prints, makes noise, or needs to be plugged in are not allowed.

Whatever calculator you use should have all the following functions:

- Exponential powers

- Base-10 logarithms

- Sine, cosine, tangent

Make sure you practice performing these functions well before the day of the test. More about how to use calculators on the test follows in the next chapter.

Math IIC Scoring

Scoring on the SAT II Math IIC is very similar to the scoring for all other SAT II tests. For every right answer, you earn 1 point. For every wrong answer, you lose ¼ of a point. For every question you leave blank, you earn 0 points. Add these points up, and you get your raw score. ETS then converts your raw score to a scaled score according to a special curve. We have included a generalized version of that curve in the table below. Note that the curve changes slightly for each edition of the test, so the table shown will be close to, but not exactly the same as, the table used by the ETS for the particular test you take. You should use this chart to convert your raw scores on practice tests into a scaled score.

Scaled Score	Average Raw Score	Scaled Score	Average Raw Score
800	50	570	18
800	49	560	17
800	48	550	16
800	47	540	15
800	46	530	14
800	45	520	13
800	44	510	12
800	43	500	11
790	42	490	10
780	41	480	9
770	40	470	8
760	39	450	7
750	38	440	6
740	37	430	5
730	36	420	4
720	35	410	3
710	34	400	2
700	33	390	1
690	32	380	0
680	31	370	−1
680	30	360	−2
670	29	350	−3
660	28	340	−4
650	27	330	−5
640	26	320	−6
630	25	310	−7
630	24	300	−8
620	23	300	−9
610	22	290	−10
600	21	290	−11
590	20	280	−12
580	19	280	−13

Content and Format

In addition to its function as a conversion table, this chart contains crucial information: it tells you that you can do very well on the SAT II Math IIC without answering every question correctly. In fact, you could skip some questions and get some other questions wrong and still earn a "perfect" score of 800.

For example, in a test of 50 questions, you could score:

- 800 if you answered 44 right, 4 wrong, and left 2 blank

- 750 if you answered 40 right, 8 wrong, and left 2 blank

- 700 if you answered 35 right, 8 wrong, and left 7 blank

- 650 if you answered 30 right, 12 wrong, and left 8 blank

- 600 if you answered 25 right, 16 wrong, and left 9 blank

This chart should prove to you that when you're taking the test you should not imagine your score plummeting with every question you can't confidently answer. You can do very well on this test without knowing or answering everything. So don't get unnecessarily wound up if you run into a difficult question. The key to doing well on the SAT II Math IIC is to take the whole test well, and to follow a strategy that ensures you will answer all the questions you can, while intelligently guessing on the questions you feel less certain about. We will talk about such strategies in the next chapter.

Strategies for the SAT II Math IIC

A MACHINE, NOT A PERSON, WILL SCORE your SAT II Math IIC test. The tabulating machine sees only the filled-in ovals on your answer sheet. It does not care how you came to these answers; it cares only if your answers are correct. So whether you knew the right answer or just took a lucky guess, the machine will award you one point. Think of this scoring system as a message to you from the ETS: "We care only about your answers, and not about any of the thought behind them."

It's obvious that the SAT II Math IIC test allows you to show off your knowledge of math; but the test gives you the same opportunity to show off your fox-like cunning by figuring out what strategies will allow you to best display that knowledge. Remember, the SAT II test is your tool to get into college, so treat it as your tool. It wants right answers? Give it right answers, following whatever strategies you can.

Basic Rules of SAT II Test-Taking

There are some rules that apply to all SAT II tests. These rules are so obvious that we hesitate to call them "strategies." Some of these rules will seem more like common sense to you than anything else. We don't disagree. However, given the cruel ways a timed test can warp and mangle common sense, we offer this list.

Avoid Carelessness

There are two types of carelessness, both of which will cost you points. The first type of carelessness results from moving too fast on the test, whether that speed is caused by overconfidence or frantic fear. In speeding through the test, you make yourself vulnerable to misinterpreting the question, overlooking one of the answer choices, or making a logical or mathematical mistake. As you take the test, make a conscious effort to approach the test calmly, and not to move so quickly that you become prone to making mistakes.

Whereas the first type of carelessness can be caused by overconfidence, the second type of carelessness results from frustration or lack of confidence. Some students take a defeatist attitude toward tests, assuming they won't be able to answer many of the questions. Such an attitude is a form of carelessness, because it causes the student to ignore reality. Just as the overconfident student assumes she can't be tricked and therefore gets tricked, the student without confidence assumes he can't answer questions and therefore at the first sign of difficulty gives up.

Both kinds of carelessness steal points from you. Avoid them.

Be Careful Gridding In Your Answers

The computer that scores SAT II tests is unmerciful. If you answered a question correctly, but somehow made a mistake in marking your answer grid, the computer will mark that question as wrong. If you skipped question 5, but put the answer to question 6 in row 5, and the answer to question 7 in row 6, etc., thereby throwing off your answers for an entire section . . . it gets ugly.

Some test prep books advise you to fill in your answer sheet five questions at a time rather than one at a time. Some suggest that you do one question and then fill in the corresponding bubble. We think you should fill out the answer sheet whatever way feels most natural to you; just make sure you're careful while doing it. In our opinion, the best way to ensure that you're being careful is to talk silently to yourself. As you figure out an answer in the test booklet and transfer it over to the answer sheet, say to yourself: "Number 23, B. Number 24, E. Number 25, A."

Know What's in the Reference Area

At the beginning of the SAT II Math IIC there is a reference area that provides you with basic geometric formulas and information.

THE FOLLOWING INFORMATION IS FOR YOUR REFERENCE IN ANSWERING SOME OF THE QUESTIONS IN THIS TEST.

Volume of a right circular cone with radius r and height h: $V = \frac{1}{3}\pi r^2 h$

Lateral area of a right circular cone with circumference of the base c and slant height ℓ: $S = \frac{1}{2}c\ell$

Volume of a sphere with radius r: $V = \frac{4}{3}\pi^3$

Surface area of a sphere with radius r: $S = 4\pi r^2$

Volume of a pyramid with base area B and height h: $V = \frac{1}{3}Bh$

You should know all of these formulas without the reference; don't neglect to memorize and understand the formulas just because you have the reference area as a crutch. Instead, view the reference area as a guide to the formulas that will likely be on the test. If you know those formulas without having to flip back to the reference area, you'll save time, which puts you one step ahead.

Write All Over Your Test Booklet . . .

Draw diagrams or write out equations to help you think. Mark up graphs or charts as necessary. Cross out answers that can't be right. The test booklet is yours to write on, and writing can often help clarify your thoughts so that you can work more quickly with fewer mistakes.

. . . But Remember That the SAT Rewards Answers, Not Work

Having told you to write in your test book, we're going to qualify that advice. Doing math scratchwork can definitely help you avoid careless errors, but doing pristine work, or more work than necessary, can be more time consuming than it's worth. You must find a balance between speed and accuracy. You need to be able to follow and understand your work, but others don't. Nobody will see your work, so don't write it out as if you're being judged.

The Importance of the Order of Difficulty

Imagine that you are taking a test that consists of two questions. After your teacher hands out the test, and before you set to work, a helpful little gnome whispers, "The first problem is very simple, the second is much harder." Would the gnome's statement affect the way you approach the two problems? The answer, of course, is yes. For a "very simple" question, it seems likely that you should be able to answer it quickly and without much, or any, agonized second-guessing. On a "much harder" question, you will probably have to spend much more time, both to come up with an answer and to check your work to make sure you didn't make an error somewhere along the way.

What about all the other students who didn't hear the gnome? They might labor over the first, easy question, exhaustively checking their work, and wasting time that they'll need for the tricky second problem. Then, when those other students do get to the second problem, they might not check their work or be wary of traps, since they have no idea that the problem is so difficult.

Because Math IIC questions are ordered by difficulty, it's as if you have that helpful little gnome sitting next to you for the entire test.

Knowing When to Be Wary

Most students answer the easy Math IIC questions correctly. Only some students get moderate questions right. Very few students get difficult questions right. What does this mean to you? It means that when you are going through the test, you can often trust your first instincts on an easy question. With difficult questions, however, you should be more cautious. There is a reason most people get these questions wrong: not only are they more difficult, containing more sophisticated vocabulary or mathematical concepts, they are also often tricky, full of enticing wrong answers that seem correct. But because the SAT orders its questions by difficulty, the test tells when to take a few extra seconds to make sure you haven't been fooled by an answer that only *seems* right.

The tricky answers seem right because they are actually the answers you would get if you were to make a mathematical or logical mistake while working on the problem. For example, let's say you're flying through the test and have to multiply $6 \times 8 \times 3$. So you quickly multiply 6 and 8 to get 42 and then multiply by 3 to get 126. You look down at the answers and there's 126! That's the answer you came to, and there it is among the answer choices like a little stamp of approval, so you mark it down as your answer and get the question wrong: $6 \times 8 = 48$, not 42, making the correct answer 144.

From this example you should learn that just because the answer you got is among the answers listed *does not* mean you definitely have it right. The SAT is designed to punish those who make careless errors. Don't be one of them. After you get an answer, quickly check your work again.

Math Questions and Time

There are often several ways to answer a Math IIC question. You can use trial and error, you can set up and solve an equation, and, for some questions, you might be able to answer the question quickly, intuitively, and elegantly, if you can just spot how. These different approaches to answering questions vary in the amount of time they take. Trial and error generally takes the longest, while the elegant method of relying on an intuitive understanding of conceptual knowledge takes the least amount of time.

Take, for example, the following problem:

> Which has a greater area, a square with sides measuring 4 cm, or a circle with a radius of the same length?

The most obvious way to solve this problem is simply to plug 4 into the formula for the area of a square and area of a circle. Let's do it: Area of a square = s^2, so the area of this square = $4^2 = 16$. Area of a circle = πr^2, so the area of this circle must therefore be $\pi 4^2 = 16\pi$. 16π is obviously bigger than 16, so the circle must be bigger. That worked nicely. But a faster approach would have been to draw a quick to-scale diagram with the square and circle superimposed.

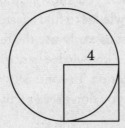

An even quicker way would have been to understand the equations of area for a square and circle so well that it was just *obvious* that the circle was bigger, since the equation for the circle will square the 4 and multiply it by π whereas the equation for the square will only square the 4.

While you may not be able to become a math whiz and just *know* the answer, you can learn to look for a quicker route, such as choosing to draw a diagram instead of working out the equation. And, as with the example above, a quicker route is not necessarily a less accurate one. Making such choices comes down to practice, being aware that those other routes are out there, and basic mathematical ability.

The value of timesaving strategies is obvious: less time spent on some questions allows you to devote more time to difficult problems. It is this issue of time that separates the students who do terrifically on the test and those who merely do well. Whether or not the ability to find accurate shortcuts is an actual measure of mathematical prowess is not for us to say, but the ability to find those shortcuts absolutely matters on this test.

Shortcuts Are Really Math Intuition

Now that you know all about shortcuts, you should use them wisely. Don't go into every question searching for a shortcut; it might end up taking longer than the normal route. Instead of seeking out math shortcuts, you should simply be mindful of the possibility that one might exist. If you go into each question knowing there could be a shortcut and keep your mind open as you think about the question, you will find the shortcuts you need.

To some extent, with practice you can teach yourself to recognize when a question might contain a shortcut. For example, simply from the problem above, you know that there will probably be a shortcut for questions that give you the dimensions of two shapes and ask you to compare them: you can just draw a diagram. A frantic test taker might see the information given and then seize on the simplest route and work out the equations. But with some calm and perspective you can see that drawing a diagram is the best idea.

The fact that we advocate using shortcuts doesn't mean you shouldn't focus on learning how to work a problem out. In fact, we can guarantee that you're not going to find a shortcut for a problem *unless* you know how to work it out the long way. After all, a shortcut just uses your knowledge to find a faster way to answer the question. To put it another way, we could just as easily use the term math intuition instead of the word shortcut. You have to have a knowledge base to work from in order to have anything on which to base your intuition. In contrast, you might be able to figure out an answer by trial and error even if you don't see exactly how to answer the problem.

Making Your Calculator Work for You

As we've already mentioned, the calculator is a very important part of the Math IIC test. You need to have the right kind of calculator, be familiar with its operations, and above all, know how to use it intelligently.

There are four types of questions on the test: calculator-friendly, calculator-neutral, calculator-unfriendly, and calculator-useless. According to the ETS, about 60 percent of the test falls under the calculator-neutral and -friendly categories. That is, calculators are useful or necessary on 30 out of the 50 questions on the SAT II Math IIC. The other 20 questions are calculator-unfriendly and -useless. The trick is to be able to identify the different types of questions on the test. Here's a breakdown of each of the four types, with examples. If you're not certain about the math discussed in the examples, don't worry. We cover all of these topics in this book.

Calculator-Friendly Questions

A calculator is extremely helpful and often necessary to solve calculator-friendly questions. Problems demanding exact values for exponents, logarithms, or trigonometric functions will most likely need a calculator. Computations that you wouldn't be able to do easily in your head are prime suspects for a calculator. Here's an example:

If $f(x) = \sqrt{x} - 2x^2 + 5$, then what is $f(3.4)$?

    (A)   −18.73
    (B)   −16.55
    (C)   −16.28
    (D)   −13.32
    (E)   −8.42

This is a simple function question in which you are asked to evaluate $f(x)$ at the value 3.4. As you will learn in the Functions chapter, all you have to do to solve this problem is plug in 3.4 for the variable x and carry out the operations in the function. But unless you know the square root and square of 3.4 off the top of your head, which most test-takers probably wouldn't (and shouldn't), then this problem is extremely difficult to answer without a calculator.

But with a calculator, all you need to do is take the square root of 3.4, subtract twice the square of 3.4, and then add 5. You get answer choice (C), −16.28.

Calculator-Neutral Questions

You have two different choices when faced with a calculator-neutral question. A calculator is useful for these types of problems, but it's probably just as quick and easy to work the problem out by hand.

If $8^x = 4^3 \times 2^3$, what is the value of x?

    (A)   2
    (B)   3
    (C)   5
    (D)   7
    (E)   8

When you see the variable x as a power, you should think logarithms. A logarithm is the power to which you must raise a given number to equal another number, so in this case, we need to find the exponent x, such that $8^x = 4^3 \times 2^3$. From the definition of logarithms, we know that given an equation of the form $a^x = b$, $\log_a b = x$. So you could type in $\log_8 (4^3 \times 2^3)$ on your trusty calculator and find that $x = 3$.

Or, you could recognize that 2 and 4 are both factors of 8, and thinking a step further, that $2^3 = 8$ and $4^3 = 64 = 8^2$. Put together, $4^3 \times 2^3 = 8^2 \times 8 = 8^3$. We come to the same answer that $x = 3$, and that (B) is the right answer.

These two processes take about the same amount of time, so choosing one over the other is more a matter of personal preference than one of strategy. If you feel quite comfortable with your calculator, then you might not want to risk the possibility of making a mental math mistake and should choose the first method. But if you're more prone to error when working with a calculator, then you should choose the second method.

Calculator-Unfriendly Questions

It is possible to answer calculator-unfriendly questions by using a calculator. But while it's possible, it isn't a good idea. These types of problems often have built-in shortcuts —if you know and understand the principle being tested, you can bypass potentially tedious computation with a few simple calculations. Here's a problem that you could solve much more quickly and effectively without the use of a calculator:

$$\frac{\{\cos^2(3 \times 63°) + \sin^2(3 \times 63°)\}^4}{2} =$$

(A) .3261
(B) .5
(C) .6467
(D) .7598
(E) .9238

If you didn't take a moment to think about this problem, you might just rush into it wielding your calculator, calculating the cosine and sine functions, squaring them each and then adding them together, etc. But if you take a closer look, you'll see that $\cos^2(3 \times 63°) + \sin^2(3 \times 63°)$ is a trigonometric identity. More specifically, it is a Pythagorean Identity: $\sin^2\theta + \cos^2\theta = 1$ for any angle θ. So, the expression $\{\cos^2(3 \times 63°) + \sin^2(3 \times 63°)\}^4/2$ simplifies down to $1^4/2 = \frac{1}{2} = .5$. Answer choice (B) is correct.

Calculator-Useless Questions

Even if you wanted to, you wouldn't be able to use your calculator on calculator-useless problems. For the most part, problems involving algebraic manipulation or problems lacking actual numerical values would fall under this category. You should easily be able to identify problems that can't be solved with a calculator. Quite often, the answers for these questions will be variables rather than numbers. Take a look at the following example:

$$(x + y - 1)(x + y + 1) =$$

(A) $(x + y)^2$
(B) $(x + y)^2 - 1$
(C) $x^2 - y^2$
(D) $x^2 + x - y + y^2 + 1$
(E) $x^2 + y^2 + 1$

This question tests you on an algebraic topic—that is, how to find the product of two polynomials—and requires knowledge of algebraic principles rather than calculator acumen. You're asked to manipulate variables, not produce a specific value. A calculator would be of no use here.

Strategies

To solve this problem, you would have to notice that the two polynomials are in the format of a Difference of Two Squares: $(a + b)(a - b) = a^2 - b^2$. In our case, $a = x + y$ and $b = 1$. As a result, $(x + y - 1)(x + y + 1) = (x + y)^2 - 1$. Answer choice (B) is correct.

Don't Immediately Use Your Calculator

The fact that the test contains all four of these question types means that you shouldn't get trigger-happy with your calculator. Just because you've got an awesome shiny hammer doesn't mean you should try to use it to pound in thumbtacks. Using your calculator to try to answer every question on the test would be just as unhelpful.

Instead of reaching instinctively for your calculator, you should come up with a problem-solving plan for each question. Take a brief look at each question so that you understand what it's asking you to do, and then decide whether you should use a calculator to solve the problem at all. That brief instant of time invested in making such decisions will save you a great deal of time later on. For example, what if you came upon the question:

If $(3, y)$ is a point on the graph of $f(x) = \dfrac{x^2 - 5x - 4}{11x - 44}$, then what is y?

(A) -3
(B) -1.45
(C) 0
(D) $.182$
(E) 4.87

A trigger-happy calculator user might immediately plug in 3 for x. But the student who takes a moment to think about the problem will probably see that the calculation would be much simpler if the function were simplified first. To start, factor 11 out of the denominator:

$$f(x) = \frac{x^2 - 5x - 4}{11x - 44} = \frac{x^2 - 5x - 4}{11(x - 4)}$$

Then, factor the numerator to its simplest form:

$$f(x) = \frac{x^2 - 5x - 4}{11(x - 4)} = \frac{(x - 4)(x - 1)}{11(x - 4)}$$

The $(x - 4)$ cancels out, and the function becomes $f(x) = (x - 1)/11$. At this point you could shift to the calculator and calculate $f(x) = (3 - 1)/11 = \frac{2}{11} = .182$, which is answer (D). If you were very comfortable with math, however, you would see that you don't even have to work out this final calculation. $\frac{2}{11}$ can't work out to any answer other than (D), since you know that $\frac{2}{11}$ isn't a negative number, won't be equal to zero, and also won't be greater than 1.

Approaching Math IIC Questions

Though there are four different types of questions on the Math IIC, there is a standard procedure that you should use to approach all of them.

1. Read the question without looking at the answers. Determine what the question is asking and come to some conclusion about how to solve it. Do not look at the answers unless you decide that using the process of elimination is the best way to go (we describe how to use the process of elimination below).

2. If you think you can solve the problem, go ahead. Once you've derived an answer, only then see if your answer matches one of the choices.

3. Once you've decided on an answer, test it quickly to make sure it's correct, and move on.

Working Backward: The Process of Elimination

If you run into difficulty while trying to solve a regular multiple-choice problem, you might want to try the process of elimination. On every question the answer is right in front of you, hidden among those five answer choices. So if you can't solve the problem directly, you might be able to plug each answer into the question to see which one works.

Not only can this process help you when you can't figure out a question, there are times when it can actually be faster than setting up an equation, especially if you work strategically. Take the following example:

A classroom contains 31 chairs, some of which have arms and some of which do not. If the room contains 5 more armchairs than chairs without arms, how many armchairs does it contain?

(A)   10
(B)   13
(C)   16
(D)   18
(E)   21

Given this question, you could build the equations:

$$\text{total chairs } (31) = \text{armchairs } (x) + \text{normal chairs } (y)$$
$$\text{normal chairs } (y) = \text{armchairs } (x) - 5$$

Then, since $y = (x - 5)$, you can make the equation:

$$31 = x + (x - 5)$$
$$31 = 2x - 5$$
$$36 = 2x$$
$$x = 18$$

This approach of building and working out the equations will produce the right answer, but it takes a long time! What if you strategically plugged in the answers instead? Since the numbers ascend in value, let's choose the one in the middle: (C) 16. This is a smart strategic move because if we plug in 16 and discover that it was too small a number to satisfy the equation, we can eliminate (A) and (B) along with (C). Alternatively, if 16 is too big, we can eliminate (D) and (E) along with (C).

So our strategy is in place. Now let's work it out. If you have 16 armchairs, then you would have 11 normal chairs and the room would contain 27 total chairs. We needed the total numbers of chairs to equal 31, so clearly (C) is not the right answer. But because the total number of chairs was too few, you can also eliminate (A) and (B), the answer choices with smaller numbers of armchairs. If you then plug in (D) 18, you have 13 normal chairs and 31 total chairs. There's your answer. In this instance, plugging in the answers takes less time, and, in general, just seems easier.

Notice that the last sentence began with the words "in this instance." Working backward and plugging in is not always the best method. For some questions it won't be possible to work backward at all. For the test, you will need to build up a sense of when working backward can most help you. A good rule of thumb for deciding whether to work backward is:

- Work backward when the question describes an equation of some sort and the answer choices are all simple numbers.

If the answer choices contain variables, working backward will often be quite difficult —more difficult than working out the problem would be. If the answer choices are complicated, with hard fractions or radicals, plugging in might prove so complex that it's a waste of time.

Substituting Numbers

Substituting numbers is a lot like working backward, except the numbers you plug into the equation *aren't* in the answer choices. Instead, you have to strategically decide on numbers to substitute into the question to take the place of variables.

For example, take the question:

If p and q are odd integers, then which of the following must be odd?

(A) $p + q$
(B) $p - q$
(C) $p^2 + q^2$
(D) $p^2 \times q^2$
(E) $p^2 + q$

It might be hard to conceptualize how the two variables in this problem interact. But what if you chose two odd numbers, let's say 5 and 3, to represent the two variables? Once you begin this substitution it quickly becomes clear that

(A) $p + q = 5 + 3 = 8$

(B) $p - q = 5 - 3 = 2$

(C) $p^2 + q^2 = 25 + 9 = 34$

(D) $p^2 \times q^2 = 25 \times 9 = 225$

(E) $p + q^2 = 5 + 9 = 14$

By picking two numbers that fit the definition of the variables provided by the question, it becomes clear that the answer has to be (D) $p^2 \times q^2$ since it multiplies to 225. By the way, you could have answered this question without doing the multiplication to 225 since two odd numbers, such as 9 and 25, when multiplied, will always result in an odd number.

Substituting numbers can help you transform problems from the abstract into the concrete. However, you have to remember to keep the substitution consistent. If you're using a 5 to represent p, don't suddenly start using 3. Also, when picking numbers to use as substitutes, pick wisely. Choose numbers that are easy to work with and that fit the definitions provided by the question.

Guessing and the Math IIC

Should you guess on the SAT II Math IIC? We'll begin to answer this question by posing a question of our own:

> G. O. Metry is holding five cards, numbered 1-5. Without telling you, he has selected one of the numbers as the "correct" card. If you pick a single card, what is the probability that you will choose the "correct" card?

The answer, of course, is ⅕. But just as important, you should recognize that the question precisely describes the situation you're in when you blindly guess the answer to any SAT II Math IIC question: you have a ⅕ chance of getting the question right. If you were to guess on ten questions, you would, according to probability, get two questions right and eight questions wrong.

- 2 right answers gets you 2 raw points

- 8 wrong answers gets you $8 \times -\frac{1}{4}$ points $= -2$ raw points

Those ten answers, therefore, net you a total of 0 points. Your guessing was a complete waste of time, which is precisely what the ETS wants. They designed the scoring system so that blind guessing is pointless.

Educated Guessing

But what if your guessing isn't blind? Consider the following question:

$x + 2x = 6$, what is the value of x?

    (A) -2
    (B) 2
    (C) 3
    (D) 0
    (E) 1

Let's say you had no idea how to solve this problem, but you did realize that 0 multiplied by any number equals 0, and that $0 + 2 \times 0$ cannot add up to 6. This means that you can eliminate "0" as a possible answer, and now have four choices from which to choose. Is it now worth it to guess? Probability states that if you are guessing between four choices you will get one question right for every three you get wrong. For that one correct answer you'll get 1 point, and for the three incorrect answers you'll lose a total of $\frac{3}{4}$ of a point. $1 - \frac{3}{4} = \frac{1}{4}$, meaning that if you can eliminate even one answer, the odds of guessing turn in your favor: you become more likely to gain points than to lose points.

Therefore, the rule for guessing on the Math IIC test is simple: *if you can eliminate even one answer-choice on a question, you should definitely guess*. And if you follow the critical thinking methods we described above about how to eliminate answer choices, you should be able to eliminate at least one answer from almost every question.

Guessing As Partial Credit

Some students feel that guessing is similar to cheating, that in guessing correctly credit is given where none is due. But instead of looking at guessing as an attempt to gain undeserved points, you should look at it as a form of partial credit. Take the example of the question above. Most people taking the test will see that adding two zeroes will never equal six, and will only be able to throw out that choice as a possible answer. But let's say that you also knew that negative numbers added together cannot equal a positive number 6. Don't you deserve something for that extra knowledge? Well, you do get something: when you look at this question, you can throw out both "0" and "−2" as answer choices, leaving you with a $\frac{1}{3}$ chance of getting the question right if you guess. Your extra knowledge gives you better odds of getting this question right, exactly as extra knowledge should.

Pacing

As we said earlier, the questions on the SAT II Math IIC are organized from least to most difficult: the basic material appears near the beginning, and the advanced topics show up at the end. You can always have a sense of what is awaiting you later on in the test. Use this information. Part of your job is to make sure you don't spend too much time on the easiest questions. Don't put yourself in the position of having to leave blank those questions near the end of the test that you could have answered *if only you had more time*.

True, answering 50 math questions in 60 minutes is not the easiest of tasks, but if you learn how to pace yourself, you should be able to look at every single question on the test. Note that we said "look at" every question on the test. We didn't say "answer" every question on the test. There is a very big difference between the two.

It is unlikely that you will be able to answer every question on the test.

Some questions will stump you, completely resisting your efforts to eliminate even one possible answer choice. Others might demand so much of your time that answering them becomes more trouble than it's worth. While taking five minutes to solve a particularly difficult question might strike you as a moral victory when you're taking the test, it's quite possible that you could have used that same time to answer six other questions that would have vastly increased your score. Instead of getting bogged down in individual questions, you will do better if you learn to skip, and leave for later, the very difficult questions that you either can't answer or that will take an extremely long time to answer.

By perfecting your pacing on practice tests, you can make sure that you will see every question on the test. And this way, you can select which questions you will and won't answer, rather than running out of time before reaching the end of the test. You're no longer allowing the test to decide, by default, which questions you won't answer.

There are a few simple rules that, if followed, will make pacing yourself much easier.

- Make sure not to get bogged down in any one question.

- Answer every question to which you know the answer, and make an educated guess for every question in which you can quickly eliminate at least one answer choice.

- Skip questions that refer to concepts completely foreign to you. If you look at the question and answers and have no idea what topics they cover, you have little chance of even coming up with an educated guess. Mark the question in some way to indicate that it is very difficult. Return to it only if you have answered everything else. Remember to skip that line on your answer sheet!

Setting a Target Score

You can make the job of pacing yourself much easier if you go into the test knowing how many questions you have to answer correctly in order to earn the score that you want. So, what score do you want to get? Obviously, you should strive for the best score possible, but be realistic: consider how much you know about math and how well you do in general on SAT-type tests. You should also consider what exactly defines a good score at the colleges to which you're applying: is it a 680? A 740? Talk to the admissions offices of the colleges you might want to attend, do a little research in college guidebooks, or talk to your guidance counselor. No matter how you do it, you should find out what the average score is of a student going to the schools you want to attend. Take that number and set your target score above it (you want to be above average, right?). Then take a look at the chart we showed you before:

You will get:

- 800 if you answered 44 right, 4 wrong, and left 2 blank

- 750 if you answered 40 right, 8 wrong, and left 2 blank

- 700 if you answered 35 right, 8 wrong, and left 7 blank

- 650 if you answered 30 right, 12 wrong, and left 8 blank

- 600 if you answered 25 right, 16 wrong, and left 9 blank

So let's say the average score for the SAT II Math IIC for the school you want to attend is a 700. You should set your target at about 750. Looking at this chart, you can see that in order to get that score, you need to get 40 questions right, can get 8 wrong, and can leave 2 blank.

If you know all these numbers going into the test, you can pace yourself accordingly. You should use practice tests to teach yourself the proper pace, increasing your speed if you find that you aren't getting to answer all the questions you need to, or decreasing your pace if you find that you're rushing and making careless mistakes. If you reach your target score during preparation, give yourself a cookie and take a break for the day. But just because you hit your target score doesn't mean you should stop working altogether. In fact, you should view reaching your target score as a clue that you can do *better* than that score: set a new target 50-100 points above your original, and work to pick up your pace a little bit and skip fewer questions.

By working to improve in manageable increments, you can slowly work up to your top speed, integrating your new knowledge about how to take the test and the subjects it covers without overwhelming yourself by trying to take on too much too soon. If you can handle working just a little faster without becoming careless and losing points, your score will certainly go up. If you meet your new target score again, repeat the process.

SAT II
MATH IIC
REVIEW

Math IIC
Fundamentals

ONLY A FEW QUESTIONS ON THE MATH IIC will directly test basic math—a mere 2-5% of the questions. But knowledge of basic math is vital for the test, since almost all of the 50 questions *assume* you know these topics. In other words, you'll need to understand these concepts and be able to apply them to everything from algebra to trigonometry problems.

You probably know some of these topics like the back of your hand. On others, you may need a refresher. Either way, it can't hurt to thumb through this chapter and make sure you're still sound on math fundamentals.

Order of Operations

One of the most instrumental and basic principles of arithmetic is the order of operations, which refers to the order in which you must perform the various operations in a given mathematical expression. The addition, subtraction, multiplication, division, and exponentiation found in an expression need to be done in a specific order. There is a simple reason for the strictness of this protocol. If operations in an expression could be performed in any random order, a single expression would take on a vast array of values. Take a look:

Evaluate the expression $3 \times 2^3 + 6 \div 4$.

One student might perform the operations from left to right:

$$3 \times 2^3 + 6 \div 4 = 6^3 + 6 \div 4 = 216 + 6 \div 4 = 222 \div 4 = 55.5$$

Another student chooses to add before executing the multiplication or division:

$$3 \times 2^3 + 6 \div 4 = 3 \times 8 + 6 \div 4 = 3 \times 14 \div 4 = 10.5$$

As you can see, there are a great many possible evaluations of this expression depending on the order in which we perform the required operations. That's why we have PEMDAS: a catchy acronym for determining the correct order of operations in any expression. PEMDAS stands for:

- **P**arentheses—first, perform the operations in the innermost parentheses. A set of parentheses supercedes any other operation.

- **E**xponents—before you do any other operation, raise all the required bases to the prescribed exponent. Exponents include square roots and cube roots, since those two operations are the equivalent of raising a base to the ½ and ⅓ power, respectively.

- **M**ultiplication and **D**ivision—perform multiplication and division.

- **A**ddition and **S**ubtraction—perform addition and subtraction.

Let's work through a few examples to see how order of operations and PEMDAS work. First, we should find out the proper way to evaluate the expression $3 \times 2^3 + 6 \div 4$. Since nothing is enclosed in parentheses, the first operation we carry out is exponentiation:

$$3 \times 2^3 + 6 \div 4 = 3 \times 8 + 6 \div 4$$

Next, we do all the necessary multiplication and division:

$$3 \times 8 + 6 \div 4 = 24 + 1.5$$

Last, we perform the required addition and subtraction. Our final answer is:

$$24 + 1.5 = 25.5$$

Here's another example, which is a bit trickier. Try it on your own, and then compare your results to the explanation that follows:

Evaluate $6\sqrt{2^3 + 4(5-3)}$.

First, resolve the operations under the square root, which is symbolized by $\sqrt{}$ and is also called a radical.

But wait, you may be thinking to yourself, I thought we were supposed to do everything within a parentheses before performing exponentiation. Expressions under a radical are special exceptions because they are really an expression within parentheses that has been raised to a fractional power. In terms of math, $6\sqrt{2^3 + 4(5-3)} = 6(2^3 + 4(5-3))^{1/2}$. The radical effectively acts as a large set of parentheses, so the rules of PEMDAS still apply.

To work out this expression, first execute the operations within the innermost set of parentheses:

$$6\sqrt{2^3 + 4(5-3)} = 6\sqrt{2^3 + 4(2)}$$

Next perform the required exponentiation:

$$6\sqrt{2^3 + 4(2)} = 6\sqrt{8 + 4(2)}$$

Then, multiply:

$$6\sqrt{2^3 + 4(2)} = 6\sqrt{8 + 8}$$

Finally, add:

$$6\sqrt{8 + 8} = 6\sqrt{16}$$

Now that the operations under the radical have been resolved, we can take the square root.

$$6\sqrt{16} = 6 \times 4 = 24$$

One additional note is important for the division step in the order of operations. When the division symbol ÷ is replaced by a fraction bar (i.e. the expression includes a fraction), you must evaluate the **numerator** and the **denominator** separately before you divide the numerator by the denominator. The fraction bar is the equivalent of placing a set of parentheses around the whole numerator and another for the whole denominator. For example, in the fraction

$$\frac{5 - 2^2}{6 + 4} =$$

you must work out the numerator and denominator before actually dividing:

$$\frac{5 - 4}{10} = \frac{1}{10} = .1$$

Order of Operations and Your Calculator

There are two ways to deal with the order of operations while using a calculator:

1. Work out operations one by one on your calculator while keeping track of the entire equation on paper. This is a slow but accurate process.

2. If you have a graphing calculator, you can type the whole expression into your calculator. This method will be faster, but it is vulnerable to careless errors.

If you want to type full expressions into your graphing calculator, you must be familiar with how your calculator works. In particular, you need to be able to type the full expression into your calculator correctly, so that the calculator follows the right order of operations. You can't enter fractions and exponents into your calculator the way they appear on paper. Instead, you have to be sure to recognize and preserve the order of operations. So acquaint yourself by practicing with the following expression:

$$\frac{(2^2) + 3 \times 4}{\frac{1}{2} \div 2} = ?$$

How would you enter this into your calculator? It should look like this:

$$(2^2 + (3 \times 4)) \div ((1 \div 2) \div 2)$$

Numbers

Before you take the Math IIC, you should become familiar with some common types of numbers. Understand their properties and you will be well served.

- **Whole Numbers:** the set of counting numbers, including zero {0, 1, 2, 3, . . .}.

- **Natural Numbers:** the set of all whole numbers except zero {1, 2, 3, 4, 5, . . .}.

- **Integers:** the set of all positive and negative whole numbers, including zero. Fractions and decimals are not included {. . . , –3, –2, –1, 0, 1, 2, 3, . . .}.

- **Rational Numbers:** the set of all numbers that can be expressed as a quotient of integers. That is, any numbers that can be expressed in the form m/n, where m and n are integers. The set of rational numbers includes all integers, and all fractions that can be created using integers in the **numerator** and **denominator**.

- **Irrational Numbers:** the set of all numbers that cannot be expressed as a quotient of integers. Examples include π, $\sqrt{3}$, 1.01001000100001000001. . . . The sets of irrational numbers and rational numbers are mutually exclusive. Any given number must be either rational or irrational; no number can be both.

- **Real Numbers:** every number on the number line. The set of real numbers includes all rational and irrational numbers.

- **Imaginary Numbers:** numbers that do not appear on the real number line. We explain the ways in which imaginary numbers appear on the Math IIC in the Special Math chapter later in this book.

On the Math IIC, integers and real numbers will appear far more often than any of the other types.

Even and Odd Numbers

Even numbers are those numbers that are divisible by two with no remainder.

Only integers can be even or odd, meaning decimals and fractions cannot be even or odd. Zero, however, is an integer and divisible by two, so it is even.

$$. . . , –6, –4, –2, 0, 2, 4, 6, . . .$$

Odd numbers are those numbers not evenly divisible by two.

$$. . . , –5, –3, –1, 1, 3, 5, . . .$$

The set of even numbers and the set of odd numbers are mutually exclusive.

A more rigorous definition of even and odd numbers appears below:

- Even numbers are numbers that can be written in the form $2n$, where n is an integer. Odd numbers are numbers that can be written in the form $2n + 1$, where n is an integer.

This definition is nothing more than a technical repetition of the fact that even numbers are divisible by two, and odd numbers are not. It may come in handy, though, when you need to represent an even or odd number with a variable.

Operations of Odd and Even Numbers

There are a few basic rules regarding the operations of odd and even numbers that you should know well. If you grasp the principles behind the two types of signed numbers, these rules should come easily.

Addition

$$\text{even} + \text{even} = \text{even}$$
$$\text{odd} + \text{odd} = \text{even}$$
$$\text{even} + \text{odd} = \text{odd}$$

Subtraction

$$\text{even} - \text{even} = \text{even}$$
$$\text{odd} - \text{odd} = \text{even}$$
$$\text{even} - \text{odd} = \text{odd}$$

Multiplication

$$\text{even} \times \text{even} = \text{even}$$
$$\text{odd} \times \text{odd} = \text{odd}$$
$$\text{even} \times \text{odd} = \text{even}$$

Positive and Negative Numbers

Positive and negative numbers are governed by rules similar to those associated with even and odd numbers. First, for their quick definitions:

- Positive numbers are numbers that are greater than zero. Negative numbers are numbers that are less than zero. The number zero is neither positive nor negative.

Operations of Positive and Negative Numbers

The following rules define how positive and negative numbers operate under various operations.

Addition and Subtraction

You should already know how to add and subtract positive numbers. When adding and subtracting negative numbers, however, it helps to remember the following:

Adding a negative number is the same as subtracting its opposite. For example:

$$3 + (-2) = 3 - 2 = 1$$

Subtracting a negative number is the same as adding its opposite. Again, for example:

$$3 - (-2) = 3 + 2 = 5$$

Multiplication

$$\text{positive} \times \text{positive} = \text{positive}$$
$$\text{negative} \times \text{negative} = \text{positive}$$
$$\text{positive} \times \text{negative} = \text{negative}$$

Division

$$\text{positive} \div \text{positive} = \text{positive}$$
$$\text{negative} \div \text{negative} = \text{positive}$$
$$\text{positive} \div \text{negative} = \text{negative}$$

The rules for multiplication and division are exactly the same since any division operation can be written as a form of multiplication: $a \div b = {}^{a}/_{b} = a \times {}^{1}/_{b}$.

Absolute Value

The absolute value of a number is the distance on a number line between that number and zero. Or, you could think of it as the positive "version" of every number. The absolute value of a positive number is that same number, and the absolute value of a negative number is the opposite of that number.

The absolute value of x is symbolized by $|x|$.

$$\text{If } x = 5, |x| = 5.$$
$$\text{If } x = -4.234, |x| = 4.234.$$
$$\text{If } x = 0, |x| = 0.$$

Fundamentals

Solving an equation with an absolute value in it can be particularly tricky. As you will see, the answer is often ambiguous. Take a look at the following equation:

$$4|x| + 2 = 10$$

We can simplify the equation in order to isolate $|x|$:

$$4|x| + 2 = 10$$
$$4|x| = 8$$
$$|x| = 2$$

Knowing that $|x| = 2$ means that $x = 2$ and $x = -2$ are both possible solutions to the problem. Keep this in mind; we'll deal more with absolute values in equations later on in the algebra chapter.

Factors

A factor is an integer that divides another integer evenly. If a/b is an integer, then b is a factor of a. 3, 4, and 6, for example, are factors of 12.

Sometimes it is necessary or helpful to factor an integer completely. This means finding all the factors of that integer. It's possible that the test will directly require this skill or will make use of it in a more complicated question. In either case, it's something you should know how to do.

Factorization

To find all the factors of a number, write them down in pairs, beginning with 1 and the number you're factoring. We'll factor 24 for this example. So 1 and 24 are both factors of 24. Next, try every integer greater than 1 in increasing order. Here are the factor pairs we find for 24:

- 1 and 24 (1 × 24 = 24)

- 2 and 12 (2 × 12 = 24)

- 3 and 8 (3 × 8 = 24)

- 4 and 6 (4 × 6 = 24)

You know you've found all the factors of a number when the lesser number in each product pair exceeds the greater number. For example, after you found that 4 was a factor of 24 and 5 was not, you would see that 6, the next factor of 24, had already been included in a pair of factors. Thus, all the factors have been found.

Prime Numbers

A prime number is a number whose only factors are one and itself. All prime numbers are positive (because every negative number has −1 as a factor in addition to 1 and itself). Furthermore, all prime numbers besides 2 are odd. The first few primes, in increasing order, are:

$$2, 3, 5, 7, 11, 13, 17, 19, 23, 29, 31, 37, 41, 43, 47, 53, \ldots$$

To determine whether a number is prime, you shouldn't check whether the number is divisible by every number less than itself. Such an effort would take an incredible amount of time, and you have only an hour for the Math IIC. Instead, to decide whether a number is prime, all you need to do is estimate the square root of the number, then check all the prime numbers that fall below your estimate. For example, to see if 91 is prime, you should estimate the square root of the number: $\sqrt{91} \approx 10$. Now you should test 91 for divisibility by the prime numbers smaller than 10: 2, 3, 5 and 7.

- Is 91 divisible by 2? No, it does not end with an even number.

- Is 91 divisible by 3? No, $9 + 1 = 10$, and 10 is not divisible by 3.

- Is 91 divisible by 5? No, 91 does not end with 0 or 5.

- Is 91 divisible by 7? Yes! $91 \div 7 = 13$.

Therefore, 91 is not prime.

Prime Factorization

Another form of factorization is called **prime factorization**. The prime factorization of an integer is the listing of the prime numbers whose product is that number.

To find the prime factorization of a number, divide it and all of its factors until every integer remaining is prime. This group of prime numbers is the prime factorization of the original integer. Let's find the prime factorization of 36 as an example.

$$36 = 2 \times 18 = 2 \times 2 \times 9 = 2 \times 2 \times 3 \times 3$$

It can be helpful to think of prime factorization in the form of a tree:

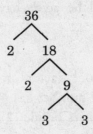

As you may already have noticed, there is more than one way to find the prime factorization of a number. We could have first resolved 36 into 6 × 6, for example, and then determined the prime factorization from there. So don't worry—you can't screw up. No matter which path you take, you will always get the same result. That is, as long as you do your arithmetic correctly. Just for practice, find the prime factorizations for 45 and 41.

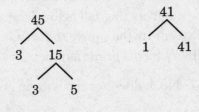

$$3 \times 3 \times 5 = 45 \qquad 1 \times 41 = 41$$

Since the only factors of 41 are 1 and 41, 41 is a prime number. It is therefore its own prime factorization.

Greatest Common Factor

The greatest common factor (GCF) of two numbers is the greatest factor that they have in common. Finding the GCF of two numbers is especially useful in certain applications, such as manipulating fractions. We'll explain why later in this section.

In order to find the greatest common factor of two numbers, we must first produce their prime factorizations. What is the greatest common factor of 18 and 24, for example?

First, their prime factorizations:

$$18 = 2 \times 9 = 2 \times 3 \times 3$$
$$24 = 2 \times 12 = 2 \times 2 \times 6 = 2 \times 2 \times 3$$

The greatest common factor is the greatest integer that can be written as a product of common prime factors. That is to say, the GCF is the "overlap," or intersection, of the two prime factorizations. In this case, both prime factorizations contain $2 \times 3 = 6$. This is their GCF.

Here's another example:

What is the GCF of 96 and 144?

First:

$$96 = 2 \times 48 = 2 \times 2 \times 24 = 2 \times 2 \times 2 \times 12 = 2 \times 2 \times 2 \times 2 \times 6 = 2 \times 2 \times 2 \times 2 \times 2 \times 3 = 2^5 \times 3$$
$$144 = 2 \times 72 = 2 \times 2 \times 36 = 2 \times 2 \times 2 \times 18 = 2 \times 2 \times 2 \times 2 \times 9 = 2 \times 2 \times 2 \times 2 \times 3 \times 3 = 2^4 \times 3^2$$

So, the product of the prime factors that they share is $2^4 \times 3 = 48$, which is their GCF.

For practice, find the GCF of the following pairs of integers:

1. 12 and 15

2. 30 and 45

3. 13 and 72

4. 14 and 49

5. 100 and 80

Compare your answers to the solutions:

1. $12 = 2^2 \times 3$
    $15 = 3 \times 5$
    The GCF is 3.

2. $30 = 2 \times 3 \times 5$
    $45 = 3^2 \times 5$
    The GCF is $3 \times 5 = 15$.

3. $13 = 1 \times 13$
    $72 = 2^3 \times 3^2$
    There are no common prime factors. The GCF is 1.

4. $14 = 2 \times 7$
    $49 = 7^2$
    The GCF is 7.

5. $100 = 2^2 \times 5^2$
    $80 = 2^4 \times 5$
    The GCF is $2^2 \times 5 = 20$.

Fundamentals

Relatively Prime Numbers

Two numbers are called relatively prime if they have no common prime factors (i.e., if their GCF is 1). This doesn't mean, however, that each number is itself. 8 and 15 are relatively prime, because they have no common primes in their prime factorizations (8 = 2 × 2 × 2 and 15 = 3 × 5), but neither number is prime. It might be a good idea to know the definition of relatively prime numbers, in case it pops up somewhere on the test.

Multiples

A multiple is an integer that can be evenly divided by another integer. If c/d is an integer, then c is a multiple of d. 45, 27, and 18, for example, are all multiples of 9. Alternatively, you could define a multiple as an integer with at least one factor. All that really matters is that you understand the concept of multiples, and this is best done with a simple example.

What are some multiples of 4?

- 12, 20, and 96 are all multiples of 4.

How do we know these numbers are multiples of 4?

$$12 = 4 \times 3$$
$$20 = 4 \times 5$$
$$96 = 4 \times 24$$

Also, note that any integer, n, is a multiple of 1 and n, because $1 \times n = n$.

Least Common Multiple

The least common multiple (LCM) of two integers is the smallest multiple that the two numbers have in common. Like the GCF, the least common multiple of two numbers is useful when manipulating fractions.

To find the LCM of two integers, you must first find the integers' prime factorizations. The least common multiple is the smallest prime factorization that contains every prime number in each of the two prime factorizations. If the same prime factor appears in the prime factorizations of both integers, multiply the factor by the greatest number of times it appears in the factorization of either number. For example, what is the least common multiple of 4 and 6? We must first find their prime factorizations.

$$4 = 2 \times 2$$
$$6 = 2 \times 3$$

In this example, 2 appears as a prime factor of both integers. It appears twice in the prime factorization in which it is more prevalent, so to find the LCM we will use two 2s. We will also use the 3 from the prime factorization of 6. The LCM of 4 and 6 is therefore

$$2 \times 2 \times 3 = 12$$

Let's try a harder example. What is the LCM of 14 and 38? Again, we start by finding the prime factorizations of both numbers:

$$14 = 2 \times 7$$
$$38 = 2 \times 19$$

In this example, 2 appears in both prime factorizations, but not more than once in each, so we only need to use one 2. Therefore, the LCM of 7 and 38 is

$$2 \times 7 \times 19 = 266$$

For practice, find the LCM of the following pairs of integers:

1. 12 and 32

2. 15 and 26

3. 34 and 40

4. 3 and 17

5. 18 and 16

Compare your answers to the solutions:

1. $12 = 2^3 \times 3$
    $32 = 2^5$
    The LCM is $2^5 \times 3 = 96$.

2. $15 = 3 \times 5$
    $26 = 2 \times 13$
    The LCM is $2 \times 3 \times 5 \times 13 = 390$.

3. $34 = 2 \times 17$
    $40 = 2^3 \times 5$
    The LCM is $2^3 \times 5 \times 17 = 680$.

4. $3 = 1 \times 3$
   $17 = 1 \times 17$
   The LCM is $3 \times 17 = 51$.

5. $18 = 2 \times 3^2$
   $16 = 2^4$
   The LCM is $2^4 \times 3^2 = 144$.

Fractions

The ability to efficiently and correctly manipulate fractions is essential to doing well on the Math IIC test. A fraction describes a part of a whole. It is composed of two expressions, a numerator and a denominator. The numerator of a fraction is the quantity above the fraction bar, and the denominator is the quantity below the fraction bar. For example, in the fraction ½, 1 is the numerator and 2 is the denominator.

Equivalent Fractions

Two fractions are equivalent if they describe equal parts of the same whole. To determine if two fractions are equivalent, multiply the denominator and numerator of one fraction so that the denominators of the two fractions are equal. For example, ½ = ³⁄₆ because if you multiply the numerator and denominator of ½ by 3, you get

$$\frac{1 \times 3}{2 \times 3} = \frac{3}{6}$$

As long as you multiply or divide *both* the numerator and denominator of a fraction by the *same* non-zero number, you will not change the overall value of the fraction. Since fractions represent a part of a whole, increasing both the part and whole by the same multiple will not change the fundamental relationship between the part and the whole.

Reducing Fractions

Reducing fractions makes life with fractions much simpler. It makes unwieldy fractions, such as ⁴⁵⁰⁄₆₀₀, smaller and easier to work with.

To reduce a fraction to lowest terms, divide the numerator and denominator by their greatest common factor. For example, for ⁴⁵⁰⁄₆₀₀, the GCF of 450 and 600 is 150. The fraction reduces to ¾.

A fraction is in reduced form if its numerator and denominator are relatively prime (their GCF is 1). Therefore, it makes sense that the equivalent fractions we studied in the previous section all reduce to the same fraction. For example, the equivalent fractions $\frac{4}{6}$ and $\frac{8}{12}$ both reduce to $\frac{2}{3}$.

Comparing Fractions

When dealing with integers, a large positive number with a lot of digits, like 5,000,000 means that it is greater than a number with fewer digits, such as 5. Fractions, on the other hand, do not work the same way. For example, $\frac{200}{20,000}$ might seem like a nice, big, impressive fraction, but $\frac{2}{3}$ is actually larger because 2 is a much bigger part of 3 than 200 is a part of 20,000.

In certain cases, comparing two fractions can be very simple. If they have the same denominator, then the fraction with the larger numerator is bigger. If they have the same numerator, the fraction with the smaller denominator is bigger.

However, you'll most likely be dealing with two fractions that have different numerators and denominators, such as $\frac{200}{20,000}$ and $\frac{2}{3}$. When faced with this situation, an easy way to compare these two fractions is to use cross-multiplication. Simply multiply the numerator of each fraction by the denominator of the other, then write the product of each multiplication next to the numerator you used to get it. We'll cross-multiply $\frac{200}{20,000}$ and $\frac{2}{3}$:

$$600 = \frac{200}{20,000} \quad\diagdown\!\!\!\!\!\diagup\quad \frac{2}{3} = 40,000$$

Since 40,000 > 600, $\frac{2}{3}$ is the greater fraction.

Adding and Subtracting Fractions

On the SAT II Math IIC, you will need to know how to add and subtract two different types of fractions. The fractions will either have the same or different denominators.

Fractions with the Same Denominators

Fractions are extremely easy to add and subtract if they have the same denominator. All you have to do is add up the numerators:

$$\frac{1}{20} + \frac{3}{20} + \frac{13}{20} = \frac{17}{20}$$

Subtraction works similarly. If the denominators of the fractions are equal, then you simply subtract one numerator from the other:

$$\frac{13}{20} - \frac{2}{20} = \frac{11}{20}$$

Fractions with Different Denominators

If the fractions do not have equal denominators, the process becomes somewhat more involved. The first step is to make the denominators the same, and then to subtract as described above. The best way to do this is to find the Least Common Denominator (LCD), which is simply the Least Common Multiple of the two denominators. For example, the LCD of ½ and ⅔ is 6, since 6 is the LCM of 2 and 3.

The second step, after you've equalized the denominators of the two fractions, is to multiply each numerator by the same value as their respective denominator. Let's take a look at how to do this for our example, ½ + ⅔. For ½:

$$\text{denominator} = 2 \times 3 = 6$$
$$\text{numerator} = 1 \times 3 = 3$$

So, the new fraction is ³⁄₆. The same process is repeated for the second fraction, ⅔:

$$\text{denominator} = 3 \times 2 = 6$$
$$\text{numerator} = 2 \times 2 = 4$$

The new fraction is ⁴⁄₆. The final step is to perform the addition or subtraction. In this case, ³⁄₆ + ⁴⁄₆ = ⁷⁄₆.

If you think it will be faster, you can always skip finding the LCD and multiply the denominators together to get a common denominator. In some cases, such as our example, the product of the denominators will actually be the LCD (2 × 3 = 6 = LCD). Other times, however, the product of the denominators will be greater than the LCD. For example, if the two denominators are 6 and 8, you could use 6 × 8 = 48 as a denominator instead of 24 (the LCD).

There are two drawbacks to this. The first is that you will have to work with larger numbers. The second is that you will have to take the extra step of reducing your answer at the end since the test answer choices appear as reduced fractions.

Multiplying Fractions

Multiplying fractions is quite simple. The product of two fractions is the product of their numerators over the product of their denominators. Symbolically, this can be represented as:

$$\frac{a}{b} \times \frac{c}{d} = \frac{ac}{bd}$$

Or, for a numerical example:

$$\frac{3}{7} \times \frac{2}{5} = \frac{3 \times 2}{7 \times 5} = \frac{6}{35}$$

Dividing Fractions

Multiplication and division are inverse operations. It makes sense, then, that to perform division with fractions, you need to flip the second fraction over, which is also called taking its reciprocal, and then multiply:

$$\frac{a}{b} \div \frac{c}{d} = \frac{a}{b} \times \frac{d}{c} = \frac{ad}{bc}$$

Here's a numerical example:

$$\frac{1}{2} \div \frac{4}{5} = \frac{1}{2} \times \frac{5}{4} = \frac{5}{8}$$

Mixed Numbers

A mixed number is an integer followed by a fraction, like $1\frac{1}{2}$. It is another form of an improper fraction, which is a fraction greater than one. But any operation such as addition, subtraction, multiplication, or division, can be performed only on the improper fraction form, so you need to know how to convert between the two.

Let's convert the mixed number $1\frac{1}{2}$ into an improper fraction. First, you multiply the integer portion of the mixed number by the denominator, and add that product to the numerator. So $1 \times 2 + 1 = 3$ is the numerator of the improper fraction. Put the numerator over the original denominator, and you have your converted fraction, $\frac{3}{2}$.

Here's another example:

$$3\,\frac{2}{13} = \frac{(3 \times 13) + 2}{13} = \frac{39 + 2}{13} = \frac{41}{13}$$

Decimals

Decimals are just another way to express fractions. To produce a decimal, divide the numerator of a fraction by the denominator. For example, $\frac{1}{2} = 1 \div 2 = .5$.

More specifically, a **decimal number** is any number with a non-zero digit to the right of the **decimal point**. Integers are not decimal numbers, as you can see by the example below:

- 4 = 4.00000 . . . not a decimal number because there is only the zero digit to the right of the decimal point

- $\frac{3}{7}$ = 0.428571428571 . . . a decimal number because 4285 . . . is to the right of the decimal point

Comparing Decimals

As with fractions, comparing decimals can be a bit deceptive. As a general rule, when comparing two decimals such as .3 with .003, the decimal with more leading zeroes is smaller. But if asked to compare .003 with .0009, however, you might overlook the additional zero, and because 9 is the larger integer, choose .0009 as the larger decimal. That, of course, would be wrong. Take care to avoid such mistakes. One way is to line up the decimal points of the two decimals:

- .0009 is clearly smaller than
  .0030

If numbers are being added to the right of the decimal number, then it's a different story.

- .000900 is smaller than
  .000925

Converting Decimals to Fractions

Knowing how to convert decimals into fractions, and fractions into decimals, is a useful skill. Sometimes you'll produce a decimal while solving a question, and then have to choose from fractions for test choices. Other times, it may be easier to work with fractions. Whatever the case, both conversions can be done easily.

To convert a decimal number to a fraction:

1. Remove the decimal point and use the decimal number as the numerator.

2. The denominator is the number 1 followed by as many zeroes as there are decimal places in the decimal number.

3. Reduce this fraction.

Let's convert .3875 into a fraction. First, we eliminate the decimal point and place 3875 in the numerator position:

$$.3875 = \frac{3875}{?}$$

Since .3875 has four digits after the decimal point, we put four zeroes in the denominator:

$$.3875 = \frac{3875}{10000}$$

Then, by finding the greatest common factor of 3875 and 10000, 125, we can reduce the fraction:

$$\frac{3875}{10000} = \frac{31}{80}$$

To convert from fractions to decimals is a cinch. Simply carry out the necessary division on your calculator, such as for $\frac{3}{5}$:

$$\frac{3}{5} = 3 \div 5 = 0.6$$

Percents

A **percent** is another way to describe a part of a whole (which means that percents are also another way to talk about fractions or decimals). Percent literally means "of 100" in Latin, so when you attend school 25 percent of the time, that means you only go to school $\frac{25}{100}$ (or .25) of the time.

You would probably fail your classes if your attendance percentage were that low, so don't get any ideas from our example. Instead, take a look at a sample question: 3 is what percent of 15? This question presents you with a whole, 15, and then asks you to determine how much of that whole 3 represents in percentage form. Since a percent is "of 100", to solve the question you have to set the fraction $\frac{3}{15}$ equal to $\frac{x}{100}$:

$$\frac{3}{15} = \frac{x}{100}$$

You then cross-multiply and solve for x:

$$15x = 3 \times 100 = 300$$
$$x = 20$$

Converting Percents into Fractions or Decimals

You should be skilled at converting percents into fractions and decimals, because it will definitely come up on the Math IIC test.

Percents directly relate to decimal numbers. A percent is a decimal number with the decimal point moved two decimal places to the left.

For example:

$$50\% \text{ of } 12 = .50 \times 12 = 6$$
$$12\% \text{ of } 120 = .12 \times 120 = 14.4$$

To convert from a decimal number to a percent, move the decimal point two places to the right:

$$.07 \times 1100 = 7\% \text{ of } 1100 = 77$$
$$.97 \times 13 = 97\% \text{ of } 13 = 12.61$$

On an even simpler level, we can say, for example, that 50% = 0.5, or 22.346% = .22346. Percentages greater than 100 also exist. 235% = 2.35, for example.

To convert from a percent to a fraction, take the percentage number and place it as the numerator over the denominator 100. 58 percent is the same as $^{58}/_{100}$.

To convert from a fraction back to a percent, the easiest method is to convert the fraction into a decimal first, and then change the resulting decimal into a percent.

For example:

$$\frac{3}{4} = 3 \div 4 = .75 = 75\%$$

Exponents

An exponent defines the number of times a number is to be multiplied by itself. For example, in a^b, where a is the base, and b the exponent, a is multiplied by itself b times. In a numerical example, $2^5 = 2 \times 2 \times 2 \times 2 \times 2$. An exponent can also be referred to as a power: a number with an exponent of 2 is raised to the second power. The following are other terms related to exponents with which you should be familiar:

- **Base.** The base refers to the 3 in 3^5. It is the number that is being multiplied by itself however many times specified by the exponent.

- **Exponent.** The exponent is the 5 in 3^5. It indicates the number of times the base is to be multiplied with itself.

- **Squared.** Saying that a number is squared is a common term meaning that the number has been raised to the second power, i.e., that it has an exponent of 2. In the expression 6^2, 6 has been squared.

- **Cubed.** Saying that a number is cubed signifies that the number has been raised to the third power, i.e., that it has an exponent of 3. In the expression 4^3, 4 has been cubed.

Common Exponents

It may be worthwhile to memorize a few common exponents before taking the Math IIC, in order to save the time you'd take to calculate them during the test. Here is a list of squares from 1 through 10.

$$1^2 = 1$$
$$2^2 = 4$$
$$3^2 = 9$$
$$4^2 = 16$$
$$5^2 = 25$$
$$6^2 = 36$$
$$7^2 = 49$$
$$8^2 = 64$$
$$9^2 = 81$$
$$10^2 = 100$$

Memorizing the first few cubes might also be helpful:

$$1^3 = 1$$
$$2^3 = 8$$
$$3^3 = 27$$
$$4^3 = 64$$
$$5^3 = 125$$

The first few powers of two are also useful to know for many applications:

$$2^0 = 1$$
$$2^1 = 2$$
$$2^2 = 4$$
$$2^3 = 8$$
$$2^4 = 16$$
$$2^5 = 32$$
$$2^6 = 64$$
$$2^7 = 128$$
$$2^8 = 256$$
$$2^9 = 512$$
$$2^{10} = 1024$$

Adding and Subtracting Numbers with Exponents

Numbers with exponents can't be added or subtracted. Instead, you have to work out each exponent to find its value, and then add the two numbers. For example, to add $3^3 + 4^2$, you must work out the exponents to get $(3 \times 3 \times 3) + (4 \times 4)$, and then, $27 + 16 = 43$. (You probably wouldn't need to write out the $(3 \times 3 \times 3) + (4 \times 4)$ step when doing a problem like this. We included it just to be complete.)

However, algebraic expressions that have the same bases and exponents, such as $3x^4$ and $5x^4$, can be added and subtracted. For example, $3x^4 + 5x^4 = 8x^4$. The expressions $3x^5 - 4x^2$ and $2x^3 + 3y^3$ are already fully simplified.

Multiplying and Dividing Numbers with Exponents

To multiply two base exponential numbers or terms that have the same base, all you have to do is add the exponents together:

$$3^6 \times 3^2 = 3^{(6+2)} = 3^8$$
$$x^4 \times x^3 = x^{(4+3)} = x^7$$

To divide two same-base exponential numbers or terms, just subtract the exponents.

$$\frac{3^6}{3^2} = 3^{(6-2)} = 3^4$$
$$\frac{x^4}{x^3} = x^{(4-3)} = x^1$$

If you need to multiply or divide two exponential numbers that do not have the same base or exponent, you'll just have to do your work the old-fashioned way: multiply the exponential numbers out, and multiply or divide them accordingly.

Raising an Exponent to an Exponent

Occasionally you might encounter an exponent raised to another exponent, as in $(3^2)^4$ and $(x^4)^3$. In such cases, multiply the exponents:

$$(3^2)^4 = 3^{(2 \times 4)} = 3^8$$
$$(x^4)^3 = x^{(4 \times 3)} = x^{12}$$

Exponents and Fractions

To raise a fraction to an exponent, raise both the numerator and denominator to that exponent:

$$\left(\frac{1}{3}\right)^3 = \frac{1}{27}$$

Exponents and Negative Numbers

As we said in the negative numbers section, when you multiply a negative number by a negative number, you get a positive number, and when you multiply a negative number by a positive number, you get a negative number. These rules affect how negative numbers function in reference to exponents.

- When you raise a negative number to an even number exponent, you get a positive number. For example $(-2)^4 = 16$. To see why this is so, let's break down the example. $(-2)^4$ means $-2 \times -2 \times -2 \times -2$. When you multiply the first two -2s together, you get positive 4 because you are multiplying two negative numbers. Then when you multiply the $+4$ by the next -2, you get -8, since you are multiplying a positive number by a negative number. Finally, you multiply the -8 by the last -2 and get $+16$, since you're once again multiplying two negative numbers.

- When you raise a negative number to an odd power, you get a negative number. To see why, all refer to the example above and stop the process at -8, which equals -2^3.

These rules can help a great deal as you go about eliminating answer choices and checking potential correct answers. For example, if you have a negative number raised to an odd power, and you get a positive answer, you know your answer is wrong. Likewise, on that same question, you could eliminate any answer choices that are positive.

Special Exponents

There are a few special properties of certain exponents that you also should know.

Zero

Any base raised to the power of zero is equal to 1. If you see any exponent of the form x^0, you should know that its value is 1.

One

Any base raised to the power of one is equal to itself. For example, $2^1 = 2$, $-67^1 = -67$, and $x^1 = x$. This can be helpful when you're attempting an operation on exponential terms with the same base. For example:

$$3x^6 \times x = 3x^6 \times x^1 = 3x^{(6+1)} = 3x^7$$

Fractional Exponents

Exponents can be fractions, too. When a number or term is raised to a fractional power, it is called taking the **root** of that number or term. This expression can be converted into a more convenient form:

$$x^{\left(\frac{a}{b}\right)} = \sqrt[b]{x^a}$$

Or, for example, $2^{13/5}$ is equal to the fifth root of 2 to the thirteenth power:

$$\sqrt[5]{2^{13}} = 6.063$$

The $\sqrt{}$ symbol is also known as the radical, and anything under the radical, in this case 2^{13}, is called the radicand. For a more familiar example, look at $9^{1/2}$, which is the same as $\sqrt{9}$:

$$\sqrt[2]{9^1} = \sqrt{9} = 3$$

Negative Exponents

Seeing a negative number as a power may be a little strange the first time around. But the principle at work is simple. Any number or term raised to a negative power is equal to the reciprocal of that base raised to the opposite power. For example:

$$x^{-5} = \frac{1}{x^5}$$

Or a slightly more complicated example:

$$\left(\frac{2}{3}\right)^{-3} = \left(\frac{1}{\frac{2}{3}}\right)^3 = \left(\frac{3}{2}\right)^3 = \frac{27}{8}$$

You've got the four rules of special exponents. Here are some examples to firm up your knowledge:

$$5^0 = 1$$

$$x^{\frac{1}{8}} = \sqrt[8]{x^1} = \sqrt[8]{x}$$

$$4^{\frac{2}{3}} \times 4^{\frac{8}{5}} = 4^{\left(\frac{2}{3}+\frac{8}{5}\right)} = 4^{\frac{34}{15}} = \sqrt[15]{4^{34}}$$

$$(3^{-2})^x = 3^{-2x} = \frac{1}{3^{2x}}$$

$$3(xy)^0 = 3$$

$$b^{-1} = \frac{1}{b}$$

$$4^{-2} = \frac{1}{4^2} = \frac{1}{16}$$

$$x^{-\frac{2}{5}} \times z^{-\frac{2}{5}} = (xz)^{-\frac{2}{5}} = \frac{1}{(xz)^{\frac{2}{5}}} = \frac{1}{\sqrt[5]{(xz)^2}}$$

$$1^{\frac{-3v^4}{2w}} = 1 \text{ (one raised to any power is still one)}$$

Roots and Radicals

We just saw that roots express fractional exponents. But it is often easier to work with roots in a different format. When a number or term is raised to a fractional power, the expression can be converted into one involving a root in the following way:

$$x^{\frac{a}{b}} = \sqrt[b]{x^a}$$

with the $\sqrt{}$ sign as the radical sign, and x^a as the radicand.

Roots are like exponents, only backwards. For example, to square the number 3 is to multiple 3 by itself two times: $3^2 = 3 \times 3 = 9$. The root of 9, $\sqrt{9}$, is 3. In other words, the square root of a number is the number that, when squared, is equal to the given number.

Square roots are the most commonly used roots, but there are also cube roots (numbers raised to ⅓), fourth roots, fifth roots, etc. Each root is represented by a radical sign with the appropriate number next to it (a radical without any superscript denotes a square root). For example, cube roots are shown as $\sqrt[3]{}$, fourth roots as $\sqrt[4]{}$, and so on. These roots of higher degrees operate the same way square roots do. Because $3^3 = 27$, it follows that the cube root of 27 is 3.

Here are a few examples:

$$\sqrt{16} = 4 \text{ because } 4^2 = 16$$
$$\sqrt[4]{81} = 3 \text{ because } 3^4 = 81$$
$$\sqrt{\frac{1}{4}} = \frac{1}{2} \text{ because } \left(\frac{1}{2}\right)^2 = \frac{1}{4}$$
$$\text{If } x^n = y, \text{ then } \sqrt[n]{y} = x$$

The same rules that apply to multiplying and dividing exponential terms with the same exponent apply to roots as well. Consider these examples:

$$\sqrt[n]{x} \times \sqrt[n]{y} = \sqrt[n]{x \times y}$$
$$\sqrt{8} \times \sqrt{2} = \sqrt{8 \times 2} = \sqrt{16} = 4$$

Just be sure that the roots are of the same degree (i.e. you are multiplying or dividing all square roots, or all roots of the fifth power).

Scientific Notation

Scientific notation is a convention used to express large numbers. A number written in scientific notation has two parts:

1. A number between 1 and 10.

2. The power of 10 by which you must multiply the first number in order to obtain the large number that is being represented.

The following examples express numbers in scientific notation:

$$3,000,000 = 3.0 \times 10^6$$
$$4,123,452,734 = 4.123452734 \times 10^9$$
$$15 = 1.5 \times 10^1$$
$$13,598,000 = 1.3598 \times 10^7$$

Scientific notation is particularly useful when a large number contains many zeroes or needs to be approximated because of its unwieldy size. Approximating quantities in scientific notation can prevent unnecessarily messy calculations. Look at the following expression:

$$13{,}234{,}836{,}823{,}436 \times 555{,}317{,}897{,}542{,}222{,}010$$

Finding the product would be pretty nasty—even when you're using a calculator. Approximating each number using scientific notation makes the problem a lot easier:

$$13{,}234{,}836{,}823{,}436 \times 555{,}317{,}897{,}542{,}222{,}010 \approx 1.32 \times 10^{13} \times 5.55 \times 10^{17}$$
$$= (1.32 \times 5.55) \times (10^{13} \times 10^{17}) = 7.326 \times 10^{30}$$

When we compare this approximation to the actual product, we find that we were less than 1% off. Not too shabby.

Also, note the way in which we combined the terms in the last example to make the multiplication a little simpler:

$$1.32 \times 10^{13} \times 5.55 \times 10^{17} = (1.32 \times 5.55) \times (10^{13} \times 10^{17})$$

In general terms:

$$(a \times 10^{x}) \times (b \times 10^{y}) = (a \times b) \times 10^{x+y}$$

Often, this type of simplification can make your calculations easier.

Scientific Notation and Calculators

On many calculators, scientific notation is written differently than what you've seen here. Instead of 3.1×10^{33}, your calculator might read 3.1 E33. The capital letter "E" has the same role as the "$\times 10^{(\text{power})}$," only it's a little shorter. In general, scientific notation allows you to work with numbers that might either be tedious to manipulate or too large to fit on your calculator.

Logarithms

Logarithms are closely related to exponents and roots. A logarithm is the power to which you must raise a given number, called the base, to equal another number. For example, $\log_2 8 = 3$ because $2^3 = 8$. In this case, 2 is the base and 3 is the logarithm.

The Math IIC likes to use logarithms in algebra problems, mostly in simple equation solving problems (which we will cover in the next chapter). For these types of questions, the key is remembering that a logarithm problem is really an exponent problem. Keeping this in mind should help reduce the mystery that seems to surround logarithms. In fact, once you get the hang of it, you'll realize that solving logarithmic equations is actually quite easy.

Having defined a logarithm in a sentence, let's show it symbolically. The three equations below are equivalent:

$$\log_a x = b, a^b = x, \text{ and } \sqrt[b]{x} = a$$

For example, $\log_4 16 = 2$ because $4^2 = 16$ and $\sqrt{16} = 4$. You should be able to see now why the three topics of exponents, roots, and logarithms are often linked together. Each provides a way to isolate one of the three variables in these types of equations. In the example above, a is the base, b is the exponent, and x is the product. Respectively, finding the root, logarithm, and exponent isolates these values.

Logarithms and Calculators

Unless the logarithm is a very simple one, you won't be able to mentally calculate it—so the calculator becomes an important tool. But there is one critical thing you need to be aware of. On your calculator, the "LOG" button assumes a base of ten. This means that for the equation $\log_4 16 = 2$, if you punched in LOG 16, you would get $\log_{10} 16$.

Some calculators can calculate a logarithm with any base, but less advanced calculators might not. When you need to calculate a logarithm with a base other than 10, and your calculator does not have the capability, keep in mind that: $\log_b a = \log_c a / \log_c b$.

Calculate a few logarithms for practice:

$$\log_{10} 1000 = 3 \text{ because } 10^3 = 1000$$
$$\log_{\frac{1}{2}} \frac{1}{4} = 2 \text{ because } \left(\frac{1}{2}\right)^2 = \frac{1}{4}$$
$$\log_4 \frac{1}{16} = -2 \text{ because } 4^{-2} = \frac{1}{16}$$

Operations on Logarithms

You will rarely see a test question involving basic logarithms such as $\log_{10} 100$, or $\log_2 4$. In particular, on the logarithm questions you'll see in the algebra chapter, you'll need to be able to manipulate logarithms within equations. You should therefore know how to perform the basic operations on logarithms:

The Product Rule: when logarithms of the same base are multiplied, the base remains the same, and the exponents can be added:

$$\log_x jk = \log_x j + \log_x k$$
$$\log_2 4 + \log_2 3 = \log_2 12$$

The Quotient Rule: when logarithms of the same base are divided, the exponents must be subtracted:

$$\log_x \frac{j}{k} = \log_x j - \log_x k$$
$$\log \frac{1}{2} = \log 1 - \log 2$$

The Power Rule: when a logarithm is raised to a power, the exponent can be brought in front and multiplied by the logarithm:

$$\log_x c^n = n \times \log_x c$$
$$\log x^4 = 4 \log x$$

You might have noticed how similar these rules are to those for exponents and roots. This similarity results from the fact that logarithms are just another way to express an exponent.

Natural Logarithms

Natural logarithms appear on the Math IIC but not on the Math IC test. A natural logarithm is one with a base of e. The value e is a naturally occurring number, infinitely long, that can be found in growth and decay models. The natural logarithm will most likely be used in problems of growth and decay.

A common numerical approximation of e is 2.718, which you could easily discover by punching e^1 into your calculator. The symbol for a natural logarithm is ln, instead of log. The following three equations are equivalent:

$$\ln x = b$$
$$\log_e x = b$$
$$e^b = x$$

Working with natural logarithms is just like working with logarithms; the only difference is that the base for natural logarithms is always e. You might also be asked to identify the graphs of $\ln x$ and e^x. Take a good look at their general shapes:

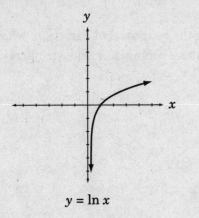

$y = \ln x$

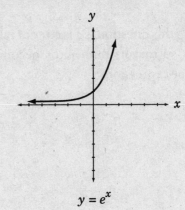

$y = e^x$

Review Questions

1. What is $\dfrac{\frac{1}{3}}{\frac{3}{2}} \times \dfrac{\frac{2}{1}}{\frac{1}{6}}$?

   (A) $\dfrac{2}{9}$ (B) $\dfrac{9}{4}$ (C) $\dfrac{15}{4}$ (D) 6   (E) 8

2. $\left| 4^{-\frac{1}{2}} - 3(8^0) \right| =$

   (A) $-\dfrac{1}{4}$ (B) $\dfrac{5}{4}$ (C) $\dfrac{5}{2}$ (D) 16   (E) 20

3. Evaluate the following expression for $x = 3$: $\dfrac{2x}{x^2} \times \left(\dfrac{x}{4} + \dfrac{x}{5} \right)$.

   (A) $\dfrac{2}{9}$ (B) $\dfrac{1}{3}$ (C) $\dfrac{1}{2}$ (D) $\dfrac{9}{10}$ (E) $\dfrac{121}{60}$

4. If x is even and positive, y is negative, and z is odd, what is a possible value of xy^z?

   (A) −24   (B) −5   (C) 1   (D) 4   (E) 25

5. Evaluate the following expression for $x = 4$: $3x^2 + x^{-1} + \log_x 64$

   (A) $\dfrac{15}{4}$

   (B)   4
   (C)   15
   (D)   32
   (E)   195

Explanations

1. **(E)**

Answering this question is a matter of taking the reciprocal of a fraction, which means flipping it so that its numerator becomes the denominator and vice versa. We can simplify the expression:

$$\frac{1}{\frac{3}{2}} \times \frac{2}{\frac{1}{6}} = \frac{2}{3} \times (2)(6)$$

$$= \frac{2}{3} \times 12$$

$$= \frac{24}{3}$$

$$= 8$$

2. **(C)**

First, before taking the absolute value of the expression, which is just the positive "version" of the resulting value, you need to carry out the expression within the absolute value signs. The first term, $4^{-1/2}$, uses the properties that any number or term raised to a negative power is equal to the reciprocal of that base raised to the opposite power and that a fractional power is equivalent to taking the root. Therefore, $4^{-1/2} = 1/\sqrt{4} = \frac{1}{2}$. The second term, $3(8^0) = 3$, since any number to the 0 power is equal to 1. So, now we can find a value for the expression:

$$\left|4^{\frac{-1}{2}} - 3(8^0)\right| = \left|\frac{1}{2} - 3\right| = \left|-\frac{5}{2}\right| = \frac{5}{2}$$

3. **(D)**

This is a simple substitution problem. Plug in 3 for x and simplify. Noticing the fact that the least common multiple of 4 and 5 is 20 makes the simplification process easier:

$$\frac{2x}{x^2} \times \left(\frac{x}{4} + \frac{x}{5}\right) = \frac{6}{9} \times \left(\frac{3}{4} + \frac{3}{5}\right)$$
$$= \frac{2}{3} \times \left(\frac{15}{20} + \frac{12}{20}\right)$$
$$= \frac{2}{3} \times \frac{27}{20}$$
$$= \frac{54}{60}$$
$$= \frac{9}{10}$$

4. **(A)**

A negative base raised to an odd power, like y^z, is negative. When this is multiplied by a positive even number, the result is negative and even. –24 is the only negative even choice among the possibilities, so it must be the right answer.

5. **(E)**

This is a simple substitution question as long as you know logarithms and remember the rules for division by a fraction. After substituting 4 into the equation in place of x, the expression simplifies to

$$3 \times 16 \div \frac{1}{4} + 3 = 48 \div \frac{1}{4} + 3$$
$$= 192 + 3$$
$$= 195$$

Algebra

AKE A MOMENT TO FLIP THROUGH this chapter. Wow, you must be thinking, it's really long. You now have an idea of how important algebra is to the Math IIC test. About 20 percent of the Math IIC questions center on algebra, in addition to the numerous other questions whose solutions indirectly rely on algebraic techniques or concepts.

Before you get overwhelmed, take a step back and look at the good news. First, the algebra tested on the math Subject Tests is not all that difficult. Second, the Math IIC test's writers focus on a limited set of algebraic topics, so you don't need to know every algebraic concept. As long as you can handle the algebra in this chapter, you'll be in fine shape for the test.

Math IIC Algebra Strategies

There are usually at least two ways to answer most algebra problems on the Math IIC. You can often try to solve a problem by setting up and solving algebraic equations. Alternatively, you can look for shortcuts in the problem that allow you to find the solution without a lot of math. Finally, you can often substitute numbers from the answer choice and use the process of elimination to discover the right answer.

None of these methods is always better than the others; the best method for solving a problem is the one that will lead you to the correct answer most quickly. Remain flexible in your approach to each question and choose the method that best suits the problem. For a problem you know how to solve, using algebra is probably the quickest method. In contrast, a problem that has you stumped might become easy if you try to plug in some answers. As you take more and more practice tests, you'll get better at recognizing patterns in the test, and you'll find yourself using more shortcuts. When you study your practice tests and look over the algebra questions you got wrong, you should think about the method you employed. To really get the most out of your practice tests, you should analyze not only the questions you get wrong, but also the questions you get right to make sure that you solved them in the quickest way.

We'll thoroughly explain the different problem-solving approaches, and you can decide for yourself which method to choose.

Let's use a sample algebra problem to illustrate these varying approaches:

> A baseball player travels from his home city, Jasonville, to Giambia City for a baseball game. He drives at 50 miles an hour. After the game, he travels back home, and takes a flight that travels at 500 miles an hour. If the distance from Jasonville to Giambia City is 250 miles, and it took him *j* hours longer to drive than to fly, what is *j*?

(A) 1
(B) 3.5
(C) 4
(D) 4.5
(E) 12

The Algebra Way

This question is a simple rate problem that can be solved with a few basic equations.

Since traveling time = distance ÷ speed, it took him:

$$250 \text{ miles} \div 50 \text{ miles an hour} = 5 \text{ hours}$$

to drive to Giambia City. To find the duration of his flight, we use the same rate formula:

$$250 \text{ miles} \div 500 \text{ miles an hour} = .5 \text{ miles an hour}$$

It took the player:

$$5 \text{ hours} - .5 \text{ hours} = 4.5 \text{ hours}$$

longer to drive. (D) is the correct answer.

Substitution

Sometimes you might be unsure about how to approach a problem, or don't have the time to think out the proper equations. In such instances, substitution might be the best method, especially with the more difficult questions at the end of the test. All you have to do is substitute the answer choices back into the problem, and see whether the given information holds true.

The process of plugging in is simple. First, you should make full use of the fact that the answer choices on the Math IIC are always presented in ascending or descending value. So you should almost always start by plugging in answer choice (C), since if it doesn't turn out to be the answer, you can usually tell whether to try a smaller or larger answer choice. Now, to solve the question: it takes the baseball player $250 \div 50 = 5$ hours to drive to Giambia City. So, if it takes him (C) 4 hours more to drive, then it takes him $5 - 4 = 1$ hour to fly back to Jasonville. But the question tells us that in 1 hour, he could fly 500 miles. Therefore, it must take him longer than 4 hours more to drive than to fly. Next, we try (D) 4.5. It takes him $5 - 4.5 = .5$ hours to fly, which means that he travels $500 \times .5 = 250$ miles on his flight. Yes, (D) is the answer.

Picking Numbers

Picking numbers is a variation of plugging in and should only be used when the answer choices contain variables. A modified version of our original sample question shows what kind of problems lend themselves to picking numbers.

> A baseball player travels from his home city, Jasonville, to Giambia City for a baseball game. He drives at m miles an hour. After the game, he flies home instead, traveling at p miles an hour. If the distance from Jasonville to Giambia City is v miles, and it took him j hours longer to drive than to fly, what is j?
>
> (A) $\dfrac{mp}{v}$ (B) $\dfrac{v+p}{v+m}$ (C) $\dfrac{pv-pj}{vj}$ (D) $\dfrac{vm-vp}{mp}$ (E) $\dfrac{5v}{m-v}$

This question asks you to figure out which set of variables correctly solves the problem. But thinking in terms of variables can sometimes be unintuitive. Picking numbers allows you to transform variables into concrete numbers.

To use the Picking Numbers method, you need to select numbers and plug them into the answer choices. You're essentially trying to eliminate the variables from the problem by replacing them with numbers that retain the relationships of the variables. It doesn't matter what specific numbers you plug into a problem. The same answer choice will always surface as long as you plug in consistently and follow all guidelines given by the problem.

For example, in the above problem, let's choose to let $m = 5$, $v = 100$, and $p = 10$. Clearly, these numbers aren't realistic (who flies at 10 miles an hour?), but your goal is to pick numbers that are easy to manipulate. Using our numbers, it takes the baseball player $100 \div 5 = 20$ hours to drive, and $100 \div 10 = 10$ hours to fly. So, it takes him $20 - 10 = 10$ hours longer to drive. Now all you have to do is replace v, p, and m in each of the answer choices with 5, 100, and 10, respectively. You are left with simple arithmetic expressions, and only (D) produces an answer of 10.

Very rarely, more than one answer choice will result in the correct answer for the first set of numbers you picked. When this occurs, simply plug in a different set of numbers. You will almost never have to plug in more than two sets of numbers.

When picking numbers, you must check through all the answer solutions with your chosen numbers. Obviously, this will slow you down, but that's the price you pay for using this method. Picking Numbers gives you a mechanical method for solving tricky problems, and also allows you to check your math for careless calculations.

Finally, when you are picking numbers, avoid 0, 1, or any numbers that already appear in the answer choices. You should also make sure that you try to use a unique number for each variable. Otherwise, you can over-simplify the expressions you are dealing with and accidentally pick the wrong answer.

The Bottom Line

As you can see, there is no "right" method to solving all algebra problems. Some methods work better than others depending on the question. Part of your practice for the Math IIC test will help get you comfortable with algebra questions so that you can quickly choose which method you want to use for each question.

Now we'll review the topics of algebra covered in the Math IIC Subject Test.

Equation Solving

There are a number of algebraic terms you should know in order to be able to talk and think about algebra.

Variable: an unknown quantity, written as a letter. x and y are the most commonly used letters for variables, but a variable can be represented by any letter in the English (or even Greek) alphabet. Variables allow you to describe general situations without specific numbers.

Constant: a quantity that does not change. In other words, a number.

Term: a constant or variable and its coefficient. In an algebraic equation, you'll find that addition and subtraction signs often separate terms from one another. For example, in the equation:

$$3x^3 + 2x^2 - 7x + 4 = x - 1$$

the left side contains four terms $\{3x^3, 2x^2, -7x, 4\}$ and the right side contains two terms $\{x, -1\}$.

Expression: any combination of terms. An expression can be as simple as a single constant term, like 5. It can also be as complicated as the sum or difference of many terms, each of which is a combination of constants and variables, such as $\{(x^2 + 2)^3 - 6x\} / 7x^5$. Expressions don't include an "equals" sign—this is what differentiates expressions from equations. Expressions therefore cannot be solved; they can only be simplified.

Equation: two expressions equated to one another.

Writing Equations

For some questions on the Math IIC test, you'll need to transform the problem from a language you're used to—English—into a more useful, albeit less familiar, language. We mean the language of math, of course, and one of your main test-taking responsibilities is to be able to write an equation based on the information given in a problem.

You'll also be asked to find an expression for a certain quantity described in a word problem. The best way to learn how to do these things quickly and effectively is to practice. Here's a sample problem:

> In a sack of 50 marbles, there are 20 more red marbles than blue marbles. All of the
> marbles in the sack are either red or blue. How many blue marbles are in the sack?

To start with, you can write $r + b = 50$, where r is the number of red marbles, and b the number of blue marbles in the sack. This equation tell us that the 50 marbles in the sack are comprised entirely of red marbles and blue marbles.

Now that you have an initial equation, you need to decipher what exactly the question is asking for. In this problem it is clear-cut: How many blue marbles are in the sack? Your mandate is clear: finding the value of b.

Unfortunately, you need more information to do that. You can create a second equation based on the knowledge that there are 20 more red marbles than blue marbles. This part of the word problem can be written in the form of an equation as $r = b + 20$ (or $b = r - 20$).

Let's list the two equations we have so far:

$$r + b = 50$$
$$b = r - 20$$

Using both of these equations, you can solve for b. After a little manipulation, which we'll cover in the coming sections, you'll find that $b = 15$ (and $r = 35$). Don't worry about the solution for now—just focus on how we translated the word problem into equations that lead to the solution.

Algebra

That problem was easy. Here's a harder one:

> Stan sells oranges for c cents apiece. The minimum number of oranges that Stan will sell to an individual is r, but the first f oranges are free ($f < r$). Find an expression for the price in dollars of 35 oranges, if $35 > r$.

According to the problem, we need to find an expression (notice, not an equation) for the price in dollars of 35 oranges. The key to a problem like this one is working step by step. First, find out how many of the 35 oranges aren't free of charge.

$$\text{number of fare oranges} = 35 - f$$

Next, find the price of those oranges.

$$\text{orange price} = (35 - f) \times c$$

But wait. Did you notice that the question asked for the price of 35 oranges in *dollars*? The writers of the Math IIC are a clever bunch, if a bit sneaky. They figure that a good number of test-takers will see only the word "price," and not notice what units are asked for. Well, be careful not to fall into their carefully laid trap.

We know there are 100 cents per dollar, so we can easily convert the price by dividing by 100.

$$35 \text{ oranges} = \frac{(35 - f)c}{100}$$

Before we move to another problem, note that the variable r didn't appear anywhere in the answer. Egad! It is yet another attempt by those devious test-writers to lower your score, and it is a common one at that. You may come across many problems, especially word problems, in which extraneous information is provided only to confuse you. Just because a variable or number appears in a problem doesn't mean that it will be useful in finding the answer.

Here's another problem:

> Gus needs to paint his house, which has a surface area of x square feet. The brand of paint he buys (at a cost of p dollars a can) comes in cans that cover y square feet each. Gus also needs to buy ten pairs of new jeans (he is uncoordinated and spills often). They cost d dollars a pair. If Gus makes these purchases, what is the difference (in dollars) between the cost of the paint and the cost of the jeans? Assume he doesn't buy any excess paint—that is, the required amount is not a fraction of a can.

This word problem is long and complicated, but you need to carry out just 4 steps to solve it:

1. Gus must buy $^{xp}\!/_y$ cans of paint to cover his house.

2. This will cost him $^{xp}\!/_y$ dollars.

3. The jeans Gus buys cost $10d$ dollars.

4. Thus, the difference, in dollars, between the cost of the paint and the cost of the jeans is $^{xp}\!/_y - 10d$.

For the rest of this chapter, we'll constantly be converting word problems into equations. If you're still uncomfortable doing this, don't worry. You'll get a lot more practice in the sections to come.

Manipulating Equations

Now that you know how to set up an equation, the next thing you need to do is solve for the value that the question asks for. Above all, the most important thing to remember when manipulating equations is that each side of the equation must be manipulated in the same way. If you divide one side of an equation by 3, you must divide the other side by 3. If you take the square root of one side of an equation, take the square root of the other. If you ask one side of the equation out on a date, ask the other. Neither side will think you're a two-timer. They'll just think you're a sound mathematician.

By treating the two sides of the equation in the same way, you won't violate the equality of the equation. You will, of course, change the *form* of the equation—that's the point of manipulating it. But the equation will always remain true as long as you do the same thing to both sides.

For example, let's look at what happens when you manipulate the equation $3x + 2 = 5$, with $x = 1$.

1. Subtract 2 from both sides:

$$3x + 2 - 2 = 5 - 2$$
$$3x + 0 = 3$$
$$3(1) = 3$$
$$3 = 3$$

2. Multiply both sides by 2:

$$2(3x + 2) = 2(5)$$
$$6x + 4 = 10$$
$$6(1) + 4 = 10$$
$$10 = 10$$

3. Add 4 to both sides:

$$3x + 2 + 4 = 5 + 4$$
$$3x + 6 = 9$$
$$3(1) + 6 = 9$$
$$9 = 9$$

These examples show that you can tamper with the equation, as long as you tamper the same way on both sides. If you follow this rule, you can manipulate the question without breaking its essential equality or affecting the values of its variables.

Solving an Equation with One Variable

To solve an equation with one variable, you must manipulate the equation to isolate that variable on one side of the equation. Then, by definition, that variable is equal to whatever is on the other side, and you have successfully "solved for the variable."

For the quickest results, take the equation apart in the opposite order of the standard order of operations. That is, first add and subtract any extra terms on the same side as the variable. Then, multiply and divide anything on the same side of the variable. Next, raise both sides of the equation to a power or take their roots. And finally, do anything inside parentheses. This process is PEMDAS in reverse (SADMEP!). The idea is to "undo" everything that is being done to the variable so that it will be isolated in the end. Let's look at an example:

$$\text{Solve for } x \text{ in the equation } \frac{(3x^2 + 5) \times 3}{4} + 1 = 61.$$

In this equation, the variable x is being squared, multiplied by 3, added to 5, etc. We need to do the opposite of all these operations in order to isolate x, and thus solve the equation.

First, subtract 1 from both sides of the equation:

$$\frac{(3x^2 + 5) \times 3}{4} + 1 - 1 = 61 - 1$$
$$\frac{(3x^2 + 5) \times 3}{4} = 60$$

Then, multiply both sides of the equation by 4:

$$\frac{(3x^2 + 5) \times 3}{4} \times 4 = 60 \times 4$$
$$(3x^2 + 5) \times 3 = 240$$

Next, divide both sides of the equation by 3:

$$(3x^2 + 5) \times 3 \div 3 = 240 \div 3$$
$$3x^2 + 5 = 80$$

Now, subtract 5 from both sides of the equation:

$$3x^2 + 5 - 5 = 80 - 5$$
$$3x^2 = 75$$

Again, divide both sides of the equation by 3:

$$3x^2 \div 3 = 75 \div 3$$
$$x^2 = 25$$

Finally, take the square root of each side of the equation:

$$\sqrt{x^2} = \sqrt{25}$$
$$x = \pm 5$$

We have isolated x to show that $x = \pm 5$.

Sometimes the variable that needs to be isolated is not located conveniently. For example, it might be in a denominator, or an exponent. Equations like these are solved the same way as any other equation, except that you may need different techniques to isolate the variable. Let's look at a couple of examples:

Algebra

Solve for x in the equation $\frac{1}{x} + 2 = 4$.

$$\frac{1}{x} + 2 = 4$$

$$\frac{1}{x} = 2$$

$$1 = 2x$$

$$x = \frac{1}{2}$$

The key step is to multiply both sides by x to extract the variable from the denominator. It is not at all uncommon to have to move the variable from one side to the other in order to isolate it. Here's another, slightly more complicated, example:

Solve for x in the equation $2^x = 3^{x+2}$.

$$2^x = 3^{x+2}$$

$$\log 2^x = \log 3^{x+2}$$

$$x \log 2 = (x + 2) \log 3$$

$$x \log 2 = x \log 3 + 2 \log 3$$

$$x \log 2 - x \log 3 = 2 \log 3$$

$$x(\log 2 - \log 3) = 2 \log 3$$

$$x = \frac{2 \log 3}{\log 2 - \log 3}$$

$$x \approx 5.42$$

This question is a good example of how it's not always simple to isolate a variable. (Don't worry about the logarithm in this problem—we'll review these later on in the chapter.) However, as you can see, even the thorniest problems can be solved systematically as long as you have the right tools. In the next section we'll discuss factoring and distributing, two techniques that were used in this example.

Having just given you a very basic introduction to solving equations, we'll reemphasize two things:

1. Do the same thing to both sides.

2. Work backwards (with respect to the order of operations).

Now we'll work with some more interesting tools you will need to solve certain equations.

Distributing and Factoring

Distributing and factoring are two of the most important techniques in algebra. They give you ways of manipulating expressions without changing the expression's value. In other words, distributing and factoring are tools of reorganization. Since they don't affect the value of the expression, you can factor or distribute one side of the equation without doing the same for the other side of the equation.

The basis for both techniques is the following property, called the distributive property:

$$a \times (b + c + \dots) = a \times b + a \times c + \dots$$

Similarly,

$$a \times (-b - c - \dots) = -a \times b - a \times c - \dots$$

a can be any kind of term, from a variable to a constant, to a combination of the two.

Distributing

When you "distribute" a factor into an expression within parentheses, you simply multiply each term inside the parentheses by the factor outside the parentheses. For example, consider the expression $3y(y^2 - 6)$:

$$3y(y^2 - 6) = 3y^3 - 18y$$

If we set the original, undistributed expression equal to another expression, you can see why distributing facilitates the solving of some equations. Solving $3y(y^2 - 6) = 3y^3 + 36$ looks quite difficult. But when you distribute the $3y$, you get:

$$3y^3 - 18y = 3y^3 + 36$$

Subtracting $3y^3$ from both sides gives us:

$$-18y = 36$$
$$y = \frac{36}{-18}$$
$$y = -2$$

Factoring

Factoring an expression is essentially the opposite of distributing. Consider the expression $4x^3 - 8x^2 + 4x$, for example. You can factor out the greatest common factor of the terms, which is $4x$:

$$4x^3 - 8x + 4x = 4x(x^2 - 2 + 1)$$

The expression simplifies further:

$$4x(x^2 - 2 + 1) = 4x(x - 1)^2$$

See how useful these techniques are? You can group or ungroup quantities in an equation to make your calculations easier. In the last example from the previous section on manipulating equations, we distributed *and* factored to solve an equation. First, we distributed the quantity log 3 into the sum of *x* and 2 (on the right side of the equation). We later factored the term *x* out of the expression *x* log 2 − *x* log 3 (on the left side of the equation).

Distributing eliminates parentheses, and factoring creates them. It's your job as a Math IIC mathematician to decide which technique will best help you solve a problem.

Let's look at a few examples:

$$3(x + y + 4) = 3x + 3y + 12 \quad \text{3 is distributed.}$$
$$2x + 4x + 6x + 8x = 2x(1 + 2 + 3 + 4) \quad \text{2}x \text{ is factored out.}$$
$$x^2(x - 1) = x^3 - x^2 \quad x^2 \text{ is distributed.}$$
$$xy^2(xy^2 + x^2y) = x^2y^4 + x^3y^3 \quad xy^2 \text{ is distributed.}$$
$$14xy^2 - 4xy + 22y = 2y(7xy - 2x + 11) \quad \text{2}y \text{ is factored out.}$$

Combining Like Terms

There are other steps you can take to simplify expressions or equations. Combining like terms is one of the simpler techniques you can use, and it involves adding or subtracting the coefficients of variables that are raised to the same power. For example, by combining like terms, the expression

$$x^2 - x^3 + 4x^2 + 3x^3$$

can be simplified to

$$(-1+3)x^3 + (1+4)x^2 = 2x^3 + 5x^2$$

by adding the coefficients of the variable x^3 together, and the coefficients of x^2 together.

The point is, you'd rather have one term, $7x^2$, instead of x^2, $3x^2$, $-3x^2$, $2x^2$, and $4x^2$ all floating around in your expression. A general formula for combining like pairs looks like this:

$$ax^k + bx^k + cx^k = x^k(a+b+c)$$

Zero Product Rule

When the product of any number of terms is zero, you know that at least one of the terms is equal to zero. For example, if $xy = 0$, you know that either:

1. $x = 0$ and $y \neq 0$,

2. $y = 0$ and $x \neq 0$, or

3. $x = y = 0$

This is useful in a situation like the following:

$$(x+4)(x-3) = 0$$
$$(x+4) = 0 \text{ or } (x-3) = 0$$

By the zero product rule, you know that $(x + 4) = 0$ or $(x - 3) = 0$. In this equation, either $x = -4$ or $x = 3$, since one of the expressions in parentheses must be equal to 0. Consider this equation:

$$3x^2(x+2) = 0$$

Again, since $3x^2$ or $(x + 2)$ must equal 0, we know that either $x = 0$ or $x = -2$.

Keep your eye out for a zero product—it's a big time-saver, especially when you have multiple-choice answers to choose from.

Algebra

Absolute Value

To solve an equation in which the variable is within absolute value brackets, you must divide the equation into two equations. The two equations are necessary because an absolute value really defines two equal values, one positive and one negative. The most basic example of this is an equation of the form $|x| = c$. In this case, either $x = c$ or $x = -c$.

A slightly more complicated example is this:

$|x + 3| = 5$. Solve for x.

In this problem, you must solve two equations: First, solve for x in the equation $x + 3 = 5$. In this case, $x = 2$. Then, solve for x in the equation $x + 3 = -5$. In this case, $x = -8$. So the solutions to the equation $|x + 3| = 5$ are $x = \{-8, 2\}$.

Generally speaking, to solve an equation in which the variable is within absolute value brackets, first isolate the expression within the absolute value brackets, and then create two equations. Keep one of these two equations the same, while in the other equation, negate one side of the equation. In either case, the absolute value of the expression within brackets will be the same. This is why there are always two solutions to absolute value problems (unless the variable is equal to 0, which is neither positive nor negative).

Here is one more example:

Solve for x in terms of y in the equation $3 \left| \dfrac{x+2}{3} \right| = y^2 - 1$.

First, isolate the expression within the absolute value brackets:

$$\left| \frac{x+2}{3} \right| = \frac{y^2 - 1}{3}$$

Then solve for the variable as if the expression within absolute value brackets were positive:

$$\frac{x+2}{3} = \frac{y^2 - 1}{3}$$
$$x + 2 = y^2 - 1$$
$$x = y^2 - 3$$

Algebra

Next, solve for the variable as if the expression within absolute value brackets were negative:

$$\frac{x+2}{3} = -\frac{y^2-1}{3}$$
$$x+2 = -y^2 + 1$$
$$x = -y^2 - 1$$

The solution set for x is $\{y^2 - 3, -y^2 - 1\}$.

Inequalities

Before you get too comfortable with expressions and equations, we should introduce inequalities. An inequality is like an equation, but instead of relating equal quantities, it specifies exactly how two expressions are unequal. There are four types of inequalities:

1. $x > y \leftrightarrow$ "x is greater than y."

2. $x < y \leftrightarrow$ "x is less than y."

3. $x \geq y \leftrightarrow$ "x is greater than or equal to y."

4. $x \leq y \leftrightarrow$ "x is less than or equal to y."

Solving inequalities is exactly like solving equations except for one very important difference: when both sides of an inequality are multiplied or divided by a negative number, the relationship between the two sides changes and so the direction of the inequality must be switched.

Here are a few examples:

Solve for x in the inequality $\frac{x}{2} - 3 < 2y$.

$$\frac{x}{2} - 3 < 2y$$
$$\frac{x}{2} < 2y + 3$$
$$x < 2(2y + 3)$$
$$x < 4y + 6$$

Solve for x in the inequality $\frac{4}{x} \geq -2$.

$$\frac{4}{x} \geq -2$$
$$4 \geq -2x$$
$$-2 \leq x$$

Notice that in the last example, the inequality had to be reversed. Another way to express the solution is $x \geq -2$. To help you remember that multiplication or division by a negative number reverses the direction of the inequality, recall that if $x > y$, then $-x < -y$, just as $5 > 4$ and $-5 < -4$. Intuitively, this makes sense, and it might help you remember this special rule of inequalities.

There is a critical difference between the solutions to equalities and solutions to inequalities. The number of solutions to an equation is usually equal to the highest power of the equation. A linear equation (highest term of x) has one solution, a quadratic equation (highest term of x^2) has two solutions, and a cubic equation (highest term of x^3) has three solutions. In an *inequality*, this rule does not hold true. As you can see from the above examples, there are often infinite solutions to inequalities: the solutions are often graphed as planes rather than points.

Absolute Value and Inequalities

An equation without any absolute values generally results in, at most, only a few different solutions. Solutions to inequalities are often large regions of the x-y plane, such as $x < 5$. The introduction of the absolute value, as we've seen before, usually introduces two sets of solutions. The same is true when absolute values are introduced to inequalities: the solutions often come in the form of two regions of the x-y plane.

If the absolute value is less than a given quantity, then the solution is a single range, with a lower and an upper bound. For example,

Solve for x in the inequality $|2x - 4| \leq 6$.

First, solve for the upper bound:

$$2x - 4 \leq 6$$
$$2x \leq 10$$
$$x \leq 5$$

Second, solve for the lower bound:

$$2x - 4 \geq -6$$
$$2x \geq -2$$
$$x \geq -1$$

Now, combine the two bounds into a range of values for x. $-1 \leq x \leq 5$ is the solution.

The other solution for an absolute value inequality involves disjoint ranges: one whose lower bound is negative infinity and whose upper bound is a real number, and one whose lower bound is a real number and whose upper bound is infinity. This occurs when the absolute value is greater than a given quantity. For example,

Solve for x in the inequality $|3x + 4| > 16$.

First, solve for the upper range:

$$3x + 4 > 16$$
$$3x > 12$$
$$x > 4$$

Then, solve for the lower range:

$$3x + 4 < -16$$
$$3x < -20$$
$$x < -\frac{20}{3}$$

Now combine the two ranges to form the solution, which is two disjoint ranges: $-\infty < x < -{}^{20}\!/_3$ or $4 < x < \infty$.

When working with absolute values, it is important to first isolate the expression within absolute value brackets. Then, and only then, should you solve separately for the cases in which the quantity is positive and negative.

Ranges

Inequalities are also used to express the range of values that a variable can take on. $a < x < b$ means that the value of x is greater than a and less than b. Consider the following word problem example:

A very complicated board game has the following recommendation on the box: "This game is appropriate for people older than 40, but no older than 65." What is the range of the age of people for which the board game is appropriate?

Let a be the age of people for which the board game is appropriate. The lower bound of a is 40, and the upper bound is 65. The range of a does not include its lower bound (it is appropriate for people "older than 40"), but it does include its upper bound ("no older than 65," i.e., 65 is appropriate, but 66 is not). Therefore, the range of the age of people for which the board game is appropriate can be expressed by the inequality:

$$40 < a \leq 65$$

Algebra

Here is another example:

> A company manufactures car parts. As is the case with any system of mass production, small errors occur on virtually every part. The key for this company to succeed in making viable car parts is to keep the errors within a specific range. The company knows that a particular piece they manufacture will not work if it weighs less than 98% of its target weight or more than 102% of its target weight. If the target weight of this piece is 21.5 grams, in what range of weights must the piece measure for it to function?

The boundary weights of this car part are .98 × 21.5 = 21.07 and 1.02 × 21.5 = 21.93 grams. The problem states that the piece cannot weigh *less* than the minimum weight or *more* than the maximum weight in order for it to work. This means that the part will function at boundary weights themselves, and the lower and upper bounds are included. The answer to the problem is $21.07 \leq x \leq 21.93$, where x is the weight of the part in grams.

Finding the range of a particular variable is essentially an exercise in close reading. Every time you come across a question involving ranges, you should carefully scrutinize the problem to pick out whether or not a particular variable's range includes its bounds. This inclusion is the difference between "less than or equal to" and simply "less than."

Operations on Ranges

Operations like addition, subtraction, and multiplication can be performed on ranges just as they are performed on variables or inequalities. For example:

> If $4 < x < 7$, what is the range of $2x + 3$?

To solve this problem, simply manipulate the range like an inequality until you have a solution. Begin with the original range:

$$4 < x < 7$$

Then multiply the inequality by 2.

$$8 < 2x < 14$$

Add 3 to the inequality, and you have the answer.

$$11 < 2x + 3 < 17$$

There is one crucial rule that you need to know about multiplying ranges: if you multiply a range by a negative number, you *must* flip the greater than or less than signs. For instance, if you multiply the range $2 < x < 8$ by -1, the new range will be $-2 > x > -8$. Math IIC questions that ask you to perform operations on ranges of one variable will often test your alertness by making you multiply the range by a negative number.

Some range problems on the Math IIC will be made slightly more difficult by the inclusion of more than one variable. In general, the same basic procedures for dealing with one-variable ranges apply to adding, subtracting, and multiplying two-variable ranges.

Addition with Ranges of Two or More Variables

If $-2 < x < 8$ and $0 < y < 5$, what is the range of $x + y$?

Simply add the ranges. The lower bound is $-2 + 0 = -2$. The upper bound is $8 + 5 = 13$. Therefore, $-2 < x + y < 13$.

Subtraction with Ranges of Two or More Variables

Suppose $4 < s < 7$ and $-3 < t < -1$. What is the range of $s - t$?

In this case, you have to find the range of $-t$. By multiplying the range of t by -1 and reversing the direction of the inequalities, we find that $1 < -t < 3$. Now we can simply add the ranges again to find the range of $s - t$. $4 + 1 = 5$, and $7 + 3 = 10$. Therefore, $5 < s - t < 10$.

In general, to subtract ranges, find the range of the *opposite* of the variable being subtracted, and then add the ranges like usual.

Multiplication with Ranges of Two or More Variables

If $-1 < j < 4$ and $6 < k < 12$, what is the range of jk?

First, multiply the lower bound of one variable by the lower and upper bounds of the other variable.

$$-1 \times 6 = -6$$
$$-1 \times 12 = -12$$

Then, multiply the upper bound of one variable with both bounds of the other variable.

$$4 \times 6 = 24$$
$$4 \times 12 = 48$$

The least of these four products becomes the lower bound, and the greatest is the upper bound. Therefore, $-12 < jk < 48$.

Algebra

Let's try one more example of performing operations on ranges:

If $3 \leq x < 7$ and $-3 \leq y \leq 4$, what is the range of $2(x + y)$?

The first step is to find the range of $x + y$. Notice that the range of y is written backwards, with the upper bound to the left of the variable. Rewrite it first:

$$-3 \leq y \leq 4$$

Next add the ranges to find the range of $x + y$:

$$3 + -3 = 0 \text{ and } 7 + 4 = 11$$

We have our bounds for the range of $x + y$, but are they included in the range? In other words, is the range $0 < x + y < 11$, $0 \leq x + y \leq 11$, or some combination of these two?

The rule to answer this question is the following: if either of the bounds that are being added, subtracted, or multiplied is non-inclusive ($<$ or $>$), then the resulting bound is non-inclusive. Only when both bounds being added, subtracted, or multiplied are inclusive ($\leq$ or $\geq$) is the resulting bound also inclusive.

The range of x includes its lower bound, 3, but not its upper bound, 7. The range of y includes both its bounds. Therefore, the range of $x + y$ is $0 \leq x + y < 11$, and the range of $2(x + y)$ is $0 \leq 2(x + y) < 22$.

Take note: an alternate way of expressing the range of a variable might appear on the Math IIC test. A range can be written by enclosing the lower and upper bounds in parentheses or brackets, depending on whether they are included in the range. Parentheses are used when the bound is not included in the range, and brackets are used when the bound is included in the range. For example, the statement $a < x < b$ can be rewritten "the range of x is (a, b)." The statement $a \leq x \leq b$ can be rewritten "the range of x is $[a, b]$." Finally, the statement $a < x \leq b$ can be rewritten "the range of x is $(a, b]$."

Systems of Equations

Sometimes a question will have a lone equation containing two variables, and using the methods we've discussed thus far will not be enough to solve for the variables. Additional information is needed, and it must come in the form of another equation.

Say, for example, that a single equation uses the two variables x and y. Try as you might, you won't be able to solve for x or y. But given another equation with the same two variables x and y, the values of both variables can be found.

These multiple equations containing the same variables are called systems of equations. For the Math IIC Subject Test, there are essentially two types of systems of equations that you will need to be able to solve. The first, easier, model involves substitution, and the second type involves manipulating equations simultaneously.

Substitution

Simply put, the substitution method involves finding the value of one variable in one equation and then substituting that value into the other equation to solve for the other variable. Here's a straightforward example:

If $x - 4 = y - 3$ and $2y = 6$, what is x?

In this case, we have two equations. The first equation contains x and y. The second contains only y. To solve for x, you must solve for y in the second equation, and then substitute that value for y in the first equation, eliminating the second variable from that equation. If $2y = 6$, then $y = 3$, and substituting that into the first equation:

$$x = y - 3 + 4$$
$$= 3 - 3 + 4$$
$$= 4$$

Here is a slightly more complicated example:

Suppose $3x = y + 5$ and $2y - 2 = 12k$. Solve for x in terms of k.

Again, you cannot solve for x in terms of k using just the first equation. Instead, you must solve for y in terms of k in the second equation, and then substitute that value in the first equation to solve for x.

$$2y - 2 = 12k$$
$$2y = 12k + 2$$
$$y = 6k + 1$$

Then substitute $y = 6k + 1$ into the equation $3x = y + 5$.

$$3x = y + 5$$
$$3x = (6k + 1) + 5$$
$$3x = 6k + 6$$
$$x = 2k + 2$$

Simultaneous Equations

Simultaneous equations refer to equations that must be added or subtracted from each other in order to find a solution. Consider the following example:

Suppose $2x + 3y = 5$ and $-1x - 3y = -7$. What is x?

In this particular problem, you can find the value of x by adding the two equations together. Observe:

$$2x + 3y = 5$$
$$\underline{+(-1x) - 3y = -7}$$
$$x = -2$$

Here is another example:

$6x + 2y = 11$ and $5x + y = 10$. What is $x + y$?

By subtracting the second equation from the first,

$$6x + 2y = 11$$
$$\underline{-(5x + y = 10)}$$
$$x + y = 1$$

we find that $x + y = 1$.

Some test-takers might have seen this problem and been tempted to immediately start trying to solve for x and y individually. The more observant and experienced test-taker would analyze the equations, then notice that by subtracting the second equation from the first, the solution is achieved.

Give this last example a try:

$2x + 3y = -6$ and $-4x + 16y = 13$. What is the value of y?

The question asks you to solve for y, which means that you should find a way to eliminate one of the variables by adding or subtracting the two equations. $4x$ is simply twice $2x$, so by multiplying the first equation by 2, you can then add the equations together to find y.

$2 \times (2x + 3y = -6) = 4x + 6y = -12$

Now add the equations and solve for y.

$$4x + 6y = -12$$
$$\underline{+(-4x) + 16y = 13}$$
$$22y = 1$$
$$y = \frac{1}{22}$$

When you solve for one variable, like we have in this last example, you can solve for the second variable using either of the original equations. If the last question had asked you to calculate the value of xy, for example, you could solve for y, as above, and then solve for x by substitution into either equation. Once you know the independent values of x and y, multiply them together.

The simultaneous equations on the Math IIC will all be this simple. They will have solutions that can be found reasonably easily by adding or subtracting the equations given. Only as a last resort should you solve for one variable in terms of the other and then plug that value into the other equation to solve for the other variable.

Common Word Problems

The writers of the math Subject Test love word problems. They force you, the test-taker, to show your range as a mathematician. They demand that you intelligently read and comprehend the problem, competently set up an equation or two, know how to manipulate these equations effectively, and utilize a good number of algebraic techniques in the process. Luckily, the Math IIC uses only a few types of word problems, and we have the nitty-gritty on all of them.

Rates

Rates are ratios that relate quantities with different units. For example, speed is a rate that relates the two quantities of distance and time. In general, all rates on the Math IIC have the same structure. There will usually be a total quantity, an interval, and the rate of quantity/interval.

The key to solving a rate problem rests in correctly identifying the total quantity, the interval, and the rate. You can then substitute the values into the specific problem. The Math IIC generally asks three different types of rate problems: speed, work, and price.

Speed

In speed rate problems, time (in units of seconds, minutes, or hours, etc.) is the interval, and distance (in units of inches, meters, or miles, etc.) is the total quantity. For example, if you traveled for 4 hours at 25 miles per hour, then:

$$4 \text{ hours} \times 25 \, \frac{\text{miles}}{\text{hour}} = 100 \text{ miles}$$

Note that the units of "hour" canceled out, since the hour in the rate is the denominator of the fraction. But you can be sure that the Math IIC test won't simply give you one of the quantities and the rate and ask you to plug it into the rate formula. Since rate questions are in the form of word problems, the information that you'll need to solve the problem will often be given in a less direct manner.

Here's an example:

> Jim rollerblades 6 miles per hour. One morning, Jim starts rollerblading and doesn't stop until he has gone 60 miles. For how many hours did he rollerblade?

As with many word problems, this question provides more information than we need to solve the problem. We know unnecessary facts such as how Jim is traveling (by rollerblades) and when he started (in the morning). Ignore them and focus on the facts you need to solve the problem.

- **Interval:** 1 hour

- **Rate:** 6 miles per hour

- **Total quantity:** 60 miles traveled

So, we can write:

$$x \text{ hours of rollerblading} = 60 \text{ miles} \div 6 \text{ miles per hour} = 10 \text{ hours}$$

Jim was rollerblading for 10 hours. Here's a slightly more difficult rate problem:

> At a cycling race, there are 50 cyclists in all, each representing a state. The cyclist from California can cycle 528,000 feet per hour. If the race is 480 miles long, how long will it take him to finish the race? (Note that 1 mile = 5280 feet)

This problem gives the rate as 528,000 feet per hour. It also tells you that a total quantity of 480 miles are traveled in the race. A complicating factor in this problem is that the problem contains inconsistent units. In the rate, the distance is measured in feet while the length of the race is given in miles. Always read over the problem carefully and don't forget to adjust the units—you can bet that the answer you would come to if you had forgotten to correct for units will be one of the answer choices.

For this question, since we know there are 5,280 feet in a mile, we can find the rate for miles per hour:

$$528{,}000 \text{ feet per hour} \div 5{,}280 \text{ feet per mile} = 100 \text{ miles per hour}$$

We can now plug the information into the rate formula to determine how many intervals passed to achieve the total quantity at the given rate:

- **Interval:** x hours cycling

- **Rate of Speed:** 100 miles per hour

- **Total Quantity:** 480 miles

$$480 \text{ miles} \div 100 \text{ miles per hour} = 4.8 \text{ hours}$$

So it takes the cyclist 4.8 hours to finish the race.

Work

In work questions, you will usually find the interval measured in units of time, the total quantity measured in units of work, and the rate measured in work per time. For example, if you knitted for 8 hours (think of this as 8 one-hour intervals) and produced 2 sweaters per hour, then:

$$8 \text{ hours} \times 2 \, \frac{\text{sweaters}}{\text{hour}} = 16 \text{ sweaters}$$

Here is a sample work problem. It is one of the harder rate questions you might come across on the Math IIC:

4 men can dig a 40-foot well in 4 days. How long would it take for 8 men to dig a 60-foot well? Assume that each of these eight men works at the same pace as each of the four men.

The first step to understanding the problem: 4 men can dig a 40-foot well in 4 days. We are given the total quantity of work of 40 feet and a time interval of 4 days. We need to create a rate, using whichever units are most convenient, to carry over to the 8-man problem. Let's try to figure out how much work each man gets done in one day. The group of men get 40 feet of work done in 4 days, so it is easy to see that the group of men gets 10 feet of work done each day. By simply dividing $10 \div 4 = 2.5$, it's clear to see that each person gets 2.5 feet of work done per day.

The question asks us to determine how long it would take 8 men to dig a 60-foot well. The total quantity is 60 feet, and the rate is 2.5 feet per man per day. The 8-man group gets 8 × 2.5 = 20 feet of work done per day.

- **Interval:** days of work

- **Rate:** 20 feet per day

- **Total Quantity:** 60 feet

60 feet ÷ 20 feet per day per 8 men = 3 days of work for 8 men

This last problem required a little bit of creativity — but nothing you can't handle. Just remember the classic rate formula and use it wisely.

Price

In rate questions dealing with price, you will usually find the total quantity measured in a number of items, the interval measured in price (usually dollars or cents), and a rate measured in price per item. For example, if you had 8 basketballs, and you knew that each basketball cost $25, you could determine the total cost of the 8 basketballs:

$$8 \text{ basketballs} \times \$25 \ \frac{\text{price}}{\text{basketball}} = \$200$$

Percent Change

Percent change questions ask you to determine how a percent increase or decrease affects the values given in the question. There are two variations of percent change questions: one where you are given the percent change and asked to find either the original value or new value; other times you will be given two of the values and asked to find the percent change. Take a look at this sample problem:

A professional golfer usually has an average score of 72, but recently went through a major slump. His new average is 20 percent worse (higher) than it used to be. What is his new average?

This is a percent change question in which you need to find how the original value is affected by a percent increase. First, to answer this question, you should multiply 72 by .20 to see what the change in score was:

$$72 \times .20 = 14.4$$

Once you know the score change, then you should add it to his original average, since his average is higher than it used to be:

$$72 + 14.4 = 86.4$$

It is also possible to solve this problem by multiplying the golfer's original score by 1.2, which allows you to combine the 20% increase and the original score in one step. Since you know that the golfer's score went up by 20% over his original score, you know that his new score is 120% higher than his old score. If you see this immediately you can skip a step and multiply $72 \times 1.2 = 86.4$.

Here's another example of a percent change problem:

> A shirt whose original price was 20 dollars has now been put on sale for 14 dollars. By what percentage did its price drop?

In this case, you have the original price and the sale price, and need to determine the percent decrease. All you need to do is divide the change by the original quantity. In this case, the shirt's price was reduced by $20 - 14 = 6$ dollars. So, $6 \div 20 = 0.3$, a 30% drop in the price of the shirt.

Double Percent Change

A slightly trickier version of the percent change question asks you to determine the cumulative effect of two percent changes in the same problem. For example:

> A bike has an original price of 300 dollars. Its price is reduced by 30%. Then, two weeks later, its price is reduced by an additional 20%. What is the final sale price of the bike?

One might be tempted to say that the bike's price is discounted 30% + 20% = 50% from its original price, and answer 50% of 300, which is 150 dollars. Unfortunately, while this is an easy calculation, it is wrong. The key to solving double percent change questions is realizing that the second percentage change is dependent on the first. For example, in the problem we just looked at, the second percent decrease is 20% of a new, lower price—not the original. Let's work through the problem carefully and see. After the first sale, the price of the bike drops 30%:

$$300 - (30\% \text{ of } 300) = 300 - .3(300) = 300 - 90 = 210 \text{ dollars}$$

The second reduction in price knocks off an additional 20% of the *sale* price, not the original price:

$$210 - (20\% \text{ of } 210) = 210 - .2(210) = 210 - 42 = 168 \text{ dollars}$$

The trickiest of the tricky percentage problems go a little something like this:

A computer has a price of 1400 dollars. Its price is raised 20%, and then lowered 20%. What is the final selling price of the computer?

It sounds too simple to be true; that's because it is. The final price is not the same as the original. Why? Because after the price was increased by 20%, the 20% reduction in price was a 20% reduction of the new, higher price. Therefore, the final price will be lower than the original. Watch and learn:

$$1400 + (20\% \text{ of } 1400) = 1400 + .2(1400) = 1400 + 280 = 1680 \text{ dollars}$$

Now, after the price is reduced by 20%,

$$1680 - (20\% \text{ of } 1680) = 1680 - .2(1680) = 1680 - 336 = 1344 \text{ dollars}$$

As you can see, double percent problems are not as simple as they seem. But once you know their tricks, they can be simply solved.

Exponential Growth and Decay

An extension of the concept of percent change is exponential growth and decay. In questions involving populations growing in size or the diminishing price of a car over time, you'll need to perform a percent change over and over again. For such a repeated percent change, exponents can be used to simplify the calculations. Here's an example problem:

If a population of 100 grows by 5% per year, how great will the population be in 50 years?

To answer this question, you might start by calculating the population after one year:

$$100 + .05 \times 100 = 100 + 5 = 105$$

Or, use the faster method we discussed in percent increase:

$$1.05 \times 100 = 105$$

After the second year, the population will have grown to:

$$100 \times 1.05 \times 1.05 = 100 \times 1.05^2 = 110.25$$

And so on and so on for 48 more years. You may already see the shortcut you can use to avoid having to do, in this case, 50 separate calculations. The final answer is simply:

$$100 \times 1.05^{50} = 1146.74 \approx 1147$$

In general, quantities like the one described in this problem are said to be growing exponentially. The formula for calculating exponential growth over a specific number of years is:

$$\text{final amount} = \text{original amount} \times 1 + \text{growth rate}^{(\text{number of changes})}$$

Exponential decay is mathematically equivalent to negative exponential growth. Instead of a quantity growing at a constant percentage, the quantity shrinks at a constant percentage. Exponential decay is a repeated percent decrease. That is why the formulas that model these two situations are so similar. To calculate exponential decay:

$$\text{final amount} = \text{original amount} \times 1 - \text{decay rate}^{(\text{time})}$$

The only difference between the two equations is that the base of the exponent in exponential decay is less than 1, which should make sense because during each unit of time the original amount is reduced by a fixed percentage. You will find that exponential decay is often used to model population decreases and the loss of physical mass over time.

Let's work through a few example questions to get a feel for both exponential growth and decay problems.

Simple Exponential Growth Problem

A population of bacteria grows by 35% every hour. If the population begins with 100 specimens, how many are there after 6 hours?

The question, with its growing population of bacteria, makes it quite clear that this is an exponential growth problem. To solve the problem you just need to plug the appropriate values into the formula for a repeated percent increase. The rate is .035; the original amount is 1000; and the time is 6 hours:

$$100 \times 1.35^6 \approx 605 \text{ specimens}$$

Simple Exponential Decay Problem

A fully inflated beach ball loses 6% of its air every day. If the beach ball originally contains 4000 cubic centimeters of air, how many cubic centimeters does it hold after 10 days?

Since the beach ball loses air, we know this is an exponential decay problem. The decay rate is .06, the original amount of air is 4000 cubic centimeters, and the length of decay is 10 days. So plug the information into the formula:

$$4000 \times (.94)^{10} \approx 2154 \text{ cubic centimeters}$$

More Complicated Exponential Growth Problem

A bank offers a 4.7% interest rate on all savings accounts, compounded monthly. If 1000 dollars are initially put into a savings account, how much money will the account hold two years later?

This problem is a bit tricky for the simple reason that the interest on the account is compounded monthly. This means that in the 2 years the question refers to, the interest will compound $2 \times 12 = 24$ times. As long as you remember to use 24 as the length of time, the answer is straightforward:

$$1000 \times 1.047^{24} \approx 3011.07 \text{ dollars}$$

Here's another compounding problem:

Sam puts 2000 dollars into a savings account that pays 5% interest compounded annually. Justin puts 2500 dollars into a different savings account that pays 4% annually. After 15 years, whose account will have more money in it, if no more money is added or subtracted from the principal?

Sam's account will have $\$2000 \times 1.05^{15} \approx \$4157.85$ in it after 15 years. Justin's account will have $\$2500 \times 1.04^{15} \approx \$4502.36$ in it. So, Justin's account will still have more money in it after 15 years.

Logarithms

Logarithms have important uses in solving problems with complicated exponential equations. Consider the following example:

The population of a small town is 1000 on January 1, 2002. It grows at a constant rate of 2% per year. In what year does the population of the town first exceed 1500?

This question is like the exponential growth problems we've just seen, but with a twist. Here, we're given the growth rate, the initial quantity, *and* the ending quantity. We need to find the length of time over which the growth rate must be applied to the initial quantity to yield the ending quantity. Logarithms provide the tool to solve this type of problem.

$$1000 \times 1.02^x = 1500$$
$$1.02^x = 1.5$$
$$\log 1.02^x = \log 1.5$$
$$x \log 1.02 = \log 1.5$$
$$x = \frac{\log 1.5}{\log 1.02}$$
$$x = 20.47$$

It will take roughly twenty and a half years for the town's population to exceed 1500. So about halfway through the year 2022, the population will first exceed 1500.

In general, to solve a problem such as the example problem in which the exponent is unknown, the first step is to isolate the exponential term. Once the exponential term has been isolated, the next step is to isolate the variable itself by taking the logarithm of both sides and then using the power rule of logarithms to bring the variable out of the exponent. It does not matter which base you use in your logarithm; you could choose a base-10 logarithm or a natural logarithm for ease of calculation

Here's a simple example to illustrate this process:

If $6^x = 5^{1000}$, then find the value of x.

This problem would be vastly more difficult if we didn't have logarithms. How would you possibly calculate 5^{1000}? And how do you solve for x when it's the exponent of a number? Fortunately, we can simply take the logarithm of each side of the equation and then apply the power rule of logarithms:

Algebra

$$\log 6^x = \log 5^{1000}$$
$$x \log 6 = 1000 \log 5$$

From here, the solution becomes much more clear.

$$x \log 6 = 1000 \log 5$$
$$x = 1000 \times \frac{\log 5}{\log 6}$$
$$x = 1000 \times \frac{.699}{.778}$$
$$x = 1000 \times .898$$
$$x = 898$$

Monomials, Binomials, and Polynomials

The rest of this chapter is concerned with operations on monomials, binomials, and polynomials. These terms have simple definitions; look them over to make sure that you're familiar with them.

- **Monomial:** an expression that contains one term.

- **Binomial:** an expression that contains two terms.

- **Polynomial:** an expression that contains three or more terms.

Of course, in order for these terms to have any valuable meaning, the expressions they describe must be in simplified form, with all like terms combined. For example, an expression like $2x^2 + 4x^2 - x^2$ would not be considered a polynomial; rather, it would be considered the monomial $5x^2$.

Multiplying Binomials

There is a simple acronym that is useful in helping to keep track of the terms as you multiply binomials: **FOIL**. It stands for **F**irst, **O**uter, **I**nner, **L**ast. This is the order in which you multiply the terms of two binomials to get the right product.

For example, if asked to multiply the binomials $(x + 1)(x - 3)$, you first multiply the first terms of each binomial:

$$x \times x = x^2$$

Next, multiply the outer terms of the binomials:

$$x \times 3 = 3x$$

Then, multiply the inner terms:

$$1 \times x = x$$

Finally, multiply the last terms:

$$1 \times 3 = 3$$

Combine like terms and you have your product:

$$2x^2 + -2x + 6x + -6 = 2x^2 + 4x - 6$$

Here are a few more examples:

$$(y + 3)(y - 7) = y^2 - 7y + 3y - 21 = y^2 - 4y - 21$$
$$(-x + 2)(4x + 6) = -4x^2 - 6x + 8x + 12 = -4x^2 + 2x + 12$$
$$(3a + 2b)(6c - d) = 18ac - 3ad + 12bc - 2bd$$

Binomial Theorem

Evaluating a binomial expression that is raised to a power, such as $(a + b)^n$, can be a dreary process when n gets to be a large number. Luckily, there is a very convenient shortcut based on Pascal's triangle (see the next section) that will save us time and reduce the risk of error.

Notice that patterns emerge when we raise the binomial $(a + b)$ to consecutive powers:

$$(a + b)^0 = 1$$
$$(a + b)^1 = a + b$$
$$(a + b)^2 = a^2 + 2ab + b^2$$
$$(a + b)^3 = a^3 + 3a^2b + 3ab^2 + b^3$$
$$(a + b)^4 = a^4 + 4a^3b + 6a^2b^2 + 4ab^3 + b^4$$

Looking at these patterns, we can make predictions about the expansion of $(a + b)^n$.

1. There are $n + 1$ terms in the expansion. For example, when the exponent, n, is 4, there are 5 terms.

2. The power to which a is raised decreases by one each term, beginning with n and ending with 0. For example, if $n = 4$, then a in the second term is raised to the third power.

3. Subsequently, the exponent of b increases by one each term, beginning with 0 and ending with n. If $n = 4$, then b in the second term is raised to the first power.

4. The sum of the exponents for each term of the expansion is n.

5. The coefficient of the nth term is equal to $_nC_x$, or the number of ways to combine n items in groups of size x, also represented as

$$\binom{n}{x}$$

where x is the power to which either variable is raised in the nth term.

These five properties of binomial expansion allow you to answer questions like:

What is the thirteenth term of the expansion of $(x + y)^{17}$?

There are 18 terms in this expansion. Because of the third property, y is raised to the $13 - 1 = 12^{th}$ power. The fourth property tells us that x is raised to the $17 - 12 = 5^{th}$ power (since the sum of the exponents must be 17). The coefficient of this term is:

$$\binom{17}{5} = 6188$$

which is also equal to

$$\binom{17}{12} = 6188$$

So the thirteenth term is $6188x^5y^{12}$.

This is a rather specific line of questioning, so if it appears on the test at all, it will probably only appear once. Nevertheless, if you have the time, study these properties and you could earn easy points.

Pascal's Triangle

Pascal's triangle is made up of patterned rows of numbers, each row containing one more number than the last. The first row contains one number, the second row contains two numbers, ..., the nth row contains n numbers. The first ten rows of Pascal's triangle look like this:

$$
\begin{array}{ccccccccccccccccccc}
 & & & & & & & & 1 & & & & & & & & & \\
 & & & & & & & 1 & & 1 & & & & & & & & \\
 & & & & & & 1 & & 2 & & 1 & & & & & & & \\
 & & & & & 1 & & 3 & & 3 & & 1 & & & & & & \\
 & & & & 1 & & 4 & & 6 & & 4 & & 1 & & & & & \\
 & & & 1 & & 5 & & 10 & & 10 & & 5 & & 1 & & & & \\
 & & 1 & & 6 & & 15 & & 20 & & 15 & & 6 & & 1 & & & \\
 & 1 & & 7 & & 21 & & 35 & & 35 & & 21 & & 7 & & 1 & & \\
1 & & 8 & & 28 & & 56 & & 70 & & 56 & & 28 & & 8 & & 1 & \\
1 & 9 & & 36 & & 84 & & 126 & & 126 & & 84 & & 36 & & 9 & & 1
\end{array}
$$

Each row of the triangle starts with the number one, and every interior number is the sum of the two numbers above it.

Pascal's triangle provides a very nice shortcut for dealing with the expansion of binomials: the numbers in the $(n + 1)^{th}$ row of Pascal's triangle mirror the coefficients of the terms in the expansion of $(a + b)^n$.

Say, for example, that you intend to expand the binomial $(f + g)^5$. The coefficients of the six terms in this expansion are the six numbers in the sixth row of Pascal's triangle, which are 1, 5, 10, 10, 5, and 1:

$$(f + g)^5 = f^5 + 5f^4g + 10f^3g^2 + 10f^2g^3 + 5fg^4 + g^5$$

Sometimes it will be easier to sketch a few rows of Pascal's triangle than to multiply all of the terms in the expansion of the binomial.

Multiplying Polynomials

Every once in a while, the Math IIC test will ask you to multiply polynomials. It may seem like a daunting task. But when the process is broken down, multiplying polynomials requires nothing more than distribution and combining like terms—and some attention to detail.

Consider the polynomials $(a + b + c)$ and $(d + e + f)$. To find their product, just distribute the terms of the first polynomial into the second polynomial individually, and combine like terms to formulate your final answer.

$$(a + b + c)(d + e + f) = a(d + e + f) + b(d + e + f) + c(d + e + f)$$
$$= ad + ae + af + bd + be + bf + cd + ce + cf$$

Here's another example:

$$(x^2 + x + 4)(2x^3 + 5x^2 - 6x - 3)$$
$$= x^2(2x^3 + 5x^2 - 6x - 3) + x(2x^3 + 5x^2 - 6x - 3) + 4(2x^3 + 5x^2 - 6x - 3)$$
$$= 2x^5 + 5x^4 - 6x^3 - 3x^2 + 2x^4 + 5x^3 - 6x^2 - 3x + 8x^3 + 20x^2 - 24x - 12$$
$$= 2x^5 + 7x^4 + 7x^3 + 11x^2 - 27x - 12$$

Quadratic Equations

A quadratic, or quadratic polynomial, is a polynomial of the form $ax^2 + bx + c$, where $a \neq 0$. The following polynomials are quadratics:

$$x^2 + 3x - 4$$
$$y^2 - 5y + 3$$
$$x^2 - 6x$$
$$x^2 + 1$$
$$t^2$$

A **quadratic equation** sets a quadratic polynomial equal to zero. That is, a quadratic equation is an equation of the form $ax^2 + bx + c = 0$. The values of x for which the equation holds are called the **roots**, or solutions, of the quadratic equation. Most of the questions on quadratic equations involve finding their roots.

There are two basic ways to find roots: by factoring and by using the **quadratic formula**. Factoring is faster, but can't always be done. The quadratic formula takes longer to work out, but works for all quadratic equations. We'll study both in detail.

Factoring

To factor a quadratic you must express it as the product of two binomials. In essence, factoring a quadratic involves a reverse-FOIL process. Here's an example quadratic expression:

$$x^2 + 10x + 21$$

If we look at the FOIL method a little more closely, we can see how each of these terms is constructed:

$$(x + a)(x + b) = x^2 + (a + b)x + ab$$

You can see that the constant term is the product of the two constants in the original binomials and the x coefficient is simply the sum of those two constants. In order to factor $x^2 + 10x + 21$ into two binomials $(x + a)(x + b)$, you must find two numbers whose sum is 10 and whose product is 21.

The pair of numbers that fits the bill for a and b are 3 and 7. Thus, $x^2 + 10x + 21 = (x + 3)(x + 7)$. The quadratic expression has now been factored and simplified.

On the Math IIC, though, you will often be presented with a quadratic *equation*. The only difference between a quadratic equation and a quadratic expression is that the equation is set equal to 0: $x^2 + 10x + 21 = 0$. If you have such an equation, then once you have factored the quadratic you can solve it quite easily. Because the product of the two terms is zero, by the zero product rule we know that one of the terms must be equal to zero. Thus, $x + 3 = 0$ or $x + 7 = 0$, and the solutions (also known as roots) of the quadratic must be $x = -3$ and $x = -7$.

This system still works even in the case where one or more terms of the quadratic is negative. For example, to factor $x^2 - 4x - 21 = 0$, we simply pick two numbers whose product is –21 and whose sum is –4. Those numbers are –7 and 3, so we have factored the quadratic: $(x - 7)(x + 3) = 0$.

Two Special Quadratic Polynomials

There are two special quadratic polynomials that pop up quite frequently on the Math IIC, and you should memorize them. They are the perfect square and the difference of two squares. If you memorize the formulas below, you may be able to avoid the time taken by factoring.

There are two kinds of perfect square quadratics. They are:

Algebra

1. $a^2 + 2ab + b^2 = (a + b)(a + b) = (a + b)^2$
   Example: $a^2 + 6ab + 9 = (a + 3)^2$

2. $a^2 - 2ab + b^2 = (a - b)(a - b) = (a - b)^2$
   Example: $a^2 - 6ab + 9 = (a - 3)^2$

Note that when you solve for the roots of a perfect square quadratic equation, the solution for the equation $(a + b)^2 = 0$ will be $-b$, while the solution for $(a - b)^2 = 0$ will be b.

The difference of two square quadratics follows the form below:

$$(a + b)(a - b) = a^2 - b^2$$
$$\text{Example: } (a + 3)(a - 3) = a^2 - 9$$

Here's an example where knowing the perfect square or difference of two square equations can help you on the Math IIC:

Solve for x: $2x^2 + 20x + 50 = 0$.

To solve this question by factoring, you would do the following:

$$2x^2 + 20x + 50 = 0$$
$$2(x^2 + 10x + 25) = 0$$
$$(x + 5)^2 = 0$$
$$(x + 5)(x + 5) = 0$$
$$x = -5$$

But if you got to the step where you had $2(x^2 + 10x + 25) = 0$ and realized that you were working with a perfect square of $2(x + 5)^2$, you could immediately have divided out the 2 from both sides of the equation and seen that the solution to the problem would be −5.

Practice Quadratics

Since the ability to factor quadratics relies in large part on your ability to "read" the information in the quadratic, the best way to master these questions is to practice, practice, practice. Just like perfecting that jump shot, repeating the same drill over and over again will make you faster and more accurate. Try to factor the following examples on your own before you look at the answers.

Algebra

$$x^2 + x - 2 = 0 \qquad \text{Roots}: \{-2, 1\}$$
$$x^2 + 13x + 42 = 0 \qquad \text{Roots}: \{-7, -6\}$$
$$x^2 - 8x + 15 = 0 \qquad \text{Roots}: \{3, 5\}$$
$$x^2 - 5x - 36 = 0 \qquad \text{Roots}: \{-4, 9\}$$
$$x^2 - 10x + 25 = 0 \qquad \text{Roots}: \{5\}$$
$$x^2 - 25 = 0 \qquad \text{Roots}: \{5, -5\}$$

The Quadratic Formula

Factoring using the reverse-FOIL method is really only practical when the roots are integers. Quadratics, however, can have decimal numbers or fractions as roots. Equations like these can be solved using the quadratic formula. For an equation of the form $ax^2 + bx + c = 0$, the quadratic formula states:

$$x = \frac{-b \pm \sqrt{b^2 - 4ac}}{2a}$$

Consider the quadratic equation $x^2 + 5x + 3 = 0$. There are no integers with a sum of 5 and product of 3. So, this quadratic can't be factored, and we must resort to the quadratic equation. We plug the values, $a = 1$, $b = 5$, and $c = 3$, into the formula:

$$x = \frac{-5 \pm \sqrt{25 - 12}}{2}$$
$$= \frac{-5 \pm \sqrt{13}}{2}$$
$$= \frac{-5 + \sqrt{13}}{2}, \frac{-5 - \sqrt{13}}{2}$$
$$= -4.303, -.697$$

The roots of the quadratic are approximately $\{-4.303, -.697\}$.

Finding the Discriminant

If you want to find out quickly how many roots an equation has without calculating the entire formula, all you need to find is an equation's discriminant. The discriminant of a quadratic is the quantity $b^2 - 4ac$. As you can see, this is the radicand in the quadratic equation. If

1. $b^2 - 4ac = 0$, the quadratic has one real root and is a perfect square.

2. $b^2 - 4ac > 0$, the quadratic has two real roots.

3. $b^2 - 4ac < 0$, the quadratic has no real roots, and two complex roots.

Algebra

This information is useful when deciding whether to crank out the quadratic formula on an equation, and can spare you some unnecessary computation. For example, say you're trying to solve for the speed of a train in a rate problem, and you find that the discriminant is less than zero. This means that there are no real roots (a train can only travel at speeds that are real numbers), and there is no reason to carry out the quadratic formula.

Key Formulas

Distributive Property

$$a(b + c + d + ...) = ab + ac + ad + ...$$
$$a(-b - c - d - ...) = -ab - ac - ad - ...$$

Perfect Square of a Binomial

$$(a + b)^2 = a^2 + 2ab + b^2$$
$$(a - b)^2 = a^2 - 2ab + b^2$$

Difference of Two Squares

$$x^2 - y^2 = (x + y)(x - y)$$

Quadratic Formula

In a quadratic equation of the form $ax^2 + bx + c = 0$, where $a \neq 0$:

$$x = \frac{-b \pm \sqrt{b^2 - 4ac}}{2a}$$

Review Questions

1. If $3 < x < 8$ and $2 > y > -5$, what is the range of $x - 2y$?

    (A) $-7 < x - 2y < 4$
    (B) $-7 < x - 2y < 12$
    (C) $-2 < x - 2y < 18$
    (D) $-1 < x - 2y < 18$
    (E) $7 < x - 2y < 18$

2. If $|5x + 2| > 3$, which of the following quantities is a possible value of x?

    (A) $x = -2$
    (B) $x = -1$
    (C) $x = -\frac{1}{5}$
    (D) $x = 0$
    (E) $x = \frac{1}{5}$

3. If $5x + 3y = 4$ and $4x + 4y = 8$, what is $x - y$?

    (A) -6
    (B) -4
    (C) 0
    (D) 4
    (E) 12

4. Tony decides to go on a two-hour run. For the first hour, he runs at a pace of 8 miles per hour. He then increases his rate by 25% for the next hour. How many total miles does Tony run?

    (A) 16
    (B) 17.5
    (C) 18
    (D) 20
    (E) 22

5. A book is originally priced at $55.00—it is a very elegant hardcover by a leading author. But the book is terrible. One month after its release, its price drops by 10%. Two months after its release, its price drops an additional 20%. Three months after its release, its price drops still more, by an additional 10%. What is the price of the book after 3 months?

    (A) $33.00
    (B) $34.10
    (C) $34.65
    (D) $35.20
    (E) $35.64

Algebra

6. A full 20,000 gallon tank is drained over the course of about a day. Every hour, 800 gallons of water pour out. During the 20th hour of draining, what fraction of the remaining water in the tank pours out?

    (A) $\frac{1}{20}$ (B) $\frac{1}{10}$ (C) $\frac{1}{8}$ (D) $\frac{1}{6}$ (E) $\frac{1}{4}$

7. What is $(2x^2 - 5xy)((3y - 2) - 14xy)$?

    (A) $420x^4y^3$
    (B) $10x^3y + 42xy^2 + 28xy$
    (C) $3x^2y - 4x^2 + 70x^2y^2$
    (D) $-28x^3y + 12x^2y - 30xy^2 + 70x^2y^2$
    (E) $-28x^3y + 70x^2y^2 + 6x^2y - 15xy^2 - 4x^2 + 10xy$

8. Solve for x in the following equation: $x^2 - 8x + 13 = 0$.

    (A) $2 \pm \dfrac{\sqrt{3}}{2}$

    (B) $4 \pm \dfrac{\sqrt{3}}{2}$

    (C) $4 \pm \dfrac{\sqrt{12}}{2}$

    (D) $\dfrac{8 \pm 3\sqrt{2}}{2}$

    (E) $8 \pm \sqrt{12}$

9. What is $\dfrac{x^2 + 5x + 6}{x^2 + x - 2}$?

    (A) $x^2 + 4x + 8$
    (B) $4x + 4$

    (C) $\dfrac{x+3}{x-1}$

    (D) $\dfrac{x+2}{x-1}$

    (E) $\dfrac{x+3}{x+2}$

10. What is the fifth term of the expansion of $(a + b)^8$?

    (A) $8ab$
    (B) $70a^5b^3$
    (C) $56a^3b^5$
    (D) $70a^4b^4$
    (E) $35a^4b^4$

Explanations

1. **(D)**

To find the range of $x - 2y$, you first need to find the range of $-2y$. You can find the range of $-y$ by multiplying the range of y by -1 (remember to switch the greater than signs to less than signs): $-2 < -y < 5$. The range of $-2y$ is the range of $-y$ multiplied by 2: $-4 < -2y < 10$. Adding the range of $-2y$ to the range of x yields the answer:

$$3 + -4 < x - 2y < 8 + 10$$
$$-1 < x - 2y < 18$$

2. **(A)**

You can solve this problem by either plugging in or by using algebraic technique. Plugging in the answer choices will get you an answer, but will probably take more time than working out the algebra (provided you have a good understanding of the algebra). To work out this problem algebraically, divide the equation into two parts to solve for x. First, let $(5x + 2)$ be positive:

$$5x + 2 > 3$$
$$5x > 1$$
$$x > \frac{1}{5}$$

Next, let $(5x + 2)$ be negative:

$$5x + 2 < -3$$
$$5x < -5$$
$$x < -1$$

The range of possible values of x has two parts: $-\infty < x < -1$ or $\frac{1}{5} < x < \infty$. $x = -2$ is the only answer choice that lies within one of these ranges.

3.   **(B)**

To answer this question quickly, use the method of simultaneous equations. Subtract the second equation from the first:

$$(5x + 3y) - (4x + 4y) = 4 - 8$$
$$5x + 3y - 4x - 4y = -4$$
$$x - y = -4$$

4.   **(C)**

This questions tests rates, but also involves percent changes. To find the total distance Tony runs you must find his two rates for each of the two hours of his run. First, we are told that Tony runs for one hour at a rate of 8 miles per hour. His second rate equals the first rate increased by 25%, which works out to:

$$1.25 \times 8 \text{ miles per hour} = 10 \text{ miles per hour}$$

Since Tony runs for one hour at each rate, the distance he runs is equal to:

$$8 \times 1 + 10 \times 1 = 8 + 10 = 18 \text{ miles}$$

5.   **(E)**

Since the price of the book does not drop by the same percent every month, you cannot solve this problem as an exponential decay problem. Instead, calculate the percent decreases one by one. After one month, the book's price is

$$55 - (.1 \times 55) = 55 - 5.5 = \$49.50$$

After two months, its price is

$$49.5 - (.2 \times 49.5) = 49.5 - 9.9 = \$39.60$$

After three months, its price is

$$39.60(.1 \times 39.6) = 39.6 - 3.96 = \$35.64$$

6. **(D)**

Be careful that you don't try to solve this problem using the exponential decay model. Every hour a constant *amount* of water drains, not a constant *percentage* of the remaining water. So the first step in answering the question is determining how much water is left after 19 hours of draining.

$$20000 - 19 \times 800 = 20000 - 15200 = 4800$$

During the 20th hour of draining, 800 of the remaining 4800 gallons drain from the tank.

$$\frac{800}{4800} = \frac{1}{6}$$

7. **(E)**

This problem tests your ability to FOIL complicated binomials. The second binomial is complicated because the first term $(3y + 2)$ is itself a binomial. Even so, you can use that term as a unit and distribute according to FOIL in the usual way:

$$(2x^2 - 5xy)((3y - 2) - 14xy) = 2x^2(3y - 2) + (-5xy(3y - 2)) + (2x^2(-14xy))$$
$$+(-5xy(-14xy)$$
$$= 6x^2y - 4x^2 - 15xy^2 + 10xy - 28x^3y + 70x^2y^2$$
$$= -28x^3y + 70x^2y^2 + 6x^2y - 15xy^2 - 4x^2 + 10xy$$

8. **(B)**

The question asks you to solve a quadratic equation, but the equation cannot be easily factored. Use the quadratic equation to solve for x:

$$x = \frac{8 \pm \sqrt{8^2 - 4(1)(13)}}{2}$$
$$= \frac{8 \pm \sqrt{12}}{2}$$
$$= \frac{8 \pm 2\sqrt{3}}{2}$$
$$= 4 \pm \frac{\sqrt{3}}{2}$$

9. **(C)**

The question asks you to simplify the fraction. To do so, factor the numerator and the denominator to see if they have any terms in common.

$$\frac{x^2 + 5x + 6}{x^2 + x - 2} = \frac{(x+2)(x+3)}{(x-1)(x+2)}$$

The $(x + 2)$ terms on the top and bottom cancel each other out, and you're left with the fraction $\frac{x+3}{x-1}$.

10. **(D)**

According to the binomial theorem, for the binomial $(a + b)^n$ there are $n + 1$ terms. So, for this question, there are $8 + 1 = 9$ terms in the expansion. Also from the theorem, we know that the power to which a is raised decreases by one each term, beginning with n and ending with 0, so the exponent of a is $9 - 5 = 4$. Since the sum of the exponents for each term of the binomial is n, the exponent of b is $8 - 4 = 4$. The coefficient of the term is the fifth number in the ninth row of Pascal's triangle, which is 70. Therefore, the term is $70a^4b^4$.

Plane Geometry

T HE MATH IIC TEST DOES NOT EXPLICITLY test plane geometry. There are absolutely no questions that exclusively ask about polygons or angles. But don't get too psyched, because you still need to have the subject down cold. The writers of the Math IIC don't write questions solely covering plane geometry because they assume you already know it. This assumption frees them to incorporate various aspects of plane geometry into questions covering 3-D geometry, coordinate geometry, and trigonometry. In all, about 40 percent of the questions on the Math IIC involve plane geometry in some way.

Because the Math IIC doesn't directly test plane geometry, this chapter does not include many sample Math IIC problems—there aren't any examples to show. Nor will there be Review Questions at the end of the chapter. Instead, this chapter provides you with the principles of plane geometry that the test assumes you know. If you understand the principles in this chapter, you'll be able to call them into play when you need to apply them to Math IIC questions covering 3-D geometry, coordinate geometry, and trigonometry.

Lines and Angles

A line is a collection of points that extends without limit in a straight formation. A line can be named by a single letter, like line l, or it can be named according to two points that it contains, like line AB. The second way of naming a line indicates an important property common to all lines: any two points in space determine a line. For example, given two points, J and K:

J

K

a line is determined:

This line is called *JK*.

Line Segments

A line segment is a section of a line. It is named and determined by its endpoints. Unlike a line, whose length is infinite, a line segment has finite length. Line segment *AB* is pictured below.

Midpoint of a Line Segment

The midpoint of a line segment is the point on the segment that is equidistant (the same distance) from each endpoint. Because a midpoint splits a line segment into two equal halves, the midpoint is said to bisect the line segment.

Angles

Technically speaking, an angle is the union of two rays (lines that extend infinitely in just one direction) that share an endpoint (called the vertex of the angle). The measure of an angle is how far you must rotate one of the rays such that it coincides with the other.

In this guide and for the Math IIC, you don't need to bother with such a technical definition. Suffice it to say, angles are used to measure rotation. One full revolution around a point creates an angle of 360 degrees. A half revolution, also known as a straight angle, is 180 degrees. A quarter revolution, or right angle, is 90 degrees.

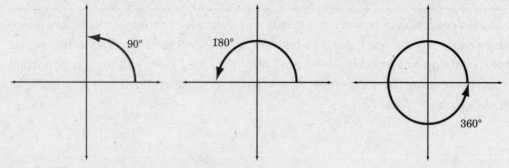

In text, angles can also be indicated through the symbol ∠.

Vertical Angles

When two lines or line segments intersect, two pairs of congruent (equal) angles are created. The angles in each pair of congruent angles created by the intersection of two lines are called vertical angles:

In this figure, angles 1 and 4 are vertical angles (and therefore congruent), as are angles 2 and 3.

Supplementary and Complementary Angles

Supplementary angles are two angles that together add up to 180°. Complementary angles are two angles that add up to 90°.

Whenever you have vertical angles, you also have supplementary angles. In the diagram of vertical angles above, angles 1 and 2, angles 1 and 3, angles 2 and 4, and angles 3 and 4 are all pairs of supplementary angles.

Parallel Lines

Lines that don't intersect are called parallel lines. The intersection of one line, called a transversal, with two parallel lines creates many interesting angle relationships. This situation is often referred to as "parallel lines cut by a transversal," where the transversal is the non-parallel line. As you can see in the diagram below of parallel lines AB and CD and transversal EF, two parallel lines cut by a transversal will form 8 angles.

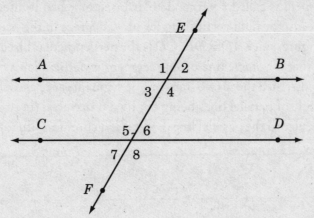

Among the eight angles formed, three special angle relationships exist:

1. **Alternate exterior angles** are pairs of congruent angles on opposite sides of the transversal, outside of the space between the parallel lines. In the figure above, there are two pairs of alternate exterior angles: angles 1 and 8, and angles 2 and 7.

2. **Alternate interior angles** are pairs of congruent angles on opposite sides of the transversal in the region between the parallel lines. In the figure above, there are two pairs of alternate interior angles: angles 3 and 6, and angles 4 and 5.

3. **Corresponding angles** are congruent angles on the same side of the transversal. Of two corresponding angles, one will always be between the parallel lines, while the other will be outside the parallel lines. In the figure above, there are four pairs of corresponding angles: $\angle 1$ and $\angle 5$, $\angle 2$ and $\angle 6$, $\angle 3$ and $\angle 7$, and $\angle 4$ and $\angle 8$.

In addition to these special relationships between angles formed by two parallel lines cut by a transversal, all adjacent angles are supplementary.

Perpendicular Lines

Two lines that intersect to form a right (90°) angle are called perpendicular lines. Line segments AB and CD are perpendicular.

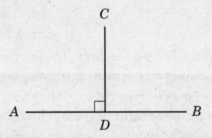

A line or line segment is called a perpendicular bisector when it intersects a line segment at the midpoint, forming vertical angles of 90 degrees in the process. For example, in the above figure, since $AD = DB$, CD is the perpendicular bisector of AB.

Keep in mind that if a single line or line segment is perpendicular to two different lines or line segments, then those two lines or line segments are parallel. This is actually just another example of parallel lines being cut by a transversal (in this case, the transversal is perpendicular to the parallel lines), but it is a common situation when dealing with polygons.

Triangles

You will also need a solid understanding of triangles in order to answer other questions about polygons, coordinate geometry, and trigonometry. Luckily for you, the essential rules governing triangles are few and easy to master.

Basic Properties

There are four main rules of triangles:

1. Sum of the Interior Angles

If you were stranded on a desert island and had to take the Math IIC test, this is the one rule about triangles you should bring along: the sum of the measures of the interior angles is 180 degrees. Now, if you know the measures of two of a triangle's angles, you will be able to find the third. Helpful rule, don't you think? This rule will help you think about triangles in a useful way.

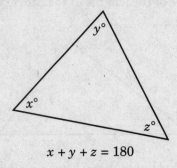

$$x + y + z = 180$$

2. Measure of an Exterior Angle

Another property of triangles is that the measure of an exterior angle of a triangle is equal to the sum of the measures of the remote interior angles.

An exterior angle of a triangle is the angle formed by extending one of the sides of the triangle past a vertex (the point at which two sides meet). An exterior angle is always supplementary to the interior angle with which it shares a vertex, and equal in measure to the sum of the measures of the remote interior angles. Take a look at the figure below, in which d, the exterior angle, is supplementary to interior angle c:

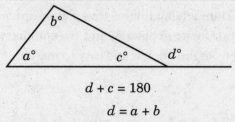

$$d + c = 180$$
$$d = a + b$$

It doesn't matter which side of a triangle you extend to create an exterior angle; the exterior angle will always be supplementary to the interior angle with which it shares a vertex, and therefore (because of the 180 degrees rule) equal to the sum of the remote interior angles.

3. Triangle Inequality

The third important property of triangles is the triangle inequality rule, which states: the length of a side of a triangle is less than the sum of the lengths of the other two sides and greater than the difference of the lengths of the other two sides.

Observe the figure below:

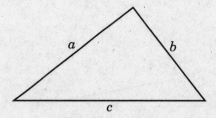

From the triangle inequality, we know that $c - b < a < c + b$. The exact length of side a depends on the measure of the angle created by sides b and c. If this angle is large (close to 180 degrees) then a will be large (close to $b + c$). If this angle is small (close to 0 degrees), then a will be small (close to $b - c$).

For an example, take a look at this triangle:

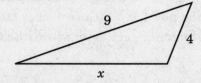

Using the triangle inequality, we can tell that $9 - 4 < x < 9 + 4$, or $5 < x < 13$. The exact value of x depends on the measure of the angle opposite side x.

4. Proportionality of Triangles:

This brings us to the last basic property of triangles, which has to do with the relationships between the angles of a triangle and the lengths of the triangle's sides. In every triangle, the longest side is opposite the largest angle and the shortest side is opposite the smallest angle.

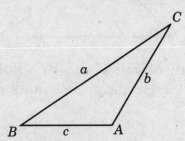

In this figure, side a is clearly the longest side and angle a is the largest angle. Conversely, side c is the shortest side and angle C is the smallest angle. It follows, therefore, that $c < b < a$ and $C < B < A$. This proportionality of side lengths and angle measures holds true for all triangles.

Special Triangles

There are several special triangles that have particular properties. Knowing these triangles and what makes each of them special can save you time and effort.

But before getting into the different types of special triangles, we must take a moment to explain the markings we use to describe the properties of each particular triangle. For example, the figure below has two pairs of sides of equal length, and three congruent angle pairs: these indicate that the sides have equal length. The arcs drawn into angles a and b indicate that these angles are congruent. In some diagrams, there might be more than one pair of equal sides or congruent angles. In this case, double hash marks or double arcs can be drawn into a pair of sides or angles to indicate that they are equal to each other, but not necessarily equal to the other pair of sides or angles.

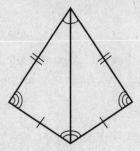

Now, on to the special triangles.

Scalene Triangles

A scalene triangle has no equal sides and no equal angles.

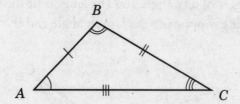

In fact, the special property of scalene triangles is that they don't really have any special properties. Scalene triangles almost never appear on the Math IIC.

Isosceles Triangles

A triangle that contains two sides of equal length is called an isosceles triangle. In an isosceles triangle, the two angles opposite the sides of equal length are congruent. These angles are usually referred to as base angles. In the isosceles triangle below, sides $a = b$ and angles $A = B$.

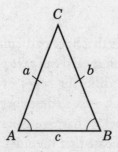

There is no such thing as a triangle with two equal sides and no congruent angles, or vice versa. From the proportionality rule, if a triangle has two equal sides, then the two angles opposite those sides are congruent, and if a triangle has two congruent angles, then the two sides opposite those angles are equal.

Equilateral Triangles

A triangle whose sides are all of equal length is called an equilateral triangle. All three angles in an equilateral triangle are congruent as well; the measure of each one is 60 degrees.

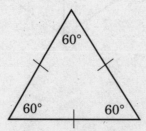

As is the case with isosceles triangles, if you know that a triangle has either three equal sides or three congruent angles, then you know that the other must also be true.

Right Triangles

A triangle that contains a right angle is called a right triangle. The side opposite the right angle is called the hypotenuse of the right triangle, and the other two sides are called legs. The angles opposite the legs of a right triangle are complementary.

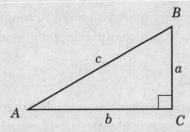

In the figure above, angle C is the right angle (as indicated by the box drawn in the angle), side c is the hypotenuse, and sides a and b are the legs.

The Pythagorean Theorem

The Pythagorean theorem is vital to most of the problems on right triangles. It will also come in handy later on as you study coordinate geometry and trigonometry. The theorem states that in a right triangle $a^2 + b^2 = c^2$,

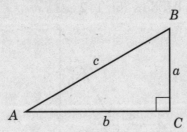

where c is the length of the hypotenuse, and a and b are the lengths of the two legs. The theorem states that the square of the hypotenuse is equal to the sum of the squares of the two legs.

Pythagorean Triples

Because right triangles obey the Pythagorean theorem, only a few have side lengths which are all integers. For example, a right triangle with legs of length 3 and 5 has a hypotenuse of length $\sqrt{3^2 + 5^2} = \sqrt{9 + 25} = \sqrt{34} = 5.83$.

The few sets of three integers that do obey the Pythagorean theorem and can therefore be the lengths of the sides of a right triangle are called Pythagorean triples. Here are some common triples:

{3, 4, 5}
{5, 12, 13}
{7, 24, 25}
{8, 15, 17}

In addition to these Pythagorean triples, you should also watch out for their multiples. For example, {6, 8, 10} is a Pythagorean triple since it's a multiple of {3, 4, 5}.

Special Right Triangles

Right triangles are pretty special in their own right. But there are two *extra*special right triangles that appear frequently on the Math IIC. They are 30-60-90 triangles and 45-45-90 triangles.

30-60-90 Triangles

A 30-60-90 triangle is a triangle with angles of 30, 60, and 90 degrees. What makes it special is the specific pattern that the lengths of the sides of a 30-60-90 triangle follow. Suppose the short leg, opposite the 30 degree angle, has length x. Then the hypotenuse has length $2x$, and the long leg, opposite the 60 degree angle, has length $x\sqrt{3}$. The sides of every 30-60-90 triangle will follow this $1 : 2 : \sqrt{3}$ ratio.

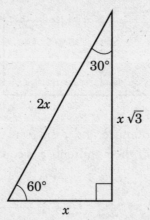

The constant ratio in the lengths of the sides of a 30-60-90 triangle means that if you know the length of one side in the triangle, you immediately know the lengths of all the sides. If, for example, you know that the side opposite the 30° angle is 2 meters long, then by using the $1 : 2 : \sqrt{3}$ ratio you know that the hypotenuse is 4 meters long, and the leg opposite the 60° angles is $2\sqrt{3}$ meters. On the Math IIC you will quite often encounter a question that will present you with an unnamed 30-60-90 triangle, allowing you to use your knowledge of this special triangle. You could solve these questions by using the Pythagorean theorem, but that method takes a lot longer than simply knowing the proper 30-60-90 ratio. The key is to be aware that there are 30-60-90 triangles lurking out there, and to strike when you see one.

45-45-90 Triangles

A 45-45-90 triangle is a triangle with two 45-degree angles, and one right angle. This type of triangle is also known as an isosceles right triangle, since it's both isosceles and right. Like the 30-60-90 triangle, the lengths of the sides of a 45-45-90 triangle follow a specific pattern that you should know. If the legs are of length x (they are always equal), then the hypotenuse has length $x \sqrt{2}$. Take a look at this diagram:

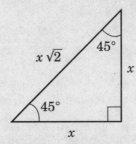

As with 30-60-90 triangles, knowing the ratio for 45-45-90 triangles can save you a great deal of time on the Math IIC.

Similar Triangles

Two triangles are called similar if the ratio of the lengths of their corresponding sides is constant. In order for this to be true, the corresponding angles of each triangle must be congruent. In essence, similar triangles have exactly the same shape, but not necessarily the same size. Take a look at a few similar triangles:

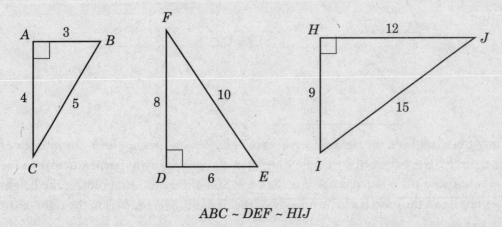

$ABC \sim DEF \sim HIJ$

As you may have assumed from the above figure, the symbol for "is similar to" is ~. So if triangle *ABC* is similar to triangle *DEF*, you could write *ABC ~ DEF*.

When you say that two triangles are similar, it is important to know which sides of each triangle correspond to each other. After all, the definition of similar triangles is that "the ratio of the lengths of their corresponding sides is constant." So, considering that *ABC ~ DEF*, you know that the ratio of the short sides equal the ratio of the larger sides. $^{AB}/_{DE} = {}^{BC}/_{EF} = {}^{CA}/_{FD}$.

Just as similar triangles have corresponding sides, they also have congruent angles. If *ABC ~ DEF*, then $\angle A = \angle D$, $\angle B = \angle E$, and $\angle C = \angle F$.

Area of a Triangle

The formula for the area of a triangle is:

$$A = \frac{1}{2}bh$$

where *b* is the length of a base of the triangle, and *h* is the height (also called the altitude).

In the previous sentence we said "a base" instead of "the base" because you can actually use any of the three sides of the triangle as the base; a triangle has no particular side that is the base until you designate one. The height of the triangle depends on the base, which is why the area formula always works, no matter which side you choose to be the base. The heights of a few triangles are pictured with their altitudes drawn in as dotted lines.

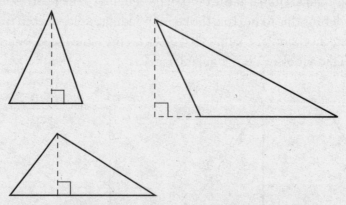

Study the triangle on the right. The measure of its height does not lie in the interior of the triangle. The height of a triangle is defined as a line segment perpendicular to *the line containing the base*, and not just the base. Sometimes the endpoint of the height does not lie on the base; it can be outside of the triangle, as is the case in the right-most triangle in the figure above.

Polygons

Polygons are enclosed geometric shapes that cannot have fewer than three sides. As this definition suggests, triangles are actually a type of polygon, but they are so important on the Math IIC that they merit their own section. Polygons are named according to the number of sides they have, as you can see in the following chart:

Number of Sides	Name
3	triangle
4	quadrilateral
5	pentagon
6	hexagon
7	heptagon
8	octagon
9	nonagon
10	decagon
12	dodecagon
n	n-gon

All polygons, no matter the number of sides they possess, share certain characteristics:

- The sum of the interior angles of a polygon with n sides is $(n-2)180$ degrees. So, for example, the sum of the interior angles of an octagon is $(8-2)180 = 6(180) = 1080$ degrees.

- The sum of the exterior angles of any polygon is 360 degrees.

- The perimeter of a polygon is the sum of the lengths of its sides. The perimeter of the hexagon below, for example, is 35.

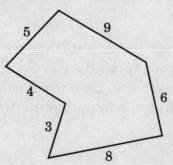

Regular Polygons

Most of the polygons with more than four sides that you'll deal with on the Math IIC will be regular polygons. A regular polygon is a polygon whose sides are all of equal length, and whose angles are all congruent (neither of these conditions can exist without the other). In the following diagram appear, from left to right, a regular pentagon, regular octagon, and a square (also known as a regular quadrilateral):

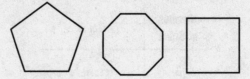

Area of a Regular Polygon

You should be familiar with one more characteristic of polygons, dealing specifically with regular hexagons. A regular hexagon can be divided into six equilateral triangles, as the figure below shows:

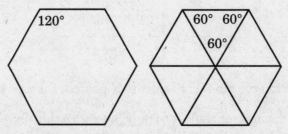

Therefore, the area of a regular hexagon can be calculated according to the length of one of its sides. The area of an equilateral triangle is $\frac{d^2 \sqrt{3}}{4}$, where d is the length of a side. So, the area of a regular hexagon is six times that, or $\frac{3d^2 \sqrt{3}}{2}$. Asking you to analyze a regular hexagon is the test-writer's favorite way of testing your ability to use properties of triangles in other polygons.

Quadrilaterals

The most frequently seen polygon on the Math IIC is the quadrilateral, which is a general term for four-sided polygons. In fact, there are five different types of quadrilateral that pop up on the test from time to time: trapezoids, parallelograms, rectangles, rhombuses, and squares. Each of these five quadrilaterals has special qualities, as you'll see in the sections below.

Trapezoids

A trapezoid is a quadrilateral with one pair of parallel sides and one pair of nonparallel sides. Below is an example of a trapezoid:

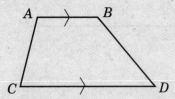

In the trapezoid pictured above, AB is parallel to CD (shown by the arrow marks), whereas AC and BD are not parallel.

The area of a trapezoid is:

$$A = \frac{s_1 + s_2}{2} h$$

where s_1 and s_2 are the lengths of the parallel sides (also called the bases of the trapezoid), and h is the height. In a trapezoid, the height is the perpendicular distance from one base to the other.

Parallelogram

A parallelogram is a quadrilateral whose opposite sides are parallel. The figure below shows an example:

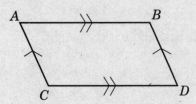

Parallelograms have three very important properties:

1. Opposite sides are equal.

2. Opposite angles are congruent.

3. Adjacent angles are supplementary (they add up to 180 degrees).

To visualize this last property, simply picture the opposite sides of the parallelogram as parallel lines, and one of the other sides as a transversal. You should then be able to see why this would be true.

The area of a parallelogram is given by the formula:

$$\text{Area} = bh$$

where b is the length of the base and h is the height.

Plane Geometry

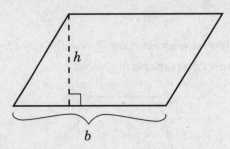

The next three quadrilaterals we'll review—rectangles, rhombuses, and squares—are all special types of parallelograms.

Rectangles

A rectangle is a quadrilateral whose opposite sides are parallel and whose interior angles are all right angles. A rectangle is essentially a parallelogram whose angles are all right angles. As with parallelograms, the opposite sides of a rectangle are equal.

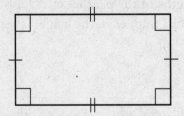

The formula for the area of a rectangle is:

$$A = bh$$

where b is the length of the base and h is the height.

Rhombuses

A rhombus is a quadrilateral whose opposite sides are parallel, and whose sides are of equal length.

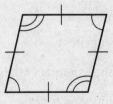

The area of a rhombus is:

$$A = bh$$

where b is the length of the base and h is the height.

Squares

A square is a quadrilateral with equal sides whose angles are all right angles. It is a special type of rhombus, rectangle, and parallelogram.

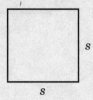

The area of a square is:

$$A = s^2$$

where s is the length of a side of the square. The perimeter of a square is $4s$.

Solving Polygons by using Triangles

It can sometimes be very helpful to think of polygons in terms of triangles. Polygons can often be cut into triangles, and if you can solve those triangles then you can solve the entire polygon. For example, if you split a square on its diagonal it forms two 45-45-90 triangles.

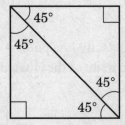

Since the hypotenuse of a 45-45-90 triangle always exists in the ratio of $\sqrt{2} : 1$ in relation to its sides, if you know the sides of a square you therefore also always know the measure of its diagonal ($d = s\sqrt{2}$). This is simply one example of the value gained by thinking about a polygon in terms of the triangles that form it. There are many other ways to use triangles when thinking about polygons. You can divide a trapezoid or a parallelogram to make two triangles and a rectangle, or you can draw a diagonal through a rectangle to make two triangles. In short, as you deal with polygons, always be aware that you can simplify the polygons by cutting them into triangles.

Circles

Circles are another popular plane geometry test topic. Unlike polygons, all circles are the same shape, and vary only in size. Circles have certain basic characteristics, and test questions will focus on your understanding of these properties.

Plane Geometry

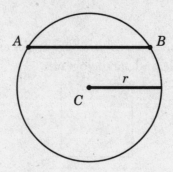

Basic Definitions of a Circle

A circle is the collection of all points equidistant from a given point, called the center. A circle is named after its center point. The distance from the center to any point on the circle is called the radius, (r), and is the most important measurement in a circle. If you know the radius of a circle, you can figure out all of its other characteristics. The diameter (d) of a circle is twice as long as the radius ($d = 2r$), and stretches between endpoints on the circle, making sure to pass through the center. A chord also extends from endpoint to endpoint on the circle, but does not pass through the center. In the figure below, point C is the center of the circle, r is the radius, and AB is a chord.

Tangent Lines

A line that intersects the circle at exactly one point is called a tangent line. The radius whose endpoint is the intersection point of the tangent line and the circle is always perpendicular to the tangent line.

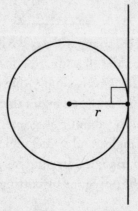

Every point in space outside the circle can extend exactly two tangent lines to the circle. The distance from the origin of the two tangents to the points of tangency are always equal. In the following figure, $XY = XZ$:

Plane Geometry

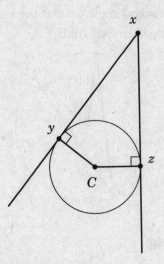

Central Angles and Inscribed Angles

An angle whose vertex is the center of the circle is called a central angle.

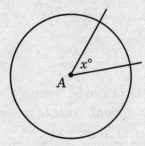

The degree of the circle (the slice of pie) cut by a central angle is equal to the measure of the angle. If a central angle is 25°, then it cuts a 25° arc in the circle.

An inscribed angle is an angle formed by two chords in a circle that originate from a single point.

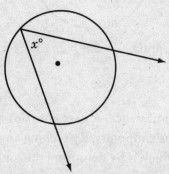

An inscribed angle will always cut out an arc in the circle that is twice the size of the degree of the inscribed angle. If an inscribed angle has a degree of 40°, it will cut an arc of 80° in the circle.

Plane Geometry

If an inscribed angle and a central angle cut out the same arc in a circle, the central angle will be twice as large as the inscribed angle.

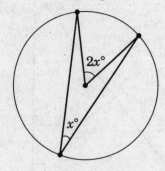

Circumference of a Circle

The circumference of a circle is the length of the 360° arc that forms the circle. In other words, if you were to trace around the edge of the circle, it is the distance from a point on the circle back to itself. The circumference is the perimeter of the circle. The formula for circumference is

$$C = 2\pi r$$

where r is the radius. The formula can also be written $C = \pi d$, where d is the diameter. Using the formula, try to find the circumference of the circle below:

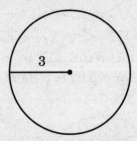

Plugging the radius into the formula, $C = 2\pi r = 2\pi (3) = 6\pi$.

Arc Length

An arc is part of a circle's circumference. An arc contains two endpoints and all of the points on the circle between the endpoints. By picking any two points on a circle, two arcs are created: a major arc, which is by definition the longer arc, and a minor arc, the shorter one.

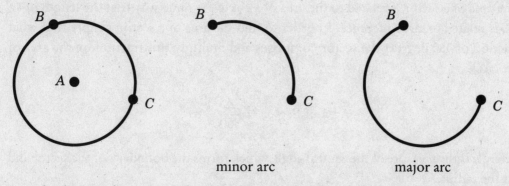

minor arc   major arc

Since the degree of an arc is defined by the central or inscribed angle that intercepts the arc's endpoints, you need only know the measure of either of those angles and the measure of the radius of the circle to calculate the arc length. The arc length formula is:

$$\text{arc length} = \frac{n}{360} \times 2\pi r$$

where n is the measure of the degree of the arc and r is the radius. The formula could be rewritten as Arc Length = $n/360$ × C, where C is the circumference of the circle.

Area of a Circle

The area of a circle depends on the radius of the circle. The formula for area is written:

$$\text{Area} = \pi r^2$$

where r is the radius. If you know the radius, you can always find the area.

Area of a Sector

A sector of a circle is the area enclosed by a central angle and the circle itself. It's shaped like a slice of pizza. The shaded region in the figure below is a sector:

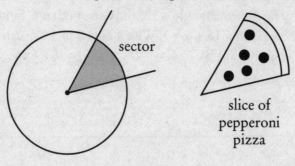

sector

slice of
pepperoni
pizza

The area of a sector is related to the area of a circle the same way that the length of an arc is related to circumference. In order to find the area of a sector, simply find what fraction of 360 degrees the sector comprises and multiply this fraction by the area of the circle.

$$\text{Area of Sector} = \frac{n}{360} \times \pi r^2$$

where n is the measure of the central angle which forms the boundary of the sector and r is the radius.

Polygons and Circles

The Math IIC test occasionally contains questions that combine polygons and circles in the same figure. These figures are really no more complicated than any other—you just have to combine your knowledge of different topics to understand them. Here's an example:

What is the length of major arc *BE* if the area of rectangle *ABCD* is 18?

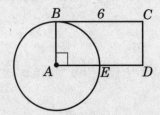

To find the length of major arc *BE*, you must know two things: the measure of the central angle that intersects the circle at its endpoints, and the radius of the circle. Because *ABCD* is a rectangle, and rectangles only have right angles, figuring out the measure of the central angle is simple. Angle *BAD* is 90°, so the measure of the central angle is $360 - 90 = 270°$.

Finding the radius of the circle is a little tougher. From the diagram, you can see that it is equal to the height of the rectangle. To find the height of the rectangle, you can use the fact that the area of the rectangle is 18, and the length is 6. Since $A = bh$, and you know both a and b, $h = A \div b = 18 \div 6 = 3$. With a radius of 3, we can use the arc length formula to find the length of arc BC. BC = $^{270}\!/_{360} \times 2\pi(3) = \frac{3}{4} \times 6\pi = {}^{9\pi}\!/_{2}$.

Key Formulas

Pythagorean Theorem

$a^2 + b^2 = c^2$, where a and b are the lengths of the legs of a right triangle, and c is the length of the hypotenuse.

Area of a Triangle

Area = ½ bh, where b is the length of the base and h is the height.

Sum of the Interior Angles of a Polygon

The sum of the interior angles of a polygon is $(n-2)180°$, where n is the number of sides in the polygon.

Area of a Trapezoid

Area = $\frac{(s_1 + s_2)h}{2}$, where s_1 and s_2 are the lengths of the bases of the trapezoid, and h is the height.

Area of a Parallelogram, Rectangle, and Rhombus

Area = bh, where b is the length of the base and h is the height.

Area of a Square

Area = s^2, where s is the length of a side of the square.

Circumference of a Circle

Circumference = $2\pi r$, where r is the radius of the circle.

Arc Length

Arc Length = $\frac{n}{360} \times 2\pi r$, where n is the measure of the degree of the arc and r is the radius of the circle.

Area of a Circle

Area = πr^2, where r is the radius of the circle.

Area of a Sector

Area of Sector = $\frac{n}{360} \times \pi r^2$, where n is the measure of the central angle which forms the boundary of the sector and r is the radius of the circle.

Plane Geometry

Solid Geometry

S OLID GEOMETRY ADDS LITERALLY another dimension to the plane geometry you've just studied—instead of squares and circles, we now have cubes and spheres. These three-dimensional shapes can be slightly more difficult to visualize, but there are only a few specific solids that you'll need to know about for the Math IIC. We'll review them one by one.

Prisms

Most of the solids you'll see on the Math IIC test are prisms, or variations on prisms. A prism is defined as a geometric solid with two congruent bases that lie in parallel planes. You can create a prism by dragging any two-dimensional triangle or polygon through space without rotating or tilting it. The three-dimensional space defined by the moving triangle or polygon is the body of the prism. The planes at which the movement the two-dimensional shape begins and ends are the two bases of the prism. The perpendicular distance between the parallel planes in which the bases lie is the height of the prism.

The figures below are all prisms. The bases of these prisms are shaded, and the height (altitude) of each prism is drawn in:

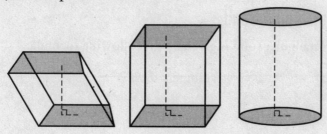

Solid Geometry

There are two main aspects of prisms that you need to be concerned with for the Math IIC: 1) volume, and 2) surface area. Some prisms have additional characteristics you should know about and which we'll cover when we discuss specific kinds of solids, but volume and surface area are fundamental to all of them.

Volume of a Prism

The volume of a prism measures the amount of space taken up by that prism. The general formula for volume of a prism is very simple:

$$\text{Volume} = Bh$$

where B is the area of the base, and h is the height.

Surface Area of a Prism

The surface area of a prism is the sum of the areas of all the sides of the prism. The formula for the surface area of a prism therefore depends on the type of prism you are dealing with. As with volume, we cover the specifics of calculating surface area as we cover each type of geometric solid.

Rectangular Solids

A rectangular solid is a prism with a rectangular base and lateral edges perpendicular to its base. In short, a rectangular solid is shaped like a box.

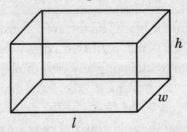

A rectangular solid has three important dimensions: length (l), width (w), and height (h). If you know these measurements, you can find the solid's surface area, volume, and diagonal length.

Volume of a Rectangular Solid

The volume of a rectangular solid is given by the following formula:

$$\text{Volume} = lwh$$

where *l* is the length, *w* is the width, and *h* is the height. Notice how this formula corresponds with the general formula for the volume of a prism: the product *lw* is the area of the base. Now, try to find the volume of the prism in the following example:

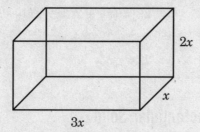

In this solid, $l = 3x$, $w = x$, and $h = 2x$. Simply plug the values into the formula given for volume, and you would find Volume $= (3x)(2x)(x) = 6x^3$.

Surface Area of a Rectangular Solid

The surface area of a rectangular solid is given by the following formula:

$$\text{Surface Area} = 2lw + 2lh + 2wh$$

where *l* is the length, *w* is the width, and *h* is the height.

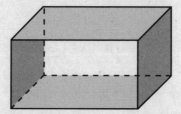

The six faces of a rectangular solid consist of three congruent pairs. The surface area formula is derived by simply adding the areas of the faces—two faces have areas of *l* × *w*, two faces have areas of *l* × *h*, and two faces have areas of *w* × *h*.

To practice, try to find the surface area of the rectangular solid we used as an example for volume. Here's the figure again:

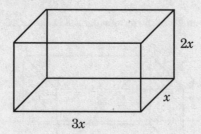

All you have to do is enter the given values into the formula for surface area:

$$\begin{aligned}
\text{Surface Area} &= 2lw + 2lh + 2wh \\
&= 2(3x)(x) + 2(3x)(2x) + 2(x)(2x) \\
&= 6x^2 + 12x^2 + 4x^2 \\
&= 22x^2
\end{aligned}$$

Diagonal Length of a Rectangular Solid

The diagonal of a rectangular solid, *d*, is the line segment whose endpoints are opposite corners of the solid. Each rectangular solid has four diagonals, all with the same length, that connect each pair of opposite vertices. Here's one diagonal drawn in:

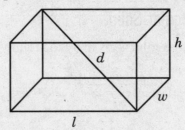

The formula for the length of a diagonal is:

$$d = \sqrt{l^2 + w^2 + h^2}$$

where *l* is the length, *w* is the width, and *h* is the height.

You can look at this formula as the Pythagorean Theorem in three dimensions. In fact, you can derive this formula using the Pythagorean Theorem. First, find the length of the diagonal along the base. This is $\sqrt{l^2 + w^2}$. Then use the Pythagorean Theorem again, incorporating height to find the length of the diagonal from one corner to the other: $d^2 = (\sqrt{l^2 + w^2})^2 + h^2$. Thus, $d^2 = l^2 + w^2 + h^2$ and $d = \sqrt{l^2 + w^2 + h^2}$. A Math IIC question might ask you:

What is the length of diagonal *AH* in the rectangular solid below if *AC* = 5, *GH* = 6, and *CG* = 3?

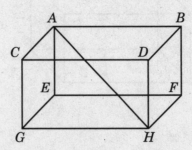

The question gives the length, width, and height of the rectangular solid, so you can just plug those numbers into the formula:

$$AH = \sqrt{5^2 + 6^2 + 3^2} = \sqrt{25 + 36 + 9} = \sqrt{70}$$

The length of the diagonal AH (as well as BG, CF, and DE) is $\sqrt{70}$.

Cubes

Just as a square is a special kind of rectangle, a cube is a special kind of rectangular solid. A cube is a rectangular solid that has edges with all the same length. In other words, the length, width, and height are equal, and each of its six faces is a square.

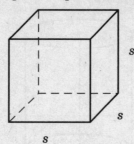

Volume of a Cube

The formula for finding the volume of a cube is essentially the same as the formula for the volume of a rectangular solid. However, in a cube the length, width, and height are all equal, so that the cube volume formula is:

$$\text{Volume of a Cube} = s^3$$

where s is the length of one edge of the cube.

Surface Area of a Cube

Since a cube is just a rectangular solid whose sides are all equal, the formula for finding the surface area of a cube is the same as for a rectangular solid, except with $s = l = w = h$:

$$\text{Surface Area of a Cube} = 6s^2$$

where s is the length of one edge of the cube.

Diagonal Length of a Cube

The same goes for the diagonal length of a cube. The formula from the rectangular solid is simply adapted from the formula for the diagonal length of a rectangular solid, with $s = l = w = h$:

$$d = \sqrt{3s^2} = s\sqrt{3}$$

where s is the length of one edge of the cube.

Cylinders

A cylinder is a prism with a circular base.

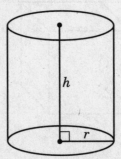

The height of a cylinder, h, is the length of the line segment whose endpoints are the centers of the bases. The radius of a cylinder, r, is the radius of its base. If you know the height and radius of a cylinder, you can calculate its volume and surface area quite easily.

Volume of a Cylinder

The volume of a cylinder is the product of the area of its base with its height. Because a cylinder has a circular base, the volume of a cylinder is:

Volume of a Cylinder $= \pi r^2 h$

where r is the radius of the circular base and h is the height. Try to find the volume of the cylinder below.

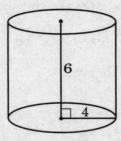

This cylinder has a radius of 4 and a height equal to 6. Using the formulas from the previous page:

$$\text{Volume} = \pi(4)^2(6) = 96\pi$$

Surface Area of a Cylinder

The surface area of a cylinder is the sum of the areas of the two bases and the lateral face of the cylinder. The bases are congruent circles, so their areas can be found easily. The lateral face is the tubing that connects the two bases. When "unrolled", the lateral base is simply a rectangle whose length is the circumference of the base, and whose width is the height of the cylinder. Therefore, the surface area of a cylinder is given by this formula:

$$\text{Surface Area} = 2\pi r^2 + 2\pi rh$$

where r is the radius and h is the height.

Go back to the cylinder example in the previous section, and now find the surface area. Plugging the values into the formula:

$$\begin{aligned} \text{Surface Area} &= 2\pi(4)^2 + 2\pi(4)(6) \\ &= 32\pi + 48\pi \\ &= 80\pi \end{aligned}$$

Solids That Aren't Prisms

The solids in this section do not have two congruent bases that lie in parallel planes, and thus, cannot be considered prisms. Like prisms, however, the two most important aspects you'll need to know for the test are 1) volume and 2) surface area.

Cones

A cone is not a prism, but it is similar to a cylinder. A cone is essentially a cylinder in which one of the bases is collapsed into a single point at the center of the base.

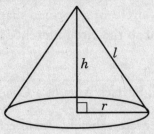

The radius of a cone is the radius of its one circular base. The height of a cone is the distance from the center of the base to the apex (the point on top). The lateral height, or slant height, of a cone is the distance from a point on the edge of the base to the apex. In the previous figure, these three measurements are denoted by r, h, and l, respectively.

Notice also that the height, radius, and lateral height of a cone make up a right triangle. This means that if you know the value for any two of these measurements, you will always be able to find the third by using the Pythagorean Theorem.

Volume of a Cone

Since a cone is similar to a cylinder, except collapsed to a single point at one end, the formula for the volume of a cone is a fraction of the formula for the volume of a cylinder:

$$\text{Volume of a Cone} = \frac{1}{3} \text{ Volume of a Cylinder} = \frac{1}{3}\pi r^2 h$$

where r is the radius and h is the height.

For practice, find the volume of the cone pictured below:

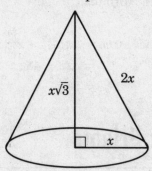

To answer this question, just use the formula for the volume of a cone with the following values plugged in: $r = x$, $l = 2x$, and $h = x\sqrt{3}$. The volume is $\frac{1}{3}\pi(x^2)(x\sqrt{3}) = \sqrt{3}x^3\pi/3$.

Surface Area of a Cone

The surface area of a cone consists of the lateral surface area and the area of the base. The base is a circle and therefore has an area of πr^2. The lateral surface is the cone "unrolled." Depending on the shape of the cone, it can be the shape of a triangle with a curved base, a half-circle, or a Pacman shape. The area of the lateral surface is a length that is related to the circumference of the circle times the lateral height, l. This is the formula:

$$\text{Lateral Surface Area of a Cone} = \pi r l$$

where r is the radius and l is the lateral height. An alternate formula for lateral surface area is:

$$\text{Lateral Surface Area of a Cone} = \pi \frac{1}{2} cl$$

where c is the circumference and l is still the lateral height. The two formulas for surface area are the same, since the circumference of a circle is equal to $2\pi r$. But knowing one or the other can save time.

The *total* surface area of a cone is the sum of the base area and lateral surface area:

$$\text{Total Surface Area of a Cone} = \pi r^2 + \pi rl$$

When you are finding the surface area of a cone, be careful not to just find the lateral surface area and then stop. Students often neglect to add the area of the circular base. Here's some practice: find the total surface area of the cone pictured below:

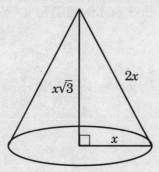

The total surface area is equal to the area of the base plus the lateral surface area. The area of the base $= \pi x^2$. The lateral surface area $= \pi x \times 2x$. The total surface area therefore equals $\pi x^2 + \pi 2x^2 = 3\pi x^2$.

Pyramids

A pyramid is like a cone, except that it has a polygon for a base. Though pyramids are not tested very often on the Math IIC test, you should be able to recognize them and calculate their volume.

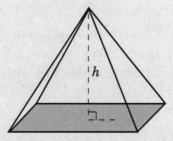

The shaded area in the figure above is the base, and the height is the perpendicular distance from the apex of the pyramid to its base.

Volume of a Pyramid

The formula for the volume of a pyramid is:

$$\text{Volume} = \frac{1}{3}Bh$$

where B is the area of the base and h is the height. Try to find the volume of the pyramid below:

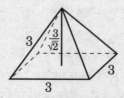

The base is just a square with side 3, and the height is $3\sqrt{2}/2$. $B = 3^2 = 9$, and the total volume of the pyramid is:

$$\begin{aligned}
\text{Volume} &= \frac{1}{3} \times (9)\left(\frac{3\sqrt{2}}{2}\right) \\
&= \frac{1}{3} \times \frac{27}{\sqrt{2}} \\
&= \frac{9\sqrt{2}}{2}
\end{aligned}$$

Surface Area of a Pyramid

The surface area of a pyramid is rarely tested on the Math IIC test. If you do come across a question that does cover the topic, you can calculate the area of each face individually using techniques from plane geometry since the base of the pyramid is a square and the sides are triangles.

Spheres

A sphere is the collection of points in three-dimensional space equidistant from a fixed point, the center of the sphere. Essentially, a sphere is a 3-D circle. The main measurement of a sphere is its radius, r, the distance from the center to any point on the sphere.

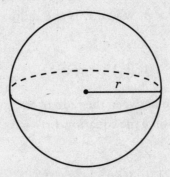

If you know the radius of a sphere you can figure out both its volume and surface area. The equation for the volume of a sphere is:

$$\text{Volume of a Sphere} = \frac{4\pi r^3}{3}$$

The equation for the surface area of a sphere is:

$$\text{Surface Area of a Sphere} = 4\pi r^2$$

Relating Length, Surface Area, and Volume

The Math IIC tests not only whether you've memorized the formulas for the different geometric solids, but also if you understand those formulas. The test gauges your understanding by asking you to calculate the lengths, surface areas, and volumes of various solids. The Math IIC will ask you about the relationship between these three properties. The exam includes two different kinds of questions that cover these relations.

Comparing Dimensions

The first way the Math IIC will test your understanding of the relationship between the basic measurements of geometric solids is by giving you the length, surface area, or volume of various figures, and asking you to compare their dimensions. The math needed to answer comparing dimensions questions isn't all that hard. But in order to get to the math you need to have a good grasp of the formulas for each type of solid, and be able to relate those formulas to each other algebraically. For example:

> The surface area of a sphere is the same as the volume of a cylinder. What is the ratio of the radius of the sphere to the radius of the cylinder?

This question tells you that the surface area of a sphere and the volume a cylinder are equal. A sphere's surface area is $4\pi(r_s)^2$, where r_s is the radius of the sphere.

A cylinder's volume is $\pi(r_c)^2 \times h$, where r_c is the radius of the cylinder, and h is its height. Therefore:

$$4\pi(r_s)^2 = \pi(r_c)^2 \times h$$

The question asks for the ratio between the radii of the sphere and cylinder. This ratio is given by r_s/r_c. Now you can solve the equation $4\pi r_s^2 = \pi r_c^2 \times h$ for the ratio r_s/r_c.

$$4\pi(r_s)^2 = \pi(r_c)^2 \times h$$
$$4(r_s)^2 = h(r_c)^2$$
$$\frac{(r_s)^2}{(r_c)^2} = \frac{h}{4}$$
$$\frac{r_s}{r_c} = \sqrt{\frac{h}{4}}$$

Changing Measurements

The second way the Math IIC will test your understanding of the relationships between length, surface area, and volume is by changing one of these measurements by a given factor, and then asking how this change will influence the other measurements.

When the solids in the question are increased by a single constant factor, a simple rule can help you come to an answer.

- If a solid's length is multiplied by a given factor, then its surface area is multiplied by the square of that factor, and its volume is multiplied by the cube of that factor.

Remember that this rule holds true if *all* of a solid's dimensions increase in length by a given factor. So for a cube or a sphere, just a side or the radius need change for the rule to hold, but for a rectangular solid, cylinder, or other solid, all of the dimensions must change. If the dimensions of the object do not increase by a constant factor, for instance if the height of a cylinder doubles but the radius of the base triples, you will have to go back to the equation for the dimension you are trying to determine and calculate by hand.

Example 1

If you double the length of the side of a square, by how much do you increase the area of that square?

If you understand the formula for the area of a square, this question is not difficult. The formula for the area of a square is $A = s^2$, where s is the length of a side. Replace s

Example 2 • 153

with $2s$, and you see that the area of a square quadruples when the length of its sides double: $(2s)^2 = 4s^2$.

Example 2

If a sphere's radius is halved, by what factor does its volume decrease?

The radius of the sphere is multiplied by a factor of $\frac{1}{2}$ (or divided by a factor of 2), and so its volume multiplies by the cube of that factor: $(\frac{1}{2})^3 = \frac{1}{8}$. Therefore, the volume of the sphere is multiplied by a factor of $\frac{1}{8}$ (divided by 8), which is the same as decreasing by a factor of 8.

Example 3

A rectangular solid has dimensions $x \times y \times z$ (these are its length, width, and height), and has a volume of 64. What is the volume of a rectangular solid of dimensions $\frac{x}{2} \times \frac{y}{2} \times z$?

If this rectangular solid had dimensions that were all one-half as large as the dimensions of the solid whose volume is 64, then its volume would be $(\frac{1}{2})^3 \times 64 = \frac{1}{8} \times 64 = 8$. But dimension z is not multiplied by $\frac{1}{2}$ like x and y. Hence, to answer a question like this one, you should turn to the volume formula for rectangular solids: volume $= l \times w \times h$. It is given in the question that $xyz = 64$. So, $\frac{x}{2} \times \frac{y}{2} \times z = \frac{1}{4} \times xyz = \frac{1}{4} \times 64 = 16$.

Inscribed Solids

An inscribed solid is a solid fit inside another solid, with the edges of the two solids touching. In the figure below, from left to right, are a cylinder inscribed in a sphere, a sphere inscribed in a cube, a rectangular solid inscribed in a sphere.

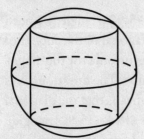 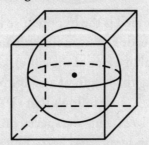 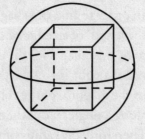

Math IIC questions that involve inscribed solids don't require any additional techniques than those you've already learned. What these questions do require is an ability to visualize inscribed solids, and the awareness of how certain line segments relate to both solids in a given figure.

Most often, an inscribed solid question will first present a figure of an inscribed solid and give information about one of the solids, such as the radius of a cylinder. Then you'd be asked to find the volume of the other solid; let's say it's a rectangular solid. What you need to do is use what you know about the radius of the cylinder to find the dimensions of the other solid (using the figure as your guide) so that you can answer the question. Here's an example:

> In the figure below, a cube is inscribed in a cylinder. If the length of the diagonal of the cube is $4\sqrt{3}$ and the height of the cylinder is 5, what is the volume of the cylinder?

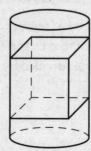

The formula for the volume of a cylinder is $\pi r^2 (h)$. It is given in the question that $h = 5$, but there is no value given for r. So in order to solve for the volume of the cylinder, we need to first find the value of r.

The key step in this problem is to recognize that the diagonal of a face of the cube is also the diameter, or twice the radius, of the cylinder. To see this, draw a diagonal, d, in either the top or bottom face of the cube.

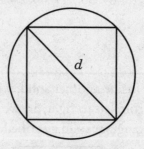

In order to find this diagonal, which is the hypotenuse in a 45-45-90 triangle, we need the length of an edge of the cube, or s. We can find s from the diagonal of the cube (not to be mistaken with the diagonal of a face of the cube), since the formula for the diagonal of a cube is $s\sqrt{3}$, with s being the length of an edge of the cube. The question gives us the diagonal of the cube as $4\sqrt{3}$, so it follows that $s = 4$. This means that the diagonal along a single face of the cube is $4\sqrt{2}$ (using the special properties of a 45-45-90 triangle). Therefore, the radius of the cylinder is $\frac{4\sqrt{2}}{2} = 2\sqrt{2}$. Plug that back into the formula for the volume of the cylinder, and you get $\pi \times (2\sqrt{2})^2 \times 5 = 40\pi$.

The Rules of Inscribed Solids

Math IIC Questions involving inscribed solids are much easier to solve when you know how the lines of different shapes relate when they are inscribed within each other. For instance, the previous example showed that when a cube is inscribed in a cylinder, the diagonal of a face of the cube is equal to the diameter of the cylinder. The better you know the rules of inscribed solids, the better you'll do on these questions. Here are the rules of inscribed solids that most commonly appear on the Math IIC.

Cylinder Inscribed in a Sphere

The diameter of the sphere is equal to the diagonal of the cylinder's height and diameter.

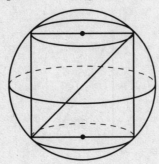

Sphere Inscribed in a Cube

The diameter of the sphere is equal to the length of cube's edge.

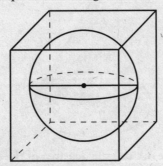

Sphere Inscribed in a Cylinder

The cylinder and sphere have the same radius.

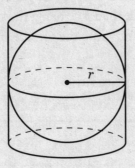

Solids Produced by Rotating Polygons

Another type of Math IIC question that you may come across involves a solid produced by the rotation of a polygon. The best way to explain this type of problem is with an example:

> What is the surface area of the geometric solid produced by the triangle below when it is rotated 360 degrees about the axis *AB*?

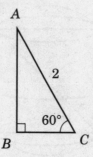

When this triangle is rotated about *AB*, a cone is formed. To solve the problem, the first thing you should do is sketch the cone that the triangle will form.

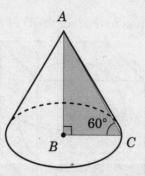

The question asks you to figure out the surface area of the cone. The formula for surface area is $\pi r^2 + \pi r l$, which means you need to know the lateral height of the cone and the radius of the circle. If you've drawn your cube correctly, you should see that the lateral height is equal to the hypotenuse of the triangle. The radius of the circle is equal to side *BC* of the triangle. You can easily calculate the length of *BC* since the triangle is a 30-60-90 triangle. If the hypotenuse is 2, then *BC*, being the side opposite the 30° angle, must be 1. Now plug both values of *l* and *r* into the surface area formula and then simplify:

$$\text{Total Surface Area} = \pi(1)^2 + \pi(1)(2)$$
$$= \pi + 2\pi$$
$$= 3\pi$$

Common Rotations

You don't need to learn any new techniques or formulas for problems dealing with rotating figures. You just have to be able to visualize the described rotation, and be aware of which parts of the polygons become which parts of the geometric solid. Below is a summary of which polygons, when rotated a specific way, produce which solids.

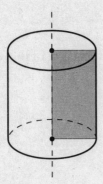
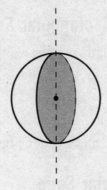
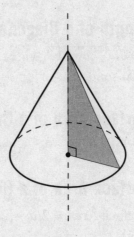

A rectangle rotated about its edge produces a cylinder.

A circle rotated about its diameter produces a sphere.

A right triangle rotated about one of its legs produces a cone.

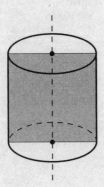
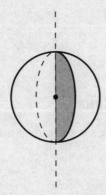
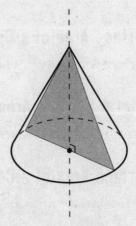

A rectangle rotated about a central axis (which must contain the midpoint of both of the sides which it intersects) produces a cylinder.

A semicircle rotated about its diameter produces a sphere.

An isosceles triangle rotated about its axis of symmetry (the altitude from the vertex of the non-congruent angle) produces a cone.

Key Formulas

Length of a Diagonal of a Cube

$d = \sqrt{3s^2} = s\sqrt{3}$, where s is the length of one edge of the cube.

Length of a Diagonal of a Rectangular Solid

$d = \sqrt{l^2 + w^2 + h^2}$, where l is the length, w is the width, and h is the height of the rectangular solid.

Surface Area of a Cube

Surface Area = $6s^2$, where s is the length of one edge.

Surface Area of a Rectangular Solid

Surface Area = $2lw + 2lh + 2wh$, where l is the length, w is the width, and h is the height.

Surface Area of a Cylinder

Surface Area = $2\pi r^2 + 2\pi rh$, where r is the radius and h is the height.

Surface Area of a Sphere

Surface Area = $4\pi r^2$, where r is the radius.

Lateral Surface Area of a Cone

Lateral Surface Area = πrl, where r is the radius and l is the lateral height of the cone.

Surface Area of a Cone

Surface Area = $\pi r^2 + \pi rl$, where r is the radius of the base, and l is the lateral height.

Volume of a Cube

Volume = s^3, where s is the length of one edge.

Volume of a Rectangular Solid

Volume = lwh, where l is the length, w is the width, and h is the height.

Solid Geometry

Volume of a Prism

Volume = Bh, where B is the area of the base and h is the height.

Volume of a Cylinder

Volume = $\pi r^2 h$, where r is the radius of the circular base and h is the height.

Volume of a Cone

Volume = $\frac{1}{3}\pi r^2 h$, where r is the radius and h is the height.

Volume of a Pyramid

Volume = $\frac{1}{3}Bh$, where B is the area of the base and h is the height.

Volume of a Sphere

Volume = $\frac{4\pi r^3}{3}$, where r is the radius.

Review Questions

1. If the length, width, and height of a rectangular solid are all doubled, by what factor is its surface area multiplied?

    (A) $\sqrt{2}$ (B) $\sqrt{3}$ (C) 4   (D) 6   (E) 8

2. A cylinder is inscribed in a sphere. If the radius of the sphere is 5, and the height of the cylinder is 8, then what is the volume of the cylinder?

    (A)   80
    (B)   110.82
    (C)   187.25
    (D)   226.19
    (E)   267.30

3. The volume of a cube is three times the volume of a sphere. What is the ratio of a side of the cube to the radius of the sphere?

    (A) $\frac{1}{3}$ (B) $\frac{1}{3\sqrt{3}}$ (C) $\sqrt[3]{4\pi}$ (D) $\frac{\sqrt{3}}{4\pi}$ (E) 3

4. A right triangle with legs 5 and 12 is rotated about the longer leg. What is the surface area of the solid formed?

    (A) 36π (B) 60π (C) 90π (D) 112π (E) 144π

Solid Geometry

Explanations

1. **(C)**

The formula for the surface area of a rectangular solid is:

$$\text{Surface Area} = 2lw + 2lh + 2wh$$

where l, w, and h are the dimensions of the solid. To answer the question, substitute $2l$, $2w$, and $2h$ for l, w, and h:

$$\begin{aligned}
\text{Surface Area} &= 2(2l)(2w) + 2(2w)(2h) + 2(2l)(2h) \\
&= 2(4lw) + 2(4wh) + 2(4lh) \\
&= 4(2lw + 2wh + 2lh)
\end{aligned}$$

When the measurements of the rectangular solid are doubled, the surface area of the solid is multiplied by 4.

2. **(D)**

The formula for the volume of a cylinder is $V = \pi r^2 h$, where r is the radius of its circular base and h is its height. The height of the cylinder is given, so we just need to find out its radius. The best way to do this is to sketch a diagram. If you look at the figure below, you can see that the diameter of the sphere, d, is the diagonal of the cylinder. The diagonal of the cylinder and its height, together with the diameter of the cylinder's circular base as the third side, make up a right triangle:

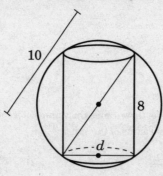

We could use the Pythagorean theorem to calculate the diameter of the cylinder base, but you should recognize that the triangle formed is a multiple of a 3-4-5 triangle, a Pythagorean triple. Therefore, since $h = 2 \times 4 = 8$ and $d = 2r = 2 \times 5 = 10$, the diameter of the cylinder base is $2 \times 3 = 6$. This means that the radius of the base is 3, and the volume of the cylinder can now be calculated:

$$\pi r^2 h = \pi(3^2)(8) = 72\pi = 226.19$$

3.   (D)
The formula for the volume of a cube is $V_c = s^3$, where s is the length of a side of the cube. The formula for the volume of a sphere is $V_s = 4\pi r^3/3$, where r is the radius of the sphere. Therefore, since we know that $V_c = 3V_s$, we can substitute in the formulas for the two solids, and solve for s/r:

$$s^3 = 3\left(\frac{4\pi r^3}{3}\right)$$
$$s^3 = 4\pi r^3$$
$$\frac{s^3}{r^3} = 4\pi$$
$$\frac{s}{r} = \sqrt[3]{4\pi}$$

4.   (C)
When the right triangle is rotated around the leg of length 12, a cone is formed with radius 5 and height 12. The formula for the surface area of a cone is $\pi r^2 + \pi r l$, where r is the radius and l is the lateral length of the cone. So, in order to calculate the surface area, we need to first find l:

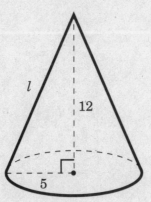

As you can see, l is just the hypotenuse of the right triangle, which is a 5-12-13 triangle (a Pythagorean triple). So $l = 13$, and we can plug in values to find the surface area of the cone:

$$\text{Surface Area} = \pi(5)^2 + \pi(5)(13) = 25\pi + 65\pi = 90\pi$$

Solid Geometry

Coordinate Geometry

COORDINATE GEOMETRY QUESTIONS make up about 10 percent of the Math IIC test. Many of the basic concepts in this chapter may be familiar to you from plane geometry, with a twist: the coordinate plane gives us new ways to analyze shapes and figures from plane geometry. There are also many topics plane geometry doesn't cover in any way: ellipses, hyperbolas, polar coordinates, the complex plane, vectors, and parametric equations.

The Coordinate Plane

The coordinate plane is a plane determined by two perpendicular lines, the *x*-axis and the *y*-axis. The *x*-axis is the horizontal axis, and the *y*-axis is the vertical axis. Any other point in the plane can be stated by a pair of coordinates that express the location of the point in terms of the two axes. The intersection of the *x*- and *y*-axes is designated as the origin, and is the point (0, 0). Following is a figure of the coordinate plane with a few points labeled with their coordinates:

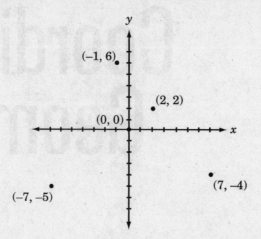

As you can see from the figure, each of the points on the coordinate plane receives a pair of coordinates: (x, y). The first coordinate in a coordinate pair is called the x-coordinate. The x-coordinate of a point is its location along the x-axis, and can be determined by the point's distance from the y-axis (where $x = 0$). If the point is to the right of the y-axis, its x-coordinate is positive, and if the point is to the left of the y-axis, its x-coordinate is negative. The second coordinate in a coordinate pair is the y-coordinate. The y-coordinate of a point is its location along the y-axis, and can be calculated as the distance from that point to the x-axis. If the point is above the x-axis, its y-coordinate is positive, and if the point is below the x-axis, its y-coordinate is negative.

The Quadrants

The coordinate plane is divided into four quadrants. Each quadrant is a specific region in the coordinate plane. The region in which $x > 0$ and $y > 0$ is Quadrant I. The region in which $x < 0$ and $y > 0$ is Quadrant II. The region in which $x < 0$ and $y < 0$ is Quadrant III. The region in which $x > 0$ and $y < 0$ is Quadrant IV.

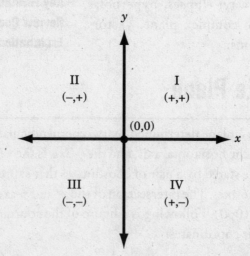

For example, the point (4, –2) lies in quadrant IV, with an *x*-coordinate 4 units to the right of the *y*-axis, and a *y*-coordinate 2 units below the *x*-axis. This is how the coordinates of a point specify its exact location. The coordinates of the origin are, by definition, (0, 0).

Lines and Distance

Lines and distance are fundamental to coordinate geometry, not to mention to the Math IIC test. Even the most complicated coordinate geometry question will use the concepts covered in the next couple sections.

Distance

Measuring distance in the coordinate plane is made possible thanks to the Pythagorean Theorem. If you are given two points, (x_1, y_1), and (x_2, y_2), their distance from each other is given by the following formula:

$$\text{Distance} = \sqrt{(x_2 - x_1)^2 + (y_2 - y_1)^2}$$

The diagram below shows how the Pythagorean Theorem plays a role in the formula. The distance between two points can be represented by the hypotenuse of a right triangle whose legs are of lengths $(x_2 - x_1)$ and $(y_2 - y_1)$.

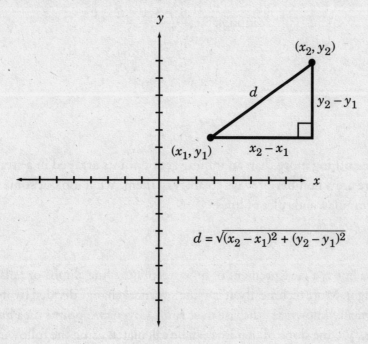

$$d = \sqrt{(x_2 - x_1)^2 + (y_2 - y_1)^2}$$

Coordinate Geometry

To calculate the distance between (4, –3) and (–3, 8):

$$\text{Distance} = \sqrt{(-3-4)^2 + (8-(-3))^2}$$
$$= \sqrt{49 + 121}$$
$$= \sqrt{170}$$

The distance between the points is $\sqrt{170}$, which equals approximately 13.04. You can double-check this answer by plugging it back into the Pythagorean Theorem.

Finding Midpoints

Like the distance between two points, the midpoint between two points in the coordinate plane can be calculated using a formula. If the endpoints of a line segment are (x_1, y_1) and (x_2, y_2), then the midpoint of the line segment is:

$$\text{Midpoint} = (\frac{x_1 + x_2}{2}, \frac{y_1 + y_2}{2})$$

In other words, the x and y coordinates of the midpoint are the averages of the x- and y-coordinates of the endpoints.

Here's a practice question:

What is the midpoint of the line segment whose endpoints are (6, 0) and (3, 7)?

To solve, all you have to do is plug the points given into the midpoint formula, $x_1 = 6$, $y_1 = 0$, $x_2 = 3$, and $y_2 = 7$:

$$\text{Midpoint} = (\frac{6+3}{2}, \frac{0+7}{2})$$
$$= (\frac{9}{2}, \frac{7}{2})$$
$$= (4.5, 3.5)$$

Lines

Lines may be nothing more than an infinite set of points arrayed in a straight formation, but there are a number of ways to analyze them. We'll look at some of the main properties, formulas, and rules of lines.

Slope

The slope of a line is a measurement of how steeply the line climbs or falls as it moves from left to right. More technically, it is a line's vertical change divided by its horizontal change, informally known as "the rise over run". Given two points on a line, call them (x_1, y_1) and (x_2, y_2), the slope of that line can be calculated using the following formula:

$$\text{Slope} = \frac{y_2 - y_1}{x_2 - x_1}$$

The symbol most often used to represent slope is m.

So, for example, the slope of a line that contains the points (–2, –4) and (6, 1) is:

$$m = \frac{1 - (-4)}{6 - (-2)} = \frac{5}{8}$$

Positive and Negative Slopes

You can easily determine whether the slope of a line is positive or negative just by look-ing at the line. If a line slopes uphill as you trace it from left to right, the slope is positive. If a line slopes downhill as you trace it from left to right, the slope is negative. You can get a sense of the magnitude of the slope of a line by looking at the line's steepness. The steeper the line, the more extreme the slope will be; the flatter the line, the smaller the slope will be. Note that an extremely positive slope is *bigger* than a moderately positive slope while an extremely negative slope is *smaller* than a moderately negative slope.

Look at the lines in the figure below and try to determine whether the slope of each line is negative or positive, and which has a greater slope:

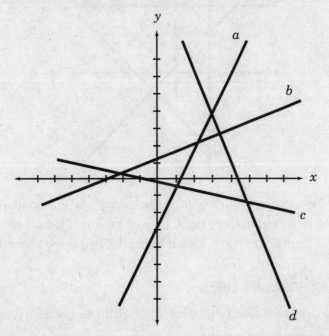

Lines l and m have a positive slope, and lines n and o have a negative slope. In terms of slope magnitude, line $m_a > m_b > m_c > m_d$.

Special Slopes

For the Math IIC, there are a few slopes you should recognize by sight. If you can simply see one of these lines and identify its slope without having to do any calculations you will save yourself a lot of time.

- A line that is horizontal has a slope of zero. Since there is no "rise," $y_2 - y_1 = 0$, and thus, $m = \frac{y_2 - y_1}{x_2 - x_1} = \frac{0}{x_2 - x_1} = 0$.

- A line that is vertical has an undefined slope. In this case, there is no "run", and $x_2 - x_1 = 0$. Thus, $m = \frac{y_2 - y_1}{x_2 - x_1} = \frac{y_2 - y_1}{0}$, and any fraction with 0 in its denominator is, by definition, undefined.

- A line that makes a 45 degree angle with a horizontal has a slope of 1 or –1. This makes sense because the "rise" equals the "run", and $y_2 - y_1 = x_2 - x_1$ or $y_2 - y_1 = -(x_2 - x_1)$.

Of the four lines pictured below, one has a slope of 0, one has a slope of 1, another has a slope of –1, and another has undefined slope. Decide which is which.

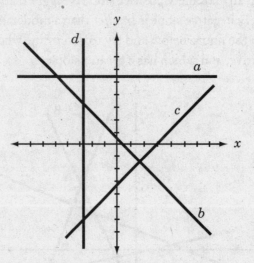

Line *a* has slope 0 because it is horizontal. Line *b* has slope –1 because it slopes downward at 45° as you move from left to right. Line *c* has slope 1 because it slopes upwards at 45°as you move from left to right. Line *d* has undefined slope because it is vertical.

Parallel and Perpendicular Lines

Parallel lines are lines that don't intersect. In coordinate geometry, they can also be described as lines with the same slope.

Perpendicular lines are lines that intersect at a right angle. In coordinate geometry, perpendicular lines have opposite, reciprocal slopes. That is, a line with slope m is perpendicular to a line with a slope of $-\frac{1}{m}$.

In the figure, lines q and r both have a slope of 2, so they are parallel. Line s is perpendicular to both lines q and r, and thus, has a slope of $-\frac{1}{2}$.

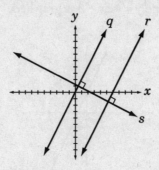

Equation of a Line

A line in coordinate geometry can be described by an equation containing the variables x and y. For the Math IIC, you need to thoroughly understand two forms of the equation of a line: the slope-intercept form and the point-slope form.

Slope-intercept Form

The slope-intercept form of the equation of a line is:

$$y = mx + b$$

where m is the slope of the line, and b is the y-intercept of the line. Both are constants.

The y-intercept of a line is the y-coordinate of the point at which the line intersects the y-axis. Likewise, the x-intercept of a line is the x-coordinate of the point at which the line intersects the x-axis. Therefore, if given the slope-intercept form of the equation of a line, you can find both intercepts.

For example, in order to find the y-intercept, simply set $x = 0$ and solve for the value of y. For the x-intercept, you set $y = 0$ and solve for x.

To sketch a line given in slope-intercept form, first plot the y-intercept, and then use the slope of the line to plot another point. Connect the two points to form your line. In the figure below the line $y = -2x + 3$ is graphed.

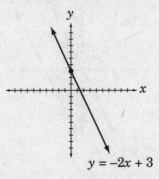

$$y = -2x + 3$$

Since the slope is equal to –2, the line descends 2 units for every 1 unit it moves in the positive x direction. The y-intercept is at 3, and so the line crosses the y-axis at (0, 3). For practice, solve for the x-intercept. First, set $y = 0$, then:

$$0 = -2x + 3$$
$$2x = 3$$
$$x = \frac{3}{2}$$

Point-slope Form

The point-slope form of the equation of a line is:

$$y - y_1 = m(x - x_1)$$

where m is the slope of the line, and (x_1, y_1) is a point on the line.

The point-slope form and slope-intercept form are just alternative ways of expressing the same equation. In fact, the slope-intercept form is the point-slope form taken at the y-intercept, or the point $(0, y_1)$:

$$y - y_1 = m(x - 0)$$
$$y - y_1 = mx$$
$$y = mx + y_1$$

Since $y_1 = b$ (the y-intercept is simply the y-coordinate of the point at which $x = 0$), the two forms are equal.

The slope-intercept form of the line equation is the more common of the two, but the point-slope form is extremely useful when all the information you have is the slope and a point (hence "point-slope").

Example Problems with Slope

The Math IIC test often asks questions that require you to understand the slope-intercept form and the point-slope form, and to be able to convert between the two.

Here's a practice question.

> What is the slope-intercept equation of the line that contains the point (3,4) and is perpendicular to the line $y = \frac{1}{3}x - 6$?

To answer this question, you need to first find the slope of the line whose equation you are trying to write. Fortunately, the question gives you the slope of a perpendicular line, and we know that the slope of a line is the opposite reciprocal of the slope of the line to which it is perpendicular. Thus, the slope is $^{-1}/\frac{1}{3} = -3$. If the line contains the point (3, 4), its point-slope equation is $y - 4 = -3(x - 3)$. To convert this to slope-intercept form, use algebra:

$$y - 4 = -3(x - 3)$$
$$y - 4 = -3x + 9$$
$$y = -3x + 13$$

Here's another question:

> What is the slope-intercept form of the equation of the line that contains the points (5, 3) and (−1, 8)?

Again, in order to solve the problem, you need to start by finding the slope of the line. You can calculate the slope with the two points you're given: $m = {}^{8-3}/_{-1-5} = -\frac{5}{6}$. To put the equation of this line in slope-intercept form, the only additional information we need is the y-intercept. To find it, plug in the x and y coordinates of a point that you know is on the line into the equation $y = -\frac{5}{6}x + b$, and solve for b. Using the point (5, 3):

$$3 = -\frac{5}{6}(5) + b$$
$$3 = -\frac{25}{6} + b$$
$$b = 3 + \frac{25}{6}$$
$$b = \frac{43}{6}$$

The slope-intercept form of the equation of this line is $y = -\frac{5}{6}x + \frac{43}{6}$.

Graphing Linear Inequalities

The graph of an inequality is a graph of a region rather than a simple graph of a line. An inequality is actually the graph of all the points on the (x, y)-plane that are either greater or less than a particular line. For this reason, while the graph of an inequality looks similar to the graph of a line but has two major differences. First, the region on one side of the line (which side depends on the inequality) is shaded. Second, the line itself is either dotted or solid depending on whether the inequality is inclusive.

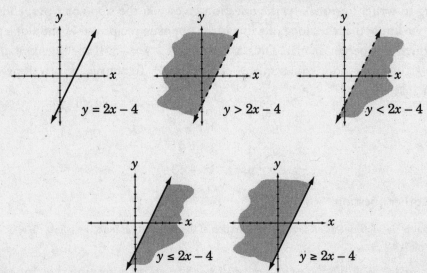

To summarize what the above graphs show: when the inequality is "greater than or equal to" or "less than or equal to," the line in the graph is solid; when the inequality is "greater than" or "less than," the line in the graph is dotted. Any point that satisfies the inequality lies in the shaded region, and any point that does not lies in the unshaded region.

And that's all you need to know about graphing inequalities for the Math IIC.

Other Important Graphs and Equations

In addition to the graphs and equations of lines, the Math IIC will test your understanding of the graphs and equations of parabolas, circles, ellipses, and hyperbolas.

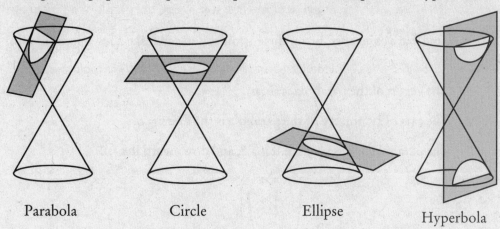

Parabola   Circle   Ellipse   Hyperbola

Questions on these topics either will ask you to match up the correct graph with the correct equation, or give you an equation and ask you to figure out certain characteristics of the graph.

Most of the questions about conic sections are straightforward. If you know the information in the sections below, you'll be able to breeze through them.

Parabolas

A parabola is a U-shaped curve that can open either upward or downward.

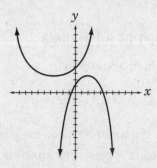

A parabola is the graph of a quadratic function, which, you may recall, is $ax^2 + bx + c$. And actually, the equation of a parabola can take on two different forms, each of which can help you determine different information about the nature of the parabola. The two ways of writing out the equation of a parabola are called the standard form and the general form.

Standard Form of the Equation of a Parabola

The standard form of the equation of a parabola is perhaps the most useful, and will be the one most used on the Math IIC test:

$$y = a(x - h)^2 + k$$

where a, h, and k are constants. From this formula, you can learn a few pieces of information:

1. The vertex of the parabola is (h, k).

2. The axis of symmetry of the parabola is the line $x = h$.

3. The parabola opens upward if $a > 0$, and downward if $a < 0$.

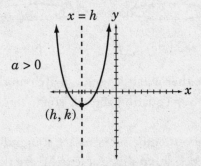

For example, if you were given the parabola equation $y = -3(x - 5)^2 + 8$, you first need to pick out what values the constants a, h, and k have. Then you can derive information about the parabola. For this example, $a = -3$, $h = 5$, and $k = 8$. So the vertex is $(5, 8)$, the axis of symmetry is the line $x = 5$, and since $-3 < 0$, the parabola opens downward.

General Form of the Equation of a Parabola

The general form of the equation of a parabola is:

$$y = ax^2 + bx + c$$

where a, b, and c are constants. If a question presents you with a parabola equation in this form, you can find out the following information about the parabola:

1. The vertex of the parabola is $(-\frac{b}{2a}, c - \frac{b^2}{4a})$.

2. The axis of symmetry of the parabola is the line $x = -\frac{b}{2a}$.

3. The parabola opens upward if $a > 0$, and downward if $a < 0$.

4. The y-intercept is the point $(0, c)$.

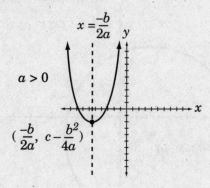

Circles

A circle is the collection of points equidistant from a given point, called the center of the circle. For the Math IIC test, there is only one equation you have to know for a circle. This equation is called the standard form:

$$(x - h)^2 + (y - k)^2 = r^2$$

where (h, k) is the center of the circle, and r is the radius. When the circle is centered at the origin, so that $h = k = 0$, then the equation simplifies to:

$$x^2 + y^2 = r^2$$

That's it. That's all you need to know about a circle in coordinate geometry. Once you know and understand this equation, you should be able to sketch a circle in its proper place on the coordinate system if given its equation. You will also be asked to figure out the equation of a circle given a picture of its graph.

To see if you know what you need to know, try to answer the following practice problem:

What is the equation of the circle pictured below?

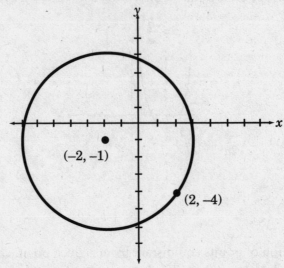

The center is given in the image: (–2 ,–1). All you need to finish the formula is the radius. We do this by finding the distance from the center and the point (2, –4) pictured on the circle:

$$r = \sqrt{(2-(-2))^2 + (-4-(-1))^2} = \sqrt{4^2 + 3^2} = 5$$

The radius of the circle is 5, so the equation of the circle can be written as $(x+2)^2 + (y+1)^2 = 25$.

Ellipses

An ellipse is a figure shaped as an oval. It looks like a circle somebody sat on, but it is actually a good deal more complicated than a circle, as you can see from the diagram with all the jargon on it.

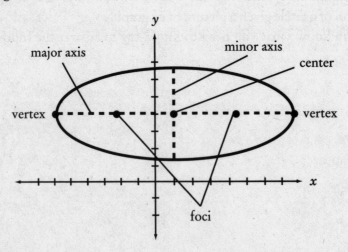

An ellipse is formed by a set of points at a constant summed distance from two fixed points called the foci. The line segment containing the foci of an ellipse with both endpoints on the ellipse is called the major axis. The endpoints of the major axis are called the vertices. The line segment perpendicular to the major axis with both endpoints on the ellipse is the minor axis. The point halfway between the foci is the center of the ellipse. When you see an ellipse, you should be able to identify where each of these components would be.

The two foci are crucial to the definition of an ellipse. The sum of the distances from both foci to any point on the ellipse is constant. For every point on the ellipse, the cumulative distance from the two foci to that point will be constant. In the image below, for example, $d_1 + d_2$ is equal to $d_3 + d_4$.

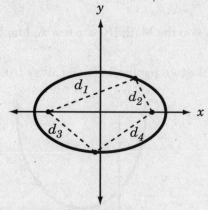

The standard form of the equation of an ellipse is:

$$\frac{(x - h)^2}{a^2} + \frac{(y - k)^2}{b^2} = 1$$

where a, b, h, and k are constants. With respect to this formula, remember that:

1. The center of the ellipse is (h, k).

2. The length of the horizontal axis is $2a$.

3. The length of the vertical axis is $2b$.

4. If $a > b$, the major axis is horizontal and the minor axis is vertical; if $b > a$, the major axis is vertical and the minor axis is horizontal.

When an ellipse is centered at the origin so that $h = k = 0$, the standard form of the equation of an ellipse becomes:

$$\frac{x^2}{a^2} + \frac{y^2}{b^2} = 1$$

On the test, you might see a question like this:

What are the coordinates of the center and vertices of an ellipse given by the following equation?

$$\frac{(x-2)^2}{16} - \frac{(y+5)^2}{36} = 1$$

First, find the center of the ellipse. By comparing this equation to the standard form, you see that $(h, k) = (2, -5)$. Since the vertices are the endpoints of the major axis, your next step should be to find the orientation and length of that axis. In this ellipse, $b > a$, so the major axis is vertical, and is $2b = 2\sqrt{36} = 12$ units long. The coordinates of the vertices are therefore $(2, -5 \pm 6)$, which works out to $(2, -11)$ and $(2, 1)$.

Hyperbolas

Though hyperbola sightings on the Math IIC are few and far between, you should still quickly review them.

A hyperbola is shaped like two parabolas facing away from each other:

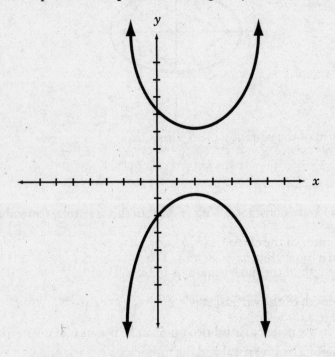

The two parts of a hyperbola can open upward and downward, like they do in the previous graph, or they can open to the sides, like the hyperbola below:

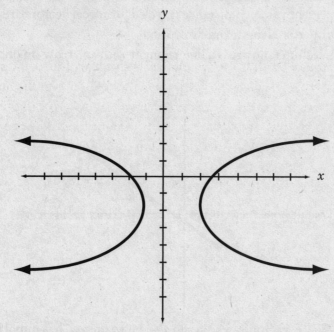

The standard form of the equation of a hyperbola that opens to the sides is:

$$\frac{(x-h)^2}{a^2} - \frac{(y-k)^2}{b^2} = 1$$

where a, b, h, and k are constants. The standard form of the equation of a hyperbola that opens upward and downward is the same as the side form except that the $(x-h)$ and $(y-k)$ terms are interchanged:

$$\frac{(y-k)^2}{a^2} - \frac{(x-h)^2}{b^2} = 1$$

The center of a hyperbola is (h, k), and the axis of symmetry is the line $x = h$ for vertical hyperbolas or $y = k$ for horizontal hyperbolas.

Similar to a circle and ellipse, the equation of a hyperbola becomes simpler for a hyperbola centered at the origin:

$$\frac{y^2}{a^2} - \frac{x^2}{b^2} = 1$$

If you see a question about a hyperbola, it will most likely concern the center of the hyperbola, which can be readily found using the equation of the hyperbola.

Vectors

Often used to represent velocity, distance traveled, or force, vectors are line segments defined by two properties: length and direction.

Graphically, a vector is shown as a line segment with an arrow on one end, to show its direction:

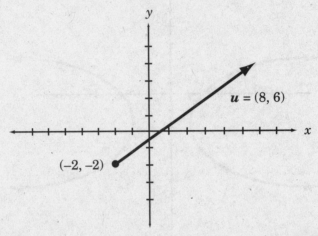

In the preceding figure, vector **u**, which can also be written $\vec{u}$, has initial point (–2, –2), and terminal point (6, 4). When you see a vector equated to a coordinate pair, say **u** = (8, 6), like in the figure above, the first coordinate is called the *x*-component of the vector, and the second coordinate is the *y*-component.

The length of a vector, also known as the magnitude, is equal to the square root of the sum of the squares of its components. Or, basically, it is a restatement of the Pythagorean Theorem. The length of the vector above, for example, is $\sqrt{6^2 + 8^2} = \sqrt{100} = 10$.

The length of a vector can be found if you know its initial point and terminal point, or if you know the components of the vector.

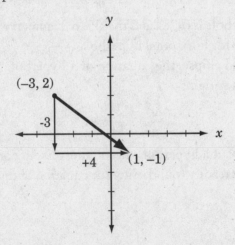

Adding and Subtracting Vectors

To add or subtract vectors, just add or subtract their respective components. For example, if $a = (2, 7)$ and $b = (-5, 2)$, $a + b = (2 + -5, 7 + 2) = (-3, 9)$. In order to graph this, you first place the second vector so that its tail starts at the tip of the first vector. Then close the triangle by drawing a vector from the tail of the first vector to the tip of the second vector. It looks like this:

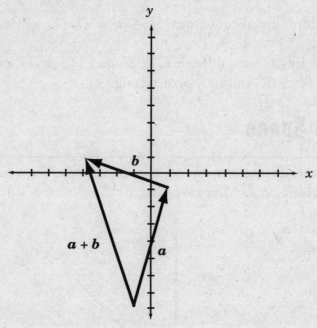

Subtracting vectors is the same process, except that you reverse the direction of the subtracted vector. $a - b = a + (-b) = (2 - (-5), 7 - 2) = (7, 5)$.

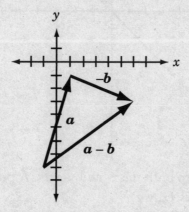

Multiplying by a Scalar

Occasionally, the Math IIC will ask you to multiply a vector by a scalar, which is a number that has magnitude but no direction. To answer this type of question, just multiply each component of the vector by the scalar. If $u = (3, 4)$, $cu = (3c, 4c)$.

Try an example problem:

If $u = (1, -5)$ and $v = (4, 2)$, what is $3u - 2v$?

It's easy—just multiply and then subtract. $3u - 2v = 3(1, -5) - 2(4, 2) = (3, -15) - (8, 4) = (-5, -19)$.

Calculating the length, sum, difference, or product of vectors and scalars is the extent of what the Math IIC will ask you on this subject.

Coordinate Space

When we add another dimension to the coordinate plane, creating a coordinate space, a new axis must be introduced. Meet the z-axis:

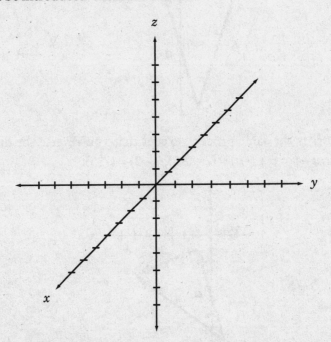

The z-axis is perpendicular to both the x- and y-axes. A point in three dimensions is specified by three coordinates: (x, y, z).

The only questions you're likely to see that involve three-dimensionsal coordinate geometry will ask you to calculate the distance between two points in space. There is a general formula that allows you to make such a calculation. If the two points are (x_1, y_1, z_1) and (x_2, y_2, z_2), then the distance between them is:

$$\text{Distance} = \sqrt{(x_2 - x_1)^2 + (y_2 - y_1)^2 + (z_2 - z_1)^2}$$

Determining the distance between two points in coordinate space is basically the same as finding the length of the diagonal of a rectangular solid. In solid geometry we were given the dimensions of the sides as measurements; for coordinate geometry we have the coordinates of the endpoints of that diagonal.

Try the example problem below:

What is the distance between the points (4, 1, –5) and (–3, 3, 6)?

Using the formula, the answer is $\sqrt{7^2 + 2^2 + 11^2} = \sqrt{174} \approx 13.19$. To see this in diagram form, take a look at the figure below:

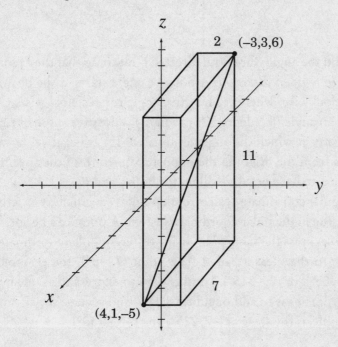

Polar Coordinates

Polar coordinates are rarely seen on the Math IIC, but will pop up every once in a while. They offer an alternate way of expressing the location of a point in the coordinate plane. Instead of measuring a given point's distance from the y and x axes, as rectangular coordinates do, polar coordinates measure the distance between a point and the origin, and the angle between the positive x-axis and the ray whose endpoint is the origin which contains the point. The distance from a point to the origin is the first coordinate, r, and the angle between the positive x-axis and the ray containing the point is the second coordinate, θ.

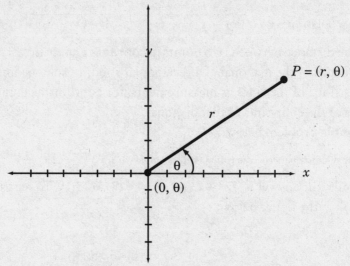

The distance r and the angle θ are both directed—meaning that they represent the distance and angle *in a given direction*. A positive angle starts at the positive x-axis and rotates counterclockwise, whereas a negative angle rotates clockwise. Once you have rotated through an angle of θ degrees (or radians), a positive value of r means that the point lies on the ray at which the angle terminated. If r is negative, however, then the point lies r units from the origin in the opposite direction of the specified angle. It is possible, therefore, to have negative values for both r and θ.

In the rectangular coordinate system, each point is specified by exactly one ordered pair. This is not true in the polar coordinate system. A point can be specified by many ordered pairs. To express the same point using different polar coordinates, simply add or subtract 360° to the measure of θ. The point (7, 45°), for example, can also be expressed as (7, 405°), or (7, –315°). Another way to express the same point using different polar coordinates is to add or subtract 180° and reverse the sign of r. The point (7, 45°), for example, is the same as (–7, 225°) and (–7, –135°).

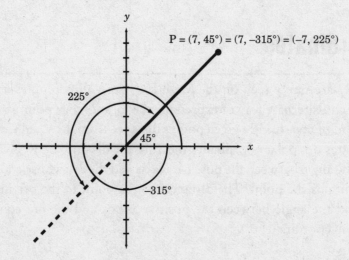

Generally speaking, any point (r, θ) is also given by the coordinates $(r, \theta + 2n\pi)$ and $(-r, \theta + (2n + 1)\pi)$, where n is an integer.

However, the usual way to express a point in polar coordinates is with a positive r and θ between 0° and 360°. A given point has only one set of polar coordinates that satisfies these conditions.

Conversions

For the test, you should know how to convert polar coordinates into rectangular coordinates and back.

To make these conversions, you have to have some knowledge of trigonometry, which we will cover in the next chapter. To find the normal rectangular coordinates of the point (r, θ), use the following two formulas:

$$x = r \cos \theta$$
$$y = r \sin \theta$$

To find the polar coordinates of the point (x, y), use these formulas:

$$r = \sqrt{x^2 + y^2}$$
$$\tan \theta = \frac{x}{y}$$

The diagram below might help you see these relationships:

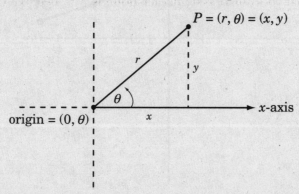

For example, the point $(12, 60°)$ can be expressed by rectangular coordinates as the point $(12 \cos 60°, 12 \sin 60°) = (6, \frac{12\sqrt{3}}{2})$. Practice this conversion by finding the polar coordinates of $(-2, -2)$.

$$r = \sqrt{4 + 4} = 2\sqrt{2}$$
$$\tan \theta = \frac{-2}{-2}; \theta = 45°$$

So the polar coordinates of $(-2, -2)$ are $(2\sqrt{2}, 45°)$.

Parametric Equations

Just like polar coordinates, parametric equations will not show up on the Math IIC test very often. However, they do show up occasionally, and knowing them might separate you from the pack.

Parametric equations are a useful way to express two variables in terms of a third variable. The third variable is called the parameter. Here is an example:

$$x = t; \; y = 2t + 1$$

As the value of t changes, the ordered pair (x, y) changes according to the parametric equations, and a graph can be drawn.

Below is a graph of the parametric equations $x = 3t - 2; \; y = -t + 4$ for the range of values $0 \le t \le 3$.

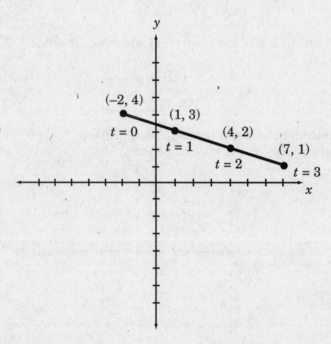

Eliminating the Parameter

As you might have guessed from the graph above, plotting parametric equations by substituting values of the parameter can be tedious. Luckily, some parametric equations can be reduced into a single equation by eliminating the parameter. All this involves is a little algebra.

Consider the parametric equations $x = 2t; \; y = t + 1$. In the first equation, we can solve for t: $t = \frac{1}{2}x$. Now we can substitute this value into the second equation to get $y = \frac{1}{2}x + 1$, which is a line we can easily sketch.

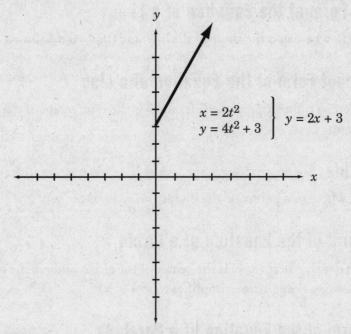

But be careful to keep the range of the original equations in mind when you eliminate the parameter in parametric equations. For example, by eliminating the parameter in the parametric equations $x = 2t^2$; $y = 4t^2 + 3$, you arrive at the equation $y = 2x + 3$. The range of this function, however, does not include x values below 0 or y values below 3 because the ranges of the original parametric equations do not include these values (take a look for yourself). So, the graph of these parametric equations actually looks like the graph of $y = 2x + 3$ cut off below the point (0, 3).

When questions on parametric equations do appear on the test, they're usually quite simple. Given a parametric equation, you should be able to recognize or sketch the proper graph, whether by plotting a few points or by eliminating the parameter.

Key Formulas

Distance in the Coordinate Plane

Distance $= \sqrt{(x_2 - x_1)^2 + (y_2 - y_1)^2}$, if you're measuring the distance between the points (x_1, y_1) and (x_2, y_2).

Midpoint Between Two Points

Midpoint $= (\frac{x_1 + x_2}{2}, \frac{y_1 + y_2}{2})$, where the endpoints of a line segment are (x_1, y_1) and (x_2, y_2).

Coordinate Geometry

Point-slope Form of the Equation of a Line

$y - y_1 = m(x - x_1)$, where m is the slope of the line, and (x_1, y_1) is a point on the line.

Slope-Intercept Form of the Equation of a Line

$y = mx + b$, where m is the slope of the line, and b is the y-intercept of the line. Both m and b are constants.

Slope of a Line

Slope $= \frac{y_2 - y_1}{x_2 - x_1}$, where two points on the line are (x_1, y_1) and (x_2, y_2).

Standard Form of the Equation of a Circle

$(x - h)^2 + (y - k)^2 = r^2$, where (h, k) is the center of the circle, and r is the radius. When centered at the origin, the equation simplifies to $x^2 + y^2 = r^2$.

Standard Form of the Equation of a Parabola

$y = a(x - h)^2 + k$, where a, h, and k are constants.

Standard Form of the Equation of a Hyperbola

$\frac{(x-h)^2}{a^2} - \frac{(y-k)^2}{b^2} = 1$, where a, b, h, and k are constants. When centered at the origin, the equation simplifies to $\frac{x^2}{a^2} - \frac{y^2}{b^2} = 1$.

Review Questions

1. An equation of line j in the figure below is:

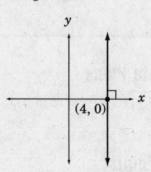

(4, 0)

(A) $x = 4y$

(B) $y = 4x$

(C) $y = 4$

(D) $x = 4$

(E)   This line is undefined.

2. Which of the following lines is perpendicular to $2y = 4x + 9$?

    (A) $y = 3x - 6$

    (B) $y = -3x + 6$

    (C) $y = -\dfrac{1}{2} x + 6$

    (D) $y = -\dfrac{1}{3} x - 2$

    (E) $y = -\dfrac{1}{3} x + 2$

3. What is the least distance between the circle $x^2 + y^2 = 2$ and the point $(3, 3)$?

    (A) 1.17   (B) 1.23   (C) 2.24   (D) 3.75   (E) 4

4. What is the least distance between the line $y = 3x + 4$ and the line that passes through the points $(1, 14)$ and $(3, 25)$?

    (A)   0
    (B)   23.67
    (C)   27.89
    (D)   45
    (E)   49

5. What is the perimeter of the triangle with vertices $(1, 0)$, $(2, \sqrt{3})$, and $(4, 0)$?

    (A) 0   (B) 7.65   (C) 8   (D) 9.32   (E) 21.77

6. What is the distance between the points $(-5, 3, -1)$ and $(2, 7, 10)$?

    (A)   10.29
    (B)   11.22
    (C)   13.64
    (D)   14.06
    (E)   16.43

7. If $\vec{a} = (-5, 3)$ and $\vec{b} = (4, 2)$, and $\vec{c} = 2\vec{b} - \vec{a}$, what is the magnitude of $\vec{c}$?

    (A)   10.21
    (B)   11.27
    (C)   12.33
    (D)   12.67
    (E)   13.04

8. a and b are points on circle O. In polar coordinates, a is the point $(3, \frac{\pi}{4})$, and b is the point $(3, \frac{2\pi}{3})$. What is the length of chord AB?

    (A)   3.65
    (B)   4.16
    (C)   4.95
    (D)   6
    (E)   7.33

Explanations

1. **(D)**

Since the line in the image is vertical, the slope is undefined, and there is no coefficient of the x in the slope-intercept form, $y = mx + b$, where m is the slope and b the y-intercept of the line. So we know that this line is in the format of $x = c$, where c is a constant. Since the line passes through the point (4, 0), the equation of the line is $x = 4$.

2. **(C)**

Before trying to answer the question, you need to put the equation into the slope-intercept form, $y = mx + b$, where m is the slope and b the y-intercept. Divide both sides of the equation by 2 to get $y = 2x + \frac{5}{2}$. Therefore, the slope is 2. A line perpendicular to this line has a slope that is the opposite of the reciprocal of 2, which is $-\frac{1}{2}$. The only answer choice with this slope is $y = -\frac{1}{2}x + 6$.

3. **(C)**

By definition, we know that all points on the circle are of equal distance from its center, in this case, (0, 0). Note that both (0, 0) and (3, 3) lie on the line $y = x$. Because a straight line is always the shortest path between two points, the point where the circle and line intersect must be the closest point to (3, 3). Since the radius of this circle is 2, this point is $(\sqrt{2}, \sqrt{2})$. The distance from (3, 3) to $(\sqrt{2}, \sqrt{2})$ can be found by the distance formula.

$$\text{distance} = \sqrt{(3 - \sqrt{2})^2 + (3 - \sqrt{2})^2}$$
$$= \sqrt{5.03}$$
$$= 2.24$$

4. **(A)**

Before trying to calculate the distance, first find the equation for the line through (1, 14) and (3, 25). The slope of the line is defined by the equation:

$$\frac{y_2 - y_1}{x_2 - x_1} = \frac{25 - 14}{3 - 1} = \frac{11}{2}$$

The slope of this line and the slope of line $y = 3x + 4$, which is 3, are not equal, which means that they are not parallel and must cross. Therefore, the least difference between the two lines is 0.

5.   **(B)**

In order to find the perimeter of this triangle, you need to know the length of each side. The side lengths are the distance between each two vertices. The distance formula is all you need. For $(1, 0)$ and $(4, 0)$:

$$\begin{aligned} \text{distance} &= \sqrt{(4-1)^2 + (0-0)^2} \\ &= \sqrt{9} \\ &= 3 \end{aligned}$$

For $(1, 0)$ and $(2, \sqrt{3})$, we get

$$\begin{aligned} \text{distance} &= \sqrt{(2-1)^2 + (\sqrt{3}-0)^2} \\ &= \sqrt{4} \\ &= 2 \end{aligned}$$

For $(4, 0)$ and $(2, \sqrt{3})$, we get

$$\begin{aligned} \text{distance} &= \sqrt{(4-2)^2 + (0-\sqrt{3})^2} \\ &= \sqrt{7} \\ &\approx 2.65 \end{aligned}$$

The perimeter is the sum of the lengths of all three sides: $3 + 2 + 2.65 = 7.65$.

6. **(C)**

Use the three-dimensional distance formula to find the distance between these two points. Recall that the distance, d, between the point (x_1, y_1, z_1) and the point (x_2, y_2, z_2) is given by $d = \sqrt{(x_2 - x_1)^2 + (y_2 - y_1)^2 + (z_2 - z_1)^2}$.

Plugging the points from the question into the equation gives you:

$$
\begin{aligned}
d &= \sqrt{(2 - (-5))^2 + (7 - 3)^2 + (10 - (-1))^2} \\
&= \sqrt{(7)^2 + (4)^2 + (11)^2} \\
&= \sqrt{186} \\
&\approx 13.64
\end{aligned}
$$

7. **(E)**

To multiply a vector by a scalar, multiply each component of the vector by the scalar. So, $2\vec{b} = 2(4, 2) = (8, 4)$. Then, to subtract these vectors, subtract their respective components: $\vec{c} = 2\vec{b} - \vec{a} = (8, 4) - (-5, 3) = (8 - (-5), 4 - 3) = (13, 1)$. The magnitude of a vector is equal to the square root of the sum of the squares of its components. In this case, the magnitude of $\vec{c}$ is $\sqrt{13^2 + 1^2} = \sqrt{170} \approx 13.04$.

8. **(A)**

First, we need to convert the points from polar coordinates to rectangular. To find the rectangular coordinates of a point (r, θ), use the conversion formulas, $x = r \cos \theta$ and $y = r \sin \theta$. In this case, for point a, $x = 3 \cos \frac{\pi}{4} \approx 2.12$ and $y = 3 \sin \frac{\pi}{4} \approx 2.12$. The rectangular coordinates for point a are $(2.12, 2.12)$. For point b, $x = 3 \cos \frac{2\pi}{3} = -1.5$ and $y = 3 \sin \frac{2\pi}{3} \approx 2.6$, so the rectangular coordinates for point b are $(-1.5, 2.6)$.

To find the length of chord AB, use the distance formula to find the distance from point a to point b: $AB = \sqrt{(-1.5 - 2.12)^2 + (2.6 - 2.12)^2} = \sqrt{13.33} \approx 3.65$.

Trigonometry

THE MATH IIC TEST RIGOROUSLY COVERS trigonometry. In fact, the depth and breath of the Math IIC test's coverage of trigonometry is one of the major differences between it and the Math IC test. If you have only a rudimentary understanding of trigonometry, the IIC test might not be the best choice for you.

But if you do have an understanding of trigonometry, the Math IIC test is the place to be (especially since it has that great scoring curve). In this chapter we'll provide the scrupulous training regimen necessary to make sure you know the necessary trigonometry. This chapter explains how to deal with radians, reviews all the basic trigonometric functions, the inverse trigonometric functions, graphs of trigonometric functions, and the use of trigonometry in oblique triangles.

Basic Functions

Most of the trigonometry on the Math IIC test has to do with the different parts of a right triangle and the relationships among these different parts. The three basic trigonometric functions—sine, cosine, and tangent—are the tools that define these connections. Given the measure of one of the non-right angles in a right triangle, you can use these tools of trigonometry to find the shape of the triangle. If you are given the measure of one of the non-right angles and one of the sides, you can find all the values of the right triangle.

Basic Functions and The Right Triangle

In more specific terms, if you're given a right triangle and know the measure of one non-right angle, the trigonometric functions tell you the ratio of the lengths of any two sides of the triangle.

In the right triangle below, the measure of one acute angle is labeled θ, and the sides of the triangle are labeled hypotenuse, opposite, and adjacent, according to their position relative to the angle of measure θ.

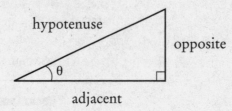

Sine

The sine of an angle is the ratio of the side opposite the angle over the hypotenuse.

$$\sin(\theta) = \frac{opposite}{hypotenuse}$$

Cosine

The cosine of an angle is the ratio of the side adjacent the angle over the hypotenuse.

$$\cos(\theta) = \frac{adjacent}{hypotenuse}$$

Tangent

The sine of an angle is the ratio of the side opposite the angle over the side adjacent to the angle.

$$\tan(\theta) = \frac{opposite}{adjacent}$$

A handy way to remember these formulas is the acronym SOHCAHTOA. The "S," "C," and "T" stand for the three different basic trigonometric functions, while the two letters after the "S," "C," and "T" refer to the sides of the triangle that are being related by that function.

- **SOH:** **S**ine is the side **O**pposite the angle divided by the **H**ypotenuse.

- **CAH:** **C**osine is the side **A**djacent to the angle divided by the **H**ypotenuse.

- **TOA:** **T**angent is the side **O**pposite divided by the **A**djacent side.

Using Your Calculator With the Basic Functions

On some questions dealing with sine, cosine, and tangent, your calculator can be extremely helpful. Using your calculator, you can quickly compute the value of one of the three trigonometric functions at any given angle. On a graphing calculator, you would find the button indicating the trigonometric function you want to perform, type in the value of the angle, and then hit Enter. To calculate the cosine of 45°, press the COS button, then type in 45, and press Enter.

$$\cos 45 = .707\ldots$$

On non-graphing calculators you may need to type in the value of the angle first and then press the trigonometric function button.

Angles Larger than 90° and the Basic Functions

Angles in a right triangle can never be larger than 90°, since the sum of all three angles must equal 180°. But on the Math IIC you may occasionally run into angles that are larger than 90°. It is often more intuitive to think of these in terms of the coordinate plane rather than in terms of a triangle.

Below are pictured four angles in the coordinate plane. The first is the acute angle we've already covered in this chapter: the next three are all larger than 90°.

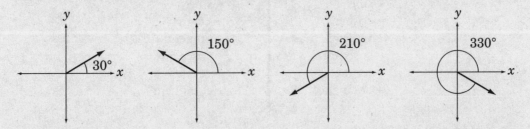

The four quadrants of the coordinate plane become very important when dealing with angles that are larger than 90°. Each angle larger than 90° can be "simplified" by looking at it in the context of its own quadrant. In the figure below, the four angles from the previous angle are defined in terms of their own quadrants:

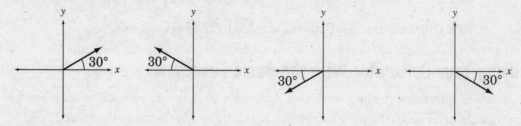

By reconsidering each angle based on its relationship to the *x*-axis, it becomes clear that each of the original angles can be treated as a reoriented 30° angle. In other words, a 210° angle is just the same as a 30° angle except that the 210° angle lives in the third quadrant. In terms of the basic trigonometric functions, this means that the value of a 210° angle is the same as the value of a 30° value, except that the sign of the trigonometric function differs based on the quadrant that the angle lives in. Depending on the quadrant of the coordinate plane in which an angle resides, the values of the trigonometric properties of that angle will be either positive or negative. Below is a figure illustrating the signs of the trigonometric functions according to the quadrant in which they lie.

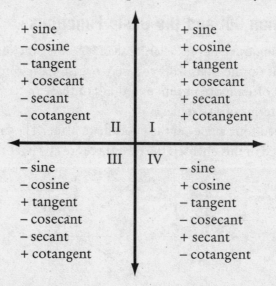

You should memorize this chart.

The Math IIC will probably test whether you know the proper sign for each quadrant in an indirect way, meaning that it's unlikely that you'll have to do any heavy calculating when dealing with this topic. Instead, you might find a question such as:

If the value of sin −θ is .5, what is the value of sin θ?

This question doesn't ask you to think about sin for any specific value of θ. Instead, it tests your understanding of the quadrant signs for the sine function. The first thing you should see is that $-\theta$ and θ have the same magnitude, even if they have different signs. This means that the magnitude of sine for $-\theta$ and θ will be the same. Immediately you should understand that sin θ must equal either .5 or $-.5$. To figure out which of these values is right, you have to decide what quadrant angle θ resides in. Based on the graph of the sine function or from the above chart, you can see that the sine function has a positive value in quadrants I and II, and negative values in quadrants III and IV. Since sin $-\theta$ is equal to a positive number, .5, you know that $-\theta$ must represent an angle in quadrant I or II. Since angle θ is simply the reflection of $-\theta$ across the y-axis, you can see that angle θ must also be in either quadrant I or II. The value of sin θ must be positive: .5 is the right answer.

Cosecant, Secant, and Cotangent

In addition to sine, cosine, and tangent, there are three other trigonometric functions you need to know for the Math IIC: cosecant, secant, and cotangent. The formulas of these functions should seem familiar to you, though, since these three functions are simply the reciprocals of sine, cosine, and tangent.

Cosecant

Cosecant is the reciprocal of sine. Its formula is:

$$csc(\theta) = \frac{\text{hypotenuse}}{\text{opposite side}} = \frac{d}{y} = \frac{1}{\sin(\theta)}$$

Secant

Secant is the reciprocal of cosine. Its formula is:

$$sec(\theta) = \frac{\text{hypotenuse}}{\text{adjacent side}} = \frac{d}{x} = \frac{1}{\cos(\theta)}$$

Cotangent

Cotangent is the reciprocal of tangent. Its formula is:

$$cot(\theta) = \frac{\text{adjacent side}}{\text{opposite side}} = \frac{x}{y} = \frac{\cos(\theta)}{\sin(\theta)}$$

The Math IIC will rarely ask you to find the values of these three functions. Most likely, it will ask you to manipulate them in algebraic equations, often with the goal of simplifying the expression down to its simplest form. For example:

What is $^{\sec \theta}/_{\csc \theta}$, if $\theta = 45$ degrees?

We can simplify the expression by eliminating the secants and cosecants because we know that they are simply the reciprocals of cosine and sine, respectively. We will also make use of the trigonometric identity $\tan \theta = ^{\sin \theta}/_{\cos \theta}$:

$$\frac{\sec \theta}{\csc \theta} = \frac{\dfrac{1}{\cos \theta}}{\dfrac{1}{\sin \theta}}$$

$$= \frac{\sin \theta}{\cos \theta}$$

$$= \tan \theta$$

Plug tan 45 into your calculator, and you get the nice, clean number 1 as an answer.

It's also possible you might have to deal with cosecant, secant, and cotangent in questions that cover trigonometric identities (we'll cover the important identities later in this chapter).

Solving Right Triangles

One of the most important applications of trigonometric functions is to "solve" a right triangle. By now, you should know that every right triangle has five unknowns: the lengths of its three sides, and the measures of its two acute angles. Solving the triangle means finding the values of these unknowns. You can use trigonometric functions to solve a right triangle if either of the following sets of information is given:

1. The length of one side and the measure of one acute angle

2. The lengths of two sides

Either situation might appear on the Math IIC, so we'll cover both.

Given: One Angle and One Side

The right triangle below has an acute angle of 35° and a side of length 7.

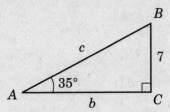

To find the measure of the other acute angle, just subtract the measures of the other two angles from 180°:

$$\angle B = 180 - 90 - 35 = 55°$$

To find the lengths of the other two sides, use trigonometric functions relating the given angle measure to the given side length. The key to problems of this type is to choose the correct trigonometric functions. In this question, you are given the measure of one angle and the length of the side opposite that angle, and two trigonometric functions relate these quantities. Since you know the length of the opposite side, the sine (opposite/hypotenuse) will allow you to solve for the length of the hypotenuse. Likewise, the tangent (opposite/adjacent) will let you solve for the length of the adjacent side.

$$\sin 35° = \frac{7}{c}$$

$$\tan 35° = \frac{7}{b}$$

You'll need your calculator to find sin 35° and tan 35°. But the basic algebra of solving right triangles is easy.

$$c = \frac{7}{\sin(35°)} = 12.2$$

$$b = \frac{7}{\tan(35°)} = 10.0$$

Given: Two Sides

The right triangle below has a leg of length 5 and a hypotenuse of length 8.

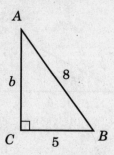

First, use the Pythagorean theorem to find the length of the third side:

$$b = \sqrt{8^2 - 5^2} = \sqrt{39} \approx 6.2$$

Next, use trigonometric functions to solve for the acute angles:

$$\sin A = \frac{5}{8}$$

$$\cos B = \frac{5}{8}$$

Now you know that $\sin A = \frac{5}{8}$, but you are looking to figure out the value of angle A, not $\sin A$. To do this, you need to use some standard algebra and isolate the angle. In other words, you have to find the inverse sine of both sides of the equation $\sin A = \frac{5}{8}$. Luckily, your calculator has inverse trigonometric function buttons labeled $\sin^{-1}$, $\cos^{-1}$, and $\tan^{-1}$. These inverse trigonometric functions are also referred to as arcsine, arccosine, and arctangent.

For this problem, use the $\sin^{-1}$ button to calculate the inverse sine of $\frac{5}{8}$. Carrying out this operation will tell you exactly which angle between 0 and 90 degrees has a sine of $\frac{5}{8}$.

$$\sin^{-}1(\sin A) = \sin^{-}1\left(\frac{5}{8}\right)$$
$$\angle A = 38.7 \text{degrees}$$

You can solve for angle b by using the $\cos^{-1}$ button and following the same steps. Try it out. You should come up with a value of 51.3 degrees.

To solve this type of problem you must know the proper math, and you also have to know how to use the inverse trigonometric function buttons on your calculator. This type of question puts the "C" in Math IIC.

General Rules of Solving Right Triangles

We've just shown you two of the different paths you can take when solving a right triangle. The actual solution will depend on the specific problem, but the same three tools are always used:

1. The trigonometric functions

2. The Pythagorean theorem

3. The fact that the sum of the angles of a triangle is 180°.

There is not necessarily a "right" way to solve a right triangle. One way that is usually "wrong", though, is solving for an angle or side in the first step, approximating that measurement, and then using that approximation to finish solving the triangle. This approximation will lead to less accurate answers, which in some cases might cause your answer not to match with the answer choices.

Trigonometric Identities

A trigonometric identity is an equation involving trigonometric functions that holds true for all angles. These identities are commonly called Pythagorean Identities, because they come from the Pythagorean theorem.

$$\tan(\theta) = \frac{\sin(\theta)}{\cos(\theta)}$$

$$\csc(\theta) = \frac{1}{\sin(\theta)}$$

$$\sec(\theta) = \frac{1}{\cos(\theta)}$$

$$\cot(\theta) = \frac{1}{\tan(\theta)} = \frac{\cos(\theta)}{\sin(\theta)}$$

In general, the Math IIC will test your knowledge of the trigonometric identities by giving you a complex expression that you have to simplify. These questions have more to do with memorizing the identities and being good with algebraic substitution than it does with the theoretical concepts of trigonometry.

For example:

What is $\dfrac{\cos\theta \times \tan\theta}{\sin\theta} - \cos^2\theta$?

To solve a problem like this, use the trigonometric identities to simplify the trigonometric into sines and cosines. After you have simplified the expression using the identities, it is quite likely that the expressions will simplify further through the canceling of terms. The simplification of the expression in the example questions proceeds as follows.

$$\frac{\cos(\theta) \times \tan(\theta)}{\sin(\theta)} - \cos^2(\theta) = \frac{\cos(\theta)\sin(\theta)}{\sin(\theta)\cos(\theta)} - \cos^2(\theta)$$
$$= 1 - \cos^2(\theta)$$
$$= sin^2(\theta)$$

Simplify the mess given to you by the problem, and you get $\sin^2\theta$.

Here's another example:

What is $\tan^2\theta \cos^2\theta + 1 - \sin^2\theta$?

$$\tan^2\theta \cos^2\theta + 1 - \sin^2\theta = \frac{\sin^2\theta \cos^2\theta}{\cos^2\theta} + 1 - \sin^2\theta$$
$$= \sin^2\theta + 1 - \sin^2\theta$$
$$= 1$$

Other Trigonometric Identities

About once a test, you may encounter a particularly complicated trigonometric expression. Such expressions *can* usually be solved using the trigonometric identities we've already covered, but the process will be laborious and difficult. However, if you know the special trigonometric identities below, these questions will be much easier and less time-consuming.

We list the special trigonometric identities in the order of usefulness, starting with the ones most likely to be used on the test.

Sum and Difference Formulas

There are three identities for the sum of two angles:

$$\sin(\alpha + \beta) = \sin(\alpha)\cos(\beta) + \cos(\alpha)\sin(\beta)$$
$$\cos(\alpha + \beta) = \cos(\alpha)\cos(\beta) - \sin(\alpha)\sin(\beta)$$
$$\tan(\alpha + \beta) = \frac{\tan(\alpha) + \tan(\beta)}{1 - \tan(\alpha)\tan(\beta)}$$

There are also three identities for the difference of two angles:

$$\sin(\alpha - \beta) = \sin(\alpha)\cos(\beta) - \cos(\alpha)\sin(\beta)$$
$$\cos(\alpha - \beta) = \cos(\alpha)\cos(\beta) + \sin(\alpha)\sin(\beta)$$
$$\tan(\alpha - \beta) = \frac{\tan(\alpha) - \tan(\beta)}{1 + \tan(\alpha)\tan(\beta)}$$

Try to use these identities in a sample problem:

Simplify the following expression: $\sin^2 x + \cos^2 x - \sec^2 x + \tan^2 x$.

Using the identities $\sin^2 x + \cos^2 x = 1$ and $1 + \tan^2 x = \sec^2 x$, the expression simplifies the following way:

$$\sin^2(x) + \cos^2(x) - \sec^2(x) + \tan^2(x) = 1 - \sec^2(x) + \tan^2(x)$$
$$= -\sec^2(x) + \sec^2(x)$$
$$= 0$$

Here's another example to practice with:

If $\sin a = -\cos b = \tfrac{3}{5}$ and a and b are both in the second quadrant, what is $\cos(a - b)$?

If $\sin a = \tfrac{3}{5}$ and the angle is in the second quadrant, then $\cos a = -\tfrac{4}{5}$. Also, if $\cos b = -\tfrac{3}{5}$ and b is in the second quadrant, then $\sin b = \tfrac{4}{5}$. See the figure below:

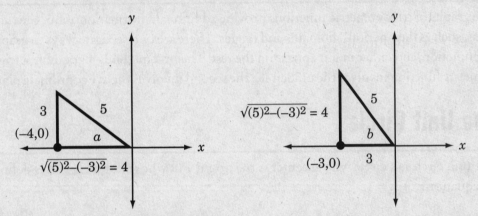

Now you can use the subtraction identity $\cos(\alpha - \beta) = \cos(\alpha)\cos(\beta) + \sin(\alpha)\sin(\beta)$ to see that $\cos(\alpha - \beta) = (-\tfrac{4}{5})(-\tfrac{3}{5}) + (\tfrac{3}{5})(\tfrac{4}{5}) = \tfrac{12}{25} + \tfrac{12}{25} = \tfrac{24}{25}$.

If you are familiar with the formula for $\cos(a - b)$ and remember the Pythagorean triple 3-4-5, you can save time on a question like this. Otherwise, you would have had to find the arcsine of $\tfrac{3}{5}$, the arccosine of $-\tfrac{3}{5}$, subtracted one from the other, and taken the cosine of the result.

Double Angle Formulas

There are three double angle formulas.

$$\sin(2x) = 2\sin(x)\cos(x)$$
$$\cos(2x) = \cos^2(x) - \sin^2(x) = 1 - 2\sin^2(x) = 2\cos^2(x) - 1$$
$$\tan(2x) = \frac{2\tan(x)}{1 - \tan^2(x)}$$

Half Angle Formulas

Of all trigonometric identities, the six half angle formulas appear most infrequently on the Math IIC.

$$\sin\frac{x}{2} = \pm\sqrt{\frac{1-\cos x}{2}}$$

$$\cos\frac{x}{2} = \pm\sqrt{\frac{1+\cos x}{2}}$$

$$\tan\frac{x}{2} = \pm\sqrt{\frac{1-\cos x}{1+\cos x}} = \frac{\sin x}{1+\cos x} = \frac{1-\cos x}{\sin x}$$

Graphing Trigonometric Functions

The graphs of trigonometric functions provide additional information about the functions, such as their periods, domains and ranges. There are two separate ways to graph a trig function, and either might appear on the test. The first method of graphing a trigonometric function involves the unit circle; the second involves the x,y coordinate plane.

The Unit Circle

The unit circle is a circle whose center is the origin and whose radius is 1. It is defined by equation $x^2 + y^2 = 1$.

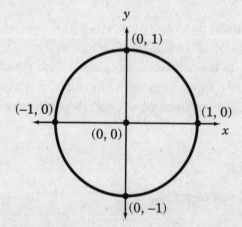

The most useful and interesting property of the unit circle is that the coordinates of a given point on the circle can be found using only the knowledge of the measure of the angle.

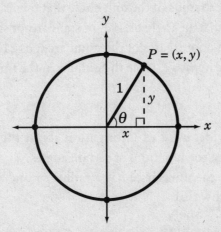

Any radius of the unit circle is the hypotenuse of a right triangle that has a (horizontal) leg of length $\cos\theta$ and a (vertical) leg of length $\sin\theta$. The angle θ is defined as the radius measured in standard position. These relationships are easy to see using the trigonometric functions:

$$\sin\theta = \frac{y}{1} = y$$
$$\cos\theta = \frac{x}{1} = x$$
$$\tan\theta = \frac{y}{x}$$

As you can see, because the radius of the unit circle is 1, the trigonometric functions sine and cosine are simplified: $\sin\theta = y$ and $\cos\theta = x$. This means that another way to write the coordinates of a point (x, y) on the unit circle is $(\cos\theta, \sin\theta)$, where θ is the measure of the angle in standard position whose terminal side contains the point.

Here's an example of a typical question on the Math IIC testing this principle:

What are the coordinates of the point P pictured below?

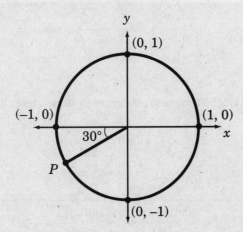

Point *P* is the endpoint of a radius of the unit circle that forms a 30° angle with the negative *x*-axis. This means that an angle of 210° in standard position would terminate in the same position. So, the coordinates of the point are (cos 210°, sin 210°) = ($-\sqrt{3}/2$, $-\frac{1}{2}$). Both coordinates must be negative, since the point is in the third quadrant.

Range

The unit circle also provides a lot of information about the range of trigonometric functions and the values of the functions at certain angles.

For example, because the unit circle has a radius of one and has points all of the form (cos θ, sin θ), we know that:

$$-1 < \sin \theta < 1 \text{ and } -1 < \cos \theta < 1$$

Tangent ranges from $-\infty$ to ∞, but is undefined at every angle whose cosine is 0. Can you guess why? Look at the formula of tan $\theta = {}^{\sin\theta}/_{\cos\theta}$. If cos $\theta = 0$, then division by 0 occurs, and the quotient, tan θ is undefined.

Radians and Degrees

Radians are another way to measure angles. Sometimes radians will be used in questions, and other times you may choose to use them since they can sometimes be more convenient to use than degrees. Radians will never appear on the Math IC test, but for the Math IIC, it is necessary to know how to convert between radians and degrees.

A degree is equal to $\frac{1}{360}$ of a circle, while a radian is equal to the angle that intercepts an arc of the same length as the radius of the circle. In the figure below, arc *AB* has length *r*, and the central angle measures one radian.

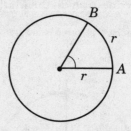

When converting between the two measurement systems, use the proportion:

$$\frac{1 \text{ degree}}{360} = \frac{1 \text{ radian}}{2\pi}$$

which can be simplified down to:

$$\frac{1 \text{ degree}}{180} = \frac{1 \text{ radian}}{\pi}$$

To convert from degrees to radians: multiply the degree measure by $^\pi/_{180}$. For example, 60 degrees is equal to $^{60\pi}/_{180} = ^\pi/_3$ radians.

To convert from radians to degrees: multiply the measure in radians by $^{180}/_\pi$. For example, $^\pi/_4$ radians is equal to $^{180\pi}/_{4\pi} = 45$ degrees.

Here are the most important angle measures in degrees and radians:

$$30° = \frac{\pi}{6} \text{ radians}$$

$$45° = \frac{\pi}{4} \text{ radians}$$

$$60° = \frac{\pi}{3} \text{ radians}$$

$$90° = \frac{\pi}{2} \text{ radians}$$

$$120° = \frac{2\pi}{3} \text{ radians}$$

$$135° = \frac{3\pi}{4} \text{ radians}$$

$$150° = \frac{5\pi}{6} \text{ radians}$$

$$180° = \pi \text{ radians}$$

$$210° = \frac{7\pi}{6} \text{ radians}$$

$$225° = \frac{5\pi}{4} \text{ radians}$$

$$240° = \frac{4\pi}{3} \text{ radians}$$

$$270° = \frac{3\pi}{2} \text{ radians}$$

$$300° = \frac{5\pi}{3} \text{ radians}$$

$$315° = \frac{7\pi}{4} \text{ radians}$$

$$330° = \frac{11\pi}{6} \text{ radians}$$

$$360° = 2\pi \text{ radians}$$

On the Math IIC, it is sometimes a better idea to work solely in radians, rather than convert back and forth between radians and degrees. Using radians is especially easy on graphing calculators that allow you to switch into radian mode.

Trigonometry

Graphing in the Entire Coordinate Plane

The functions sine, cosine, and tangent are commonly graphed in the coordinate plane, with x representing the measure of an angle (the x units are usually given in radians) and y measuring the value of a given trigonometric function at that angle. The best way to see this is to study the graphs themselves. In the image below, a) $y = \sin x$; b) $y = \cos x$; c) $y = \tan x$.

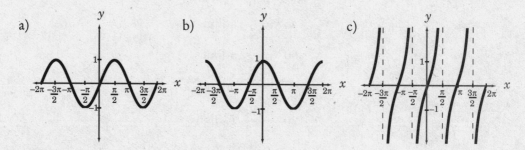

These graphs make evident a number of important characteristics of trigonometric functions.

Domain

The domain of a function is simply the x values for which the function can be calculated. In the case of the trigonometric functions, the input is an angle measure, and the output is a ratio (like $^{\text{opposite}}/_{\text{hypotenuse}}$, for example).

The domain of a trigonometric function can be seen in its graph: it is the set of all x-values for which the function is defined. For sine and cosine, the domain is the set of real numbers, because any angle measure has a sine and a cosine; there are no values of x for which sine or cosine don't produce a y-value.

The graph of the tangent function, however, tells a different story. It shows certain x-values, for which the tangent is undefined. These undefined points occur when the cosine is zero, since $\tan x = {^{\sin x}}/_{\cos x}$, and division by zero is undefined. The x-values for which tangent is undefined show up on its graph as vertical dotted lines every 180 degrees, such that $x = n(180) + 90$ degrees, where n is an integer. For example, the tangent function is undefined at the x-value $2(180) + 90 = 450$ degrees.

Range

Like the domain, the range of the trigonometric functions can be seen from their graphs. The range of a function is the set of all possible values of the function. In other words, the range is the set of all y-values of the function.

The range of sine and cosine, as you can see in its graph or by analyzing the unit circle, is $-1 \leq y \leq 1$. The graphs of these two functions never rise above 1 or fall below -1 and every point on the unit circle has a x and y values between -1 and 1. Occasionally, you may see a question in which the answer choices are possible values of sine or cosine. If any of them are greater than 1 or less than -1, you can eliminate them.

The range of tangent is the set of real numbers. To see why there are no bounds on the value of tangent, recall that the denominator ($\cos \theta$) can get arbitrarily close to zero, making the quotient get infinitely large.

The chart below summarizes what has been discussed in these previous few paragraphs. We have also included the ranges and domains of the other three trigonometric functions.

Function	Domain	Range
$y = \sin(x)$	$-\infty < x < \infty$	$-1 \leq y \leq 1$
$y = \cos(x)$	$-\infty < x < \infty$	$-1 \leq y \leq 1$
$y = \tan(x)$	$-\infty < x < \infty, x \neq n\pi + \pi/2; n$ is an integer	$-\infty < y < \infty$
$y = \csc(x)$	$-\infty < x < \infty, x \neq n\pi; n$ is an integer	$y \leq -1$ or $y \geq 1$
$y = \sec(x)$	$-\infty < x < \infty, x \neq n\pi + \pi/2; n$ is an integer	$y \leq -1$ or $y \geq 1$
$y = \cot(x)$	$-\infty < x < \infty, x \neq n\pi; n$ is an integer	$-\infty < y < \infty$

Periodic Functions

Sine, cosine, and tangent are all periodic functions, meaning that their values repeat on a regular interval. This regular interval is called the functions period. Speaking more technically, the period of a function is the smallest domain containing a full cycle of the function. Take a look at the periods for sine, cosine, and tangent:

- For $y = \sin x$ and $y = \cos x$, the period is 2π radians. This means that every 360 degrees, the values of sine and cosine repeat themselves. For example, trigonometric functions of 0 and 2π radians produce the same values.

- For $y = \tan x$, the period is π radians. Thus, the tangents of 0 degrees and 180 degrees are equal.

If a trigonometric function contains a coefficient in front of x, its period changes. In general, the period of $y = f(bx)$ is the normal period of f divided by b. For example, the period of $y = \sin \frac{1}{4}x = {}^{2\pi \text{ radians}}/\frac{1}{4} = 8\pi$ radians.

Amplitude

Another useful property of the sine and cosine curves (not tangent, though) is amplitude. The figure below shows the amplitude, a, for the sine and cosine functions:

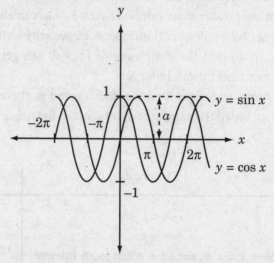

The amplitude of the sine and cosine functions is half the vertical distance between its minimum value and its maximum value. The amplitude of $y = \sin x$ and $y = \cos x$ is 1 because the minimum and maximum values of these functions are -1 and 1, respectively, and half the vertical distance between these values is 1. The tangent graph has no amplitude, because the tangent function has no minimum or maximum value. In general, the amplitude of the trigonometric function $y = af(x)$ is $|a|$. The amplitude of $\frac{1}{3} \cos x$ is $\frac{1}{3}$.

Here is an example of the type of problem you might see concerning the graphs of the trigonometric functions.

What is the period and amplitude of the function $y = 4\sin 3x$?

As we just discussed, the period of $y = f(bx)$ is the normal period of f divided by b. For the sine function, the normal period is $360°$. In this example, $b = 3$, so the period of this function is $360 \div 3 = 120°$. In general, the amplitude of the sine function $y = af(x)$ is $|a|$. In this particular case, $a = 4$. So, the amplitude is 4.

Here's another example problem:

What is the period and amplitude of the function graphed below?

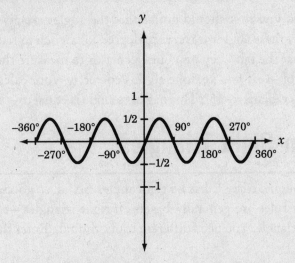

To answer this question, you simply have to read the distances off the graph. The function, which appears to be either a sine graph or a cosine graph, repeats itself every 180°. Its period is therefore 180°. Its minimum and maximum values are ±½, so its amplitude is ½.

Basically, to ably handle any question about the graphs of the trigonometric functions, you should be able to answer questions about period and amplitude based on the equation or graph of a given function.

Inverse Trigonometric Functions

We touched on the inverse trigonometric functions when we were explaining how to solve right triangles. Here, we'll go over them much more thoroughly.

The standard trig functions take an angle as input and give you the value of sine, cosine or tangent. The inverse trig functions take a sine, cosine, or tangent value as input and tell give you the measure of the angle that produces that value of sine. If you know that the cosine of an angle is equal to .866, you can use the inverse cosine function to determine the measure of the angle.

The three inverse trigonometric functions you should be familiar with are $\sin^{-1}$, $\cos^{-1}$, and $\tan^{-1}$, which are also called arcsine, arccosine, and arctangent. For the Math IIC you simply need to know how to use these functions with your calculator. Make sure you know how to use the inverse trig functions on your calculator before the test.

Since inverse trig functions are so much fun to solve, here's another example:

What angle between $-\frac{\pi}{2}$ and $\frac{\pi}{2}$ has a tangent of -1?

To find the answer, you first should notice that the angles are given in radians. You must either convert these angle measures to degrees or switch to radian mode on your calculator. Then, use the $\tan^{-1}$ key on your calculator to measure the angle that results in a tangent value of -1. If you've done all this correctly, your calculator will tell you that $\arctan{-1} = -\pi/4$ radians $= -45°$. This negative angle is equal to $-7\pi/4$ radians or $315°$.

Solving Non-Right Triangles

A non-right, or oblique, triangle has no right angles. So far, so good. Yet trigonometry—a subject whose rules are generally based on right triangles—can still be used to solve a non-right triangle. You need different tools, though. Enter the laws of sines and cosines.

In an oblique triangle, there are six unknowns: the three angle measures, and the three side lengths. To solve an oblique triangle you need one of the following sets of information:

1. Two sides and an angle opposite one of the known sides

2. Two angles and any side

3. Two sides and their included angle

4. All three sides

If you know either 1) or 2), you can use the law of sines to solve the triangle. If you know 3) or 4), you must tag-team with the law of cosines and then the law of sines to find the solution.

The Law of Sines

The law of sines is based on the proportionality of sides and angles in triangles. The law states that for the angles of a non-right triangle, each angle of the triangle has the same ratio of angle measure to sine value.

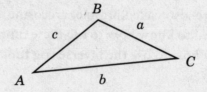

$$\frac{a}{\sin(A)} = \frac{b}{\sin(B)} = \frac{c}{\sin(C)}$$

or

$$\frac{\sin(A)}{a} = \frac{\sin(B)}{b} = \frac{\sin(C)}{c}$$

If you are given the lengths of two sides and the measure of an angle opposite one of those sides, you can use the law of sines to find the other opposite angle. The measure of the third angle can be easily found using the fact that the sum of the angles of a triangle is 180°. Finally, you can use the law of sines again to find the length of the unknown side. Here's an example:

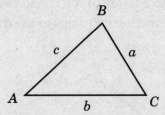

In triangle *ABC*, *a* = 5, *b* = 6, and *B* = 65°. Solve the triangle.

First, find *A* by plugging the values of *a*, *b*, and *B* into the law of sines:

$$\frac{6}{\sin(65)} = \frac{5}{\sin(A)}$$

$$\sin(A) = \frac{5\sin(65)}{6}$$

$$A = \sin^{-1}\left(\frac{5\sin(65)}{6}\right)$$

$$A \approx 49.05$$

Next, find *C*. You can do this by using the rule that all interior angles of a triangle add up to 180°:

$$C = 180 - A - B \approx 180 - 49.05 - 65 \approx 65.95$$

Last, find c by plugging in a, b, and the just calculated value of C into the law of sines:

$$\frac{6}{\sin(65)} = \frac{c}{\sin(65.95)}$$

$$c = \frac{6\sin(65.95)}{\sin(65)}$$

$$c \approx 6.05$$

The triangle is solved.

The Law of Cosines

The law of cosines offers a different way of solving non-right triangles, and can be used when you don't have the information necessary to use the law of sines. This is the law of cosines:

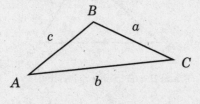

$$c^2 = a^2 + b^2 - 2ab\cos(C)$$

If you look carefully at the law of cosines, you should see a resemblance to the Pythagorean theorem. In fact, for right triangles, the law of cosines simplifies to the Pythagorean theorem. Try it yourself. The last term drops out (since cos 90 = 0) and you're left with the familiar formula of $c^2 = a^2 + b^2$. If you're curious, the $2ab \cos(C)$ term compensates for the lack of a right angle.

The law of cosines allows you to solve any triangle for which you know any three of the four unknowns in the formula. There are two ways you might know three of the four unknowns:

1. If you know two sides and their included angle, use the law of cosines to find the length of the third side. Then use the law of sines to complete the triangle.

2. If you know the lengths of all three sides, use the law of cosines to find the measure of one angle. Then use the law of sines to complete the triangle.

We'll just show one example problem, because using the law of cosines is basically just plugging values into the formula and solving it.

Solve triangle ABC if $a = 4$, $b = 7$, and $c = 10$.

First, find angle C.

$$10^2 = 4^2 + 7^2 - 2(4)(7)\cos(C)$$
$$100 = 16 + 49 - 56\cos(C)$$
$$56\cos(C) = -35$$
$$\cos(C) = -\frac{35}{56}$$
$$C \approx 128.68°$$

At this point, you can use the law of sines to find that $A \approx 18.20°$, and $B \approx 33.12°$.

Key Terms

SOHCAHTOA

$$\sin(\theta) = \frac{\text{opposite}}{\text{hypotenuse}}$$
$$\cos(\theta) = \frac{\text{adjacent}}{\text{hypotenuse}}$$
$$\tan(\theta) = \frac{\text{opposite}}{\text{adjacent}}$$

Basic Trigonometric Identities

$$\tan(\theta) = \frac{\sin(\theta)}{\cos(\theta)}$$
$$\csc(\theta) = \frac{1}{\sin(\theta)}$$
$$\sec(\theta) = \frac{1}{\cos(\theta)}$$
$$\cot(\theta) = \frac{1}{\tan(\theta)} = \frac{\cos(\theta)}{\sin(\theta)}$$

Pythagorean Identities

$$\sin^2(\theta) + \cos^2(\theta) = 1$$
$$1 + (\tan(\theta))^2 = (\sec(\theta))^2$$
$$1 + (\cot(\theta))^2 = (\csc(\theta))^2$$

Double-Angle Identities

$$\sin(2x) = 2\sin(x)\cos(x)$$
$$\cos(2x) = \cos^2(x) - \sin^2(x) = 1 - 2\sin^2(x) = 2\cos^2(x) - 1$$
$$\tan(2x) = \frac{2\tan(x)}{1 - \tan^2(x)}$$

Half-Angle Identities

$$\sin\frac{x}{2} = \pm\sqrt{\frac{1 - \cos x}{2}}$$
$$\cos\frac{x}{2} = \pm\sqrt{\frac{1 + \cos x}{2}}$$
$$\tan\frac{x}{2} = \pm\sqrt{\frac{1 - \cos x}{1 + \cos x}} = \frac{\sin x}{1 + \cos x} = \frac{1 - \cos x}{\sin x}$$

Sum and Difference Formulas

$$\sin(\alpha + \beta) = \sin(\alpha)\cos(\beta) + \cos(\alpha)\sin(\beta)$$
$$\cos(\alpha + \beta) = \cos(\alpha)\cos(\beta) - \sin(\alpha)\sin(\beta)$$
$$\tan(\alpha + \beta) = \frac{\tan(\alpha) + \tan(\beta)}{1 - \tan(\alpha)\tan(\beta)}$$
$$\sin(\alpha - \beta) = \sin(\alpha)\cos(\beta) - \cos(\alpha)\sin(\beta)$$
$$\cos(\alpha - \beta) = \cos(\alpha)\cos(\beta) + \sin(\alpha)\sin(\beta)$$
$$\tan(\alpha - \beta) = \frac{\tan(\alpha) - \tan(\beta)}{1 + \tan(\alpha)\tan(\beta)}$$

Law of Cosines

$$c^2 = a^2 + b^2 - 2ab\cos(C)$$

where a, b, and c are the lengths of the sides of a triangle, and C is the measure of the angle opposite side c.

Law of Sines

$$\frac{a}{\sin(A)} = \frac{b}{\sin(B)} = \frac{c}{\sin(C)}$$

where a, b, and c are the lengths of the sides of a triangle, and A, B, and C are the measures of the angles opposite those sides.

Review Questions

1. If $\sec^2\theta - 1 = \sin\theta$, which one of the following is a possible value for θ?

    (A) $-\frac{\pi}{2}$ (B) $-\frac{\pi}{4}$ (C) 0 (D) $\frac{\pi}{4}$ (E) $\frac{\pi}{2}$

2. Solve the following equation: $\cos(\sin^{-1}(\sin 60°))/\cos 30° = ?$

    (A) $\frac{1}{\sqrt{2}}$ (B) $\frac{1}{\sqrt{3}}$ (C) $\frac{\sqrt{2}}{\sqrt{3}}$ (D) $\sqrt{2}$ (E) $\sqrt{3}$

3. S and T are the centers of their respective circles. The two circles are mutually tangent at point U. If segment $RS = d$, what is the radius of the smaller circle in terms of d and θ?

    (A) $d\cos\theta$
    (B) $d\sin\theta$
    (C) $d(\cos\theta - \sin\theta)$
    (D) $d(\sin\theta - \cos\theta)$
    (E) $d(\sin\theta + \cos\theta)$

Trigonometry

4. In the triangle pictured below, what is the measure of BC?

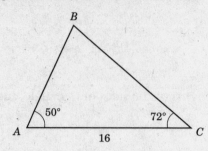

(A)   12.89
(B)   13.79
(C)   14.45
(D)   17.71
(E)   17.94

5. In the triangle pictured below, what is $\angle A$?

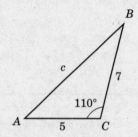

(A)   25.7°
(B)   31.2°
(C)   37.7°
(D)   39.5°
(E)   68.3°

6. Which of the following values is defined?

(A) $\sin^{-1} 2$ (B) $\tan \frac{\pi}{2}$ (C) $\sec \frac{\pi}{2}$ (D) $\tan^{-1} 0$ (E) $\cot \frac{3\pi}{2}$

7. $1 + \tan^2 x - \cos^2 x - \cos^2 x \tan^2 x$ is equivalent to which of the following expressions?

(A) $1 - \sec^2 x$
(B) $\cos^2 x$
(C) $\tan^2 x$
(D) $\cot^2 x$
(E) $\cot^2 x$

8. If $\sin 2x = \frac{1}{2}$, what is $\sin^2 x \cos^2 x$?

(A) $\frac{1}{16}$ (B) $\frac{1}{8}$ (C) $\frac{1}{2}$ (D) 1   (E) 2

Explanations

1. **(C)**

The trick to this question is knowing the identity $\tan^2\theta + 1 = \sec^2\theta$. If you didn't know it, you could have derived the identity from the base identity $\sin^2\theta + \cos^2\theta = 1$ by dividing through the equation by $\cos^2\theta$, giving $\tan^2\theta + 1 = \sec^2\theta$. Subtracting 1 from both sides gives $\tan^2\theta = \sec^2\theta - 1$.

Now, substitute into the equation from the question:

$$\sqrt{\sec^2(\theta) - 1} = \sqrt{\tan^2(\theta)}$$
$$= \tan(\theta)$$
$$= \sin(\theta)$$

The identity $\tan\theta = {}^{\sin\theta}\!/_{\cos\theta}$ allows for further simplification:

$$\frac{\sin(\theta)}{\cos(\theta)} = \sin(\theta)$$
$$\frac{1}{\cos(\theta)} = 1$$
$$\cos(\theta) = 1$$

The only answer choice for θ that yields a cosine value of 1 is 0.

2. **(B)**

For any x, $\sin^{-1}(\sin(x)) = x$. So the fraction reduces to ${}^{\cos 60°}\!/_{\cos 30°}$. Either by calculator, memorization, or using the 30-60-90 triangle, you can evaluate the trigonometric functions: $\frac{1}{2} \div \sqrt{3}/2 = {}^{1}\!/_{\sqrt{3}}$.

3. **(C)**

The first step is to calculate the length of the segment RT. To do so, use the definition of the sine function, $\sin\theta = {}^{\text{opposite}}\!/_{\text{hypotenuse}}$.

$$\sin(\theta) = \frac{\text{segment } RT}{d} \quad \text{segment } RT = d\sin(\theta)$$

Next, calculate the length of segment ST using the cosine function ($\cos\theta = {}^{\text{adjacent}}\!/_{\text{hypotenuse}}$).

$$\cos(\theta) = \frac{\text{segment } ST}{d}$$
$$\text{segment } ST = d\cos(\theta)$$

Now, the trick is to see that length segment ST is actually the sum of the radii of the two circles ($SU + UT$). Moreover, the length of segment $RT = UT$ because they are both radii of the larger circle. Since you know the length of segment RT (and so, segment UT), you can subtract this value from segment ST to get the length of segment SU (which is also the radius of the smaller circle, and the answer):

$$ST - RT = d\cos(\theta) - d\sin(\theta) = d(\cos(\theta) - \sin(\theta))$$

4. (C)

The figure gives a non-right triangle, so you can't use the basic trigonometric functions to find BC. But you are given the measures of two angles and the side between them, so you can use the law of sines: $^{AC}\!/_{\sin A} = {}^{BC}\!/_{\sin B}$.

First, find the measure of angle B, using the rule that the sum of angles in a triangle is 180: $B = 180 - 72 - 50 = 58°$. Plug the value of B into the law of sines: $^{BC}\!/_{\sin 50} = {}^{16}\!/_{\sin 58}$. By solving this proportion, you arrive at $BC \approx 14.45$.

5. (E)

Since you have the measures of two sides and the angle between them, you can start with the law of cosines to find c. Plugging the given values into the law of cosines formula: $c^2 = 5^2 + 7^2 + 2(5)(7)\cos 110°$. Working this out, you get $c \approx 7.08$. Now that you have the measure of the side opposite $\angle C$, you can use the law of sines to find a. Substitute the values into the formula, and solve the equation:

$$\frac{7.08}{\sin(110)} = \frac{7}{\sin(A)}$$
$$\sin(A) = \frac{7\sin(110)}{7.08}$$

Taking the arcsine, $A \approx 68.3°$.

6. (D)

$\sin^{-1} 2$ is undefined, because no angle exists whose sine is greater than 1. $\tan{}^{\pi}\!/_2$ is undefined, because $\cos{}^{\pi}\!/_2 = 0$. $\sec{}^{\pi}\!/_2$ is undefined because the secant function is equal to the reciprocal of the cosine function, and $\cos{}^{\pi}\!/_2 = 0$, leaving a zero in the denominator. Since $\tan^{-1} 0 = 0$, it is defined. $\cot{}^{3\pi}\!/_2$ is undefined because the cotangent function is the reciprocal of the tangent function, and $\tan{}^{3\pi}\!/_2$ is undefined.

7.   **(C)**

There are two easy ways to simplify the given expression. Both involve using identities. The first way is to immediately factor the expression into $(1 - \cos^2 x)(1 + \tan^2 x)$. Then, using the identities $1 - \cos^2 x = \sin^2 x$ and $1 + \tan^2 x = \sec^2 x$, the expression is simplified to $\sin^2 x \sec^2 x$, which can be furthered simplified:

$$\sin^2(x)\sec^2(x) = \frac{\sin^2(x)}{\cos^2(x)} = \tan^2(x)$$

The other way takes slightly longer, but requires the use of fewer identities.

$$1 + \tan^2(x) - \cos^2(x) - \cos^2(x)\tan^2(x) = 1 + \tan^2(x) - \cos^2(x) - \sin^2(x)$$
$$= 1 + \tan^2 - (\cos^2(x) + \sin^2(x))$$
$$= 1 + \tan^2(x) - 1$$
$$= \tan^2(x)$$

8.   **(A)**

Without knowing the double-angle identity for sine, you could have found the arcsine of ½, divided that angle by 2, found the sine and cosine of that angle, and then squared their product, which gives a value of ¹⁄₁₆.

Functions

$\mathbf{F}$UNCTIONS COME IN MANY SHAPES AND sizes. In fact, you've already seen quadratic functions like $f(x) = x^2 + 7x - 5$ in the algebra chapter and trigonometric functions like $f(x) = 2 \sin x + \cos^2 x$ in the trigonometry chapter. This chapter explains the specific notation, behavior, and properties of functions that you will need to know for the Math IIC test.

About 12 questions on the test cover functions. These questions can range from rather simple substitution problems, to conceptual problems about the definition of a function, to questions that test your ability to graph functions. If you find functions to be a difficult subject, you may be want to consider taking the Math IC test, which asks about half as many questions on this topic as the Math IIC does.

Characteristics of a Function

In order to be able to discuss functions, you need to have an understanding of the basic characteristics that make them, well, function how they do.

A function describes a relationship between one or more inputs and one output. The inputs to a function are variables; x is the most common variable in the functions that appear on the Math IIC, though you may also come across an occasional a, b, or some other letter. The output of the function for a particular value of x is usually represented as $f(x)$ or $g(x)$. When a function of a single variable is graphed on the xy-plane, the output of the function, $f(x)$, is graphed on the y-axis; functions are therefore commonly written as $y = x^2$ rather then $f(x) = x^2$.

Two characteristics of functions that you should become comfortable with are the domain and range. The domain is the set of inputs (x values) for which the function is defined. Consider the following two functions: $f(x) = x^2$ and $g(x) = \frac{1}{x}$. In $f(x)$, any value of x can produce a valid result since any number can be squared. In $g(x)$, though, not every value of x can generate an output: when $x = 0$, $g(x)$ is undefined.

The range of a function is closely related to the domain. Whereas the domain is the set of inputs that a function can take, the range is the set of outputs that a function can produce. To help you understand this concept, let's use the examples in the last paragraph: $f(x) = x^2$ and $g(x) = \frac{1}{x}$. Try to think of all the values that can be generated when a number is squared. Well, all squares are positive (or equal to 0), so $f(x)$ can never be negative. In the case of $g(x)$, almost every number is part of the range. In fact, the only number that cannot be generated by the function $g(x)$ is 0. Try it for yourself; there's no value of x for which $\frac{1}{x}$ equals 0. The range of the function $g(x)$ is all numbers except zero.

Once you understand the concepts of the domain and range of a function, you can see how their relationship helps to define a function. A function requires that each value of x only has one value of $f(x)$; that is, each element of the domain must be paired with exactly one element of the range. Each element of the domain and its corresponding element of the range can be written (and graphed) as a coordinate pair, $(x, f(x))$.

Now consider the set of coordinates $\{(1, 5), (3, 5), (1, 3)\}$. Does this set define a function? The answer is no, because the definition of a function requires that each element of the domain is paired with only one element of the range. Specifically, 1, has been assigned to two different values in the range, 5 and 3. This rule is easy to apply when you have the coordinates listed for you. If you are presented with a graph instead, you can use the "vertical line test," which states that any vertical line drawn anywhere along the function must not intersect the would-be function more than once.

Evaluating Functions

Evaluating a function simply means finding $f(x)$ at some specific value x. The Math IIC will likely ask you to evaluate a function at some particular constant. Take a look at the following example:

If $f(x) = x^2 - 3$, what is $f(5)$?

Evaluating a function at a constant involves nothing more than substituting the constant into the definition of the function. In this case, substitute 5 for x:

$$f(5) = 5^2 - 3 = 22$$

It's as simple as that.

The Math IIC may also ask questions in which you are asked to evaluate a function at a variable rather than a constant. For example:

If $f(x) = \frac{3x}{4-x}$, what is $f(x + 1)$?

To solve problems of this sort, follow the same method you did for evaluating a function at a constant: substitute the variable into the equation. To solve the sample question, substitute $(x + 1)$ for x in the definition of the function:

$$f(x + 1) = \frac{3(x + 1)}{4 - (x + 1)}$$
$$= \frac{3x + 3}{4 - x - 1}$$
$$= \frac{3x + 3}{3 - x}$$

Operations on Functions

Functions can be added, subtracted, multiplied, and divided just like any other quantities. There are a few rules that help make these operations easier. For any two functions $f(x)$ and $g(x)$:

Addition	$(f + g)(x) = f(x) + g(x)$	If $f(x) = \sin x$, and $g(x) = \cos x$: $(f + g)(x) = \sin x + \cos x$
Subtraction	$(f - g)(x) = f(x) - g(x)$	If $f(x) = x^2 + 5$, and $g(x) = x^2 + 2x + 1$: $(f - g)(x) = x^2 + 5 - x^2 - 2x - 1 = -2x + 4$
Multiplication	$(f \times g)(x) = f(x) \times g(x)$	If $f(x) = x$, and $g(x) = x^3 + 8$: $(f \times g)(x) = x \times (x^3 + 8) = x^4 + 8x$
Division	$\frac{f}{g}(x) = \frac{f(x)}{g(x)}, g(x) \neq 0$	If $f(x) = 2 \cos x$, and $g(x) = 2 \sin^2 x$: $(f \div g)(x) = \frac{2\cos x}{2\sin^2 x} = \frac{\cos x}{\sin^2 x}$

As usual, when dividing, you have to be aware about possible situations where you inadvertently divide by zero. Since division by zero is not allowed, you should just remember that any time you are dividing functions, like $f(x)/g(x)$, the resulting function is undefined wherever the function in the denominator equals zero.

Compound Functions

A compound function is a function that operates on another function. A compound function is written as nested functions, in the form $f(g(x))$. To evaluate a compound function, first evaluate the internal function, $g(x)$. Next, evaluate the outer function at the result of $g(x)$. Work with the inner parentheses first, and then the outer ones, just like in any other algebraic expression. Try the following example:

Suppose $h(x) = x^2 + 2x$ and $j(x) = \frac{x}{4} + 2$. What is $j(h(4))$?

To evaluate this compound function, first evaluate $h(4)$:

$$h(4) = 4^2 + 2(4)$$
$$= 16 + 8$$
$$= 24$$

Now plug 24 into the definition of j:

$$j(24) = |\frac{24}{4} + 2|$$
$$= |6 + 2|$$
$$= 8$$

It is important that you pay attention to the order in which you evaluate the compound function. Always evaluate the inner function first. For example, if we had evaluated $j(x)$ before $h(x)$ in the above question, you would get a completely different answer:

$$h(j(4)) = h(|\frac{4}{4} + 2|)$$
$$= h(|1 + 2|)$$
$$= h(3)$$
$$= 3^2 + 2(3)$$
$$= 9 + 6$$
$$= 15$$

Here's a slightly more complicated example, in which you are not given a specific point to evaluate a compound function:

Suppose $f(x) = 3x + 1$ and $g(x) = \sqrt{5x}$. What is $g(f(x))$?

In a case where you are not given a constant at which to evaluate a compound function, you should simply substitute the definition of $f(x)$ as the input to $g(x)$. This situation is exactly the same as a regular equation being evaluated at a variable rather than a constant.

$$g(f(x)) = g(3x + 1)$$
$$= \sqrt{5(3x + 1)}$$
$$= \sqrt{15x + 5}$$

Inverse Functions

The inverse of a function "undoes" that function. An example is the best way to help you understand what this means: the inverse of x^2 is $\sqrt{x}$. Let's see how $\sqrt{x}$ "undoes" x^2:

$$x = 10$$
$$10^2 = 100$$
$$\sqrt{100} = 10$$

You can think of an inverse function as one that takes the output (y) and returns the input (x). This way of looking at an inverse helps you see the graphical relationship between the graph of a function, $f(x)$ and its inverse, $f^{-1}(x)$. The graph of the inverse of a function is simply the graph of the original function reflected across the line $y = x$.

For the Math IIC, it is also important to know how to find the inverse of a simple function mathematically. For example:

What is the inverse of f(x) = 3x + 2?

The easiest way to find the inverse of a function is to break the function apart step by step. The function $f(x) = 3x + 2$ requires that for any value of x, it must be first multiplied by three and then added to 2. The inverse of this function must begin by subtracting 2 and then dividing by three, "undoing" the original function: $f^{-1}(x) = {}^{x-2}\!/_3$.

You should know how an inverse works in order to deal with any conceptual inverse questions the Math IIC might throw at you. But if you are ever asked to come up with the inverse of a particular function, there is an easy method that always works:

1. Replace the variable $f(x)$ with y.

2. Switch the places of x and y.

3. Solve for y.

4. Replace y with $f^{-1}(x)$.

Functions

Here's an example of the method in action:

What is the inverse of the function $f(x) = \sqrt{\dfrac{2x^2 - 3}{5}}$?

First, replace $f(x)$ with y. Then switch the places of x and y, and solve for y.

$$x = \sqrt{\frac{2y^2 - 3}{5}}$$

$$x^2 = \frac{2y^2 - 3}{5}$$

$$5x^2 = 2y^2 - 3$$

$$5x^2 + 3 = 2y^2$$

$$\frac{5}{2}x^2 + \frac{3}{2} = y^2$$

$$y = \sqrt{\frac{5}{2}x^2 + \frac{3}{2}}$$

Finding Whether Inverse Functions are Functions

Contrary to their name, inverse functions are not necessarily functions at all! Don't be surprised if a question on the Math IIC asks whether the inverse of a given function is a function:

Is the inverse of $f(x) = x^2$ a function?

To answer a question like this, you must, of course, first find the inverse. In this case, begin by writing $y = x^2$. Next, switch the places of x and y: $x = y^2$. Solve for y: $y = \sqrt{x}$. Now you need to analyze the inverse of the function and decide whether for every x, there is only one y. If only one y is associated with each x, you've got a function. Otherwise, you don't. In this case, since a square root can return either positive or negative numbers, there are two possible values of y for every value of x. Thus, $f^{-1}(x)$ is not a function.

Here's another sample question:

What is the inverse of $f(x) = 2|x - 1|$, and is it a function?

You know the drill:

$$x = 2|y - 1|$$

$$\frac{1}{2}x = |y - 1|$$

Now, since you're dealing with an absolute value, split the equations:

$$y - 1 = \frac{1}{2}x \text{ or } 1 - y = \frac{1}{2}x$$

Therefore,

$$y = \frac{1}{2}x + 1 \text{ or } y = -\frac{1}{2}x + 1$$

The inverse of $f(x)$ is this set of two equations. As you can see, for every value of x, except 0, the inverse of the function assigns two values of y. Consequently, $f^{-1}(x)$ is not a function.

Domain and Range

Several of the Math IIC questions about functions will focus on domain and range. These questions are quite straightforward if you understand the basic concepts and know what to look for.

Domain

We discussed the concept of a functions domain earlier in this chapter. The domain of a function is the set of inputs to the function that produce valid outputs. It is common for a domain to include only positive numbers, only negative numbers, or even all numbers except one or two points. As an example of a function that is undefined on a certain interval, consider $f(x) = \sqrt{x}$. A negative number has no square root defined in the real number system—$f(x)$ is undefined for all $x < 0$.

Finding the Domain of a Function

The Math IIC may ask you to find the domain of a given function. When you are solving a problem of this sort, you should begin by assuming that the domain is the set of real numbers. The next step is to look for any restrictions on the domain. For example, in the case, of $f(x) = \sqrt{x}$, we must restrict the domain to non-negative numbers since we know that you can't take the square root of a negative number.

In general, when finding a domain on the Math IIC there are two main restrictions to look out for:

1. Division by zero. Division by zero is mathematically impossible. A function is therefore undefined for all the values of x for which division by zero occurs. For example, $f(x) = \frac{1}{x-2}$ is undefined at $x = 2$, since when $x = 2$, the function is equal to $f(x) = \frac{1}{0}$.

2. Even roots. An even root (a square root, fourth root, etc.) of a negative number does not exist. A function is undefined for all values of x that causes a negative number to be the radicand of an even root.

Recognizing that these two situations cause the function to be undefined is the key to finding any restriction of the function's domain. Once you've discovered where the likely problem spots are, you can usually find the values to be eliminated from the domain very easily.

By now, you must be itching for a sample problem:

What is the domain of $f(x) = {}^{x}\!/(x^2 + 5x + 6)$?

In this question, $f(x)$ has variables in its denominator, which should be a big red flag that alerts you to the possibility of a division by zero. We may need to restrict the functions domain to ensure that division by zero does not occur. To find out for what values of x the denominator equals zero, set up an equation and factor the quadratic: $x^2 + 5x + 6 = (x + 2)(x + 3) = 0$. For $x = \{-2, -3\}$, the denominator is zero and $f(x)$ is undefined. Since it is defined for all other real numbers, the domain of $f(x)$ is the set of all real numbers x such that $x \neq -2, -3$. This can also be written as $\{x: x \neq -2, -3\}$.

Here's another example:

What is the domain of $f(x) = \dfrac{2\sqrt{x - 4}}{x - 7}$?

This function has both warning signs: an even root and a variable in the denominator. It's best to examine each situation separately:

1. The denominator would equal zero if $x = 7$.

2. The quantity under the square root (the radicand), $x - 4$, must be greater than or equal to zero in order for the function to be defined. Therefore, $x \geq 4$.

The domain of the function is therefore the set of real numbers x such that $x \geq 4$, $x \neq 7$.

The Domain of a Function with Two Variables

So far we have only looked at functions that take a single variable as input. Some functions on the Math IIC test take two variables, for example:

$$f(s, t) = \frac{s^2}{4} + \frac{6t}{7}$$

A two-variable function is really no different from the basic single-variable variety you've already seen. Essentially, the domain of this function is a set of ordered pairs of real numbers (s, t), rather than a set of single real numbers.

Evaluating such a function follows the same process as the evaluation of a single-variable function. Just substitute for the variables in the equation and do the algebra. Try to find $f(8, 14)$, using the definition of $f(s, t)$ above.

$$f(8, 14) = \frac{8^2}{4} + \frac{6(14)}{7}$$
$$= \frac{64}{4} + \frac{84}{7}$$
$$= 16 + 12$$
$$= 28$$

Piecewise Functions

Not all functions must have the same definition across their entire domain. Some functions have different definitions for different intervals of its domain; this type of function is called a piecewise function. Here is a typical example:

$$g(x) = 2x, \quad x < 0$$
$$x, \quad 0 \le x \le 10$$
$$-x, \quad x > 10$$

To evaluate a piecewise function, you need to find the correct interval for the given definition and evaluate as usual. For example, what is $g(6)$, using the above piecewise definition of $g(x)$?

$$0 \le 6 \le 10, \text{ so } g(6) = 6$$

Range

A function's range is the set of all values of $f(x)$ that can be generated by the function. In general, the range for most functions whose domain is unrestricted is the set of all real numbers. To help visualize the concept of range, consider two trigonometric functions, $\tan x$ and $\sin x$.

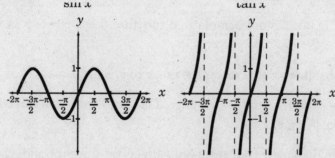

What values of the y-axis are reached on each graph? On the graph of $\tan x$, you can see that every possible value of y, from negative infinity to positive infinity, is included in the range. The range could be written as $\{y: -\infty \le y \le \infty\}$. Contrast this with the graph of sin x, where the range is actually quite limited. You'll notice that only the values between –1 and 1 are part of the range. We'll write the range using another common notation: $\{-1 \leq f(x) \leq 1\}$.

Of course, there are other ways that a function's range might be limited. For example, if a function has a limited domain (only certain x values are allowed), its range might be limited as well. In addition, there are two main causes for a function's range to be restricted:

Absolute value. Remember that by definition, the absolute value of a quantity is always positive. So, in a simple case, $f(x) = |x|$, you know that $f(x)$ must always be positive, and so the range excludes all negative numbers. Be careful, though, not to assume that any function with an absolute value symbol has the same range. For example, the range of $g(x) = -|x|$ is $\{y: -\infty \leq y \leq 0\}$ and the range of $h(x) = 10 + |x|$ is $\{10 \leq h(x) \leq \infty\}$.

Even exponents. Any time you square a number (or raise it to any multiple of 2) the resulting quantity will be positive. As in the case of the absolute value, though, don't assume that the range will always be $\{y: 0 \leq x \leq \infty\}$.

Determining the range of a complex function is very similar to finding the domain. First look for absolute values, even exponents, or other reasons that the range would be restricted. Then you simply adjust that range step-by-step as you go along. The best way to get the hang of it is to practice.

What is the range of $\frac{|x-3|}{2}$?

The absolute value around $|x-3|$ tells us that the range for that term excludes negative numbers ($y: 0 \leq y \leq \infty$). $|x-3|$ is then divided by 2, so we must also divide the range by 2: ($y: 0/2 \leq y \leq \infty/2$). Obviously, this doesn't change the range, since both zero and infinity remain the same when divided in half.

Now for a more complicated example:

What is the range of $\frac{\sqrt{|x-6|+4}}{2}$?

This example contains a more complicated function. Let's tackle it in a step-by-step fashion.

1. The absolute value restricts the range to $\{0 \leq f(x) \leq \infty\}$.

2. Add 4 to each bound of the range. This action only affects the lower bound: $\{4 \leq f(x) \leq \infty\}$.

3. Taking the square root again only affects the lower bound: $\{2 \leq f(x) \leq \infty\}$.

4. Finally, divide the bounds of the range by 2 to determine the range of the entire function: $\{1 \leq f(x) \leq \infty\}$.

Note that addition, subtraction, multiplication, division, and other mathematical operations cannot affect infinity. That's why it is particularly important that you look for absolute values and even roots. Once you can find a bound on a range, then you know the operations on the function will affect that range.

Before we move on, here is one last example that uses slightly different range notation you might come across on the Math IIC:

What is the range of $f(x) = \frac{-3x^2}{2} + 2$?

Once again, take a step-by-step approach to finding the range:

1. The range of x^2 is $[0, \infty)$.

2. The range of $-3/2 \times x^2$ is $(-\infty, 0]$.

3. The range of $-3/2 \times x^2 + 2$ is therefore $\{-\infty, 2\}$, or, simply, $f(x) \le 2$.

The Range of a Function with a Prescribed Domain

Occasionally the Math IIC will present you with a question in which the domain of a function is restricted to a given interval, and you are asked to find the range of the newly restricted function. For example:

$f(x) = 2x^2 + 4$ for $-3 < x < 5$. What is the range of f?

The best way to solve this type of problem is to manipulate the range of x in exactly the same way that x is manipulated in the function. First x is squared, then multiplied by two, then added to 4; we just need to do the same thing to the bounds of the range:

1. $-3 < x < 5$

2. $0 < x^2 < 25$

3. $0 < 2x^2 < 50$

4. $4 < 2x^2 + 4 < 54$

The range of $f(x)$ is $\{4 < f(x) < 54\}$.

Graphing Functions

While most of the function questions on the Math IIC will involve analysis and manipulation of the functions themselves, you will sometimes be asked a question about the graph of a function. A common question of this type asks you to match a function's graph to its definition. The next few topics will help prepare you questions relating to functions and their graphs.

Identifying Whether a Graph is a Function

A valuable skill for the Math IIC is the ability to determine if a given graph is indeed a function. All you need is the foolproof vertical line test: a graph only depicts a function if it is impossible to place a vertical line that intersects the graph more than once.

The vertical line test makes sense because definition of a function requires that any *x* value have only one *y* value. Since a vertical line has the same *x* value along the entire line, if it interests the graph more than once, then the graph has more than one *y* value associated with that *x* value.

The three graphs below are functions. Try the vertical line test, and check to see that a vertical line placed anywhere would touch the graph only once.

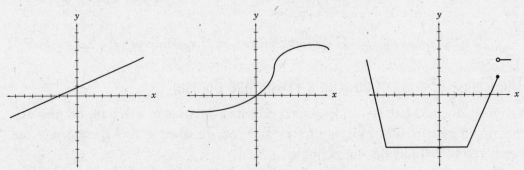

The next three graphs are not functions. In each graph, a strategically placed vertical line will intersect the graph more than once.

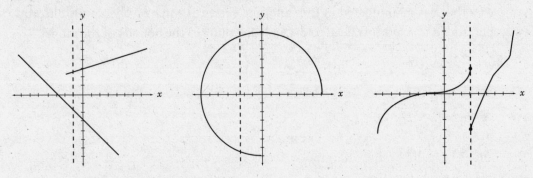

Range and Domain in Graphing

The range and domain of a function are easy enough to see in their graphs. The domain is the set of all *x* values for which the function is defined. The range is the set of all *y* values for which the function is defined. To find the domain and range of a graph, just look at which *x* and *y* values the graph includes.

Certain kinds of graphs have specific ranges and domains that are visible in their graphs. A line whose slope is not 0 (a horizontal line) or undefined (a vertical line) has the set of real numbers as its domain and range. Since a line, by definition, extends infinitely in both directions, it passes through all possible values of *x* and *y*:

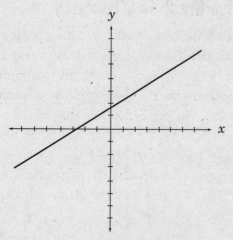

An odd-degree polynomial, which is a polynomial whose highest degree of power is an odd-number, also has the set of real numbers as its domain and range:

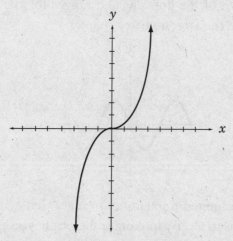

An even-degree polynomial, which is a polynomial whose highest degree of power is an even number, has the set of real numbers as its domain, but has a restricted range. The range is usually bounded at one end and unbounded at the other. The following parabola has range $(-\infty, 2]$.

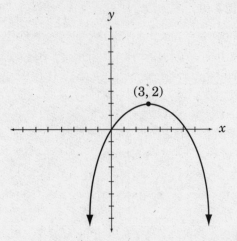

Trigonometric functions have various domains and ranges, depending on the function. Sine, for example, has the real numbers for its domain, and {−1, 1} for its range. A more detailed breakdown of the domains and ranges for the various trigonometric functions can be found in the Trigonometry chapter.

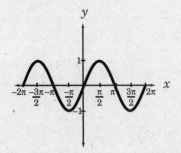

Some functions have limited domains and ranges that cannot be simply categorized, but are still obvious to see. By looking at the graph, you can see that the function below has domain {3, ∞} and range {−∞, −1}.

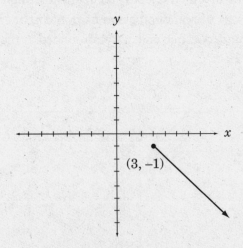

Asymptotes and Holes

There are two types of abnormalities that can further limit the domain and range of a function: asymptotes and holes. Being able to identify these abnormalities will help you to match up the domain and range of a graph to its function.

An asymptote is a line that a graph approaches but never intersects. In graphs, asymptotes are represented as dotted lines. You'll probably only see vertical and horizontal asymptotes on the Math IIC, though they can exist at other slopes as well. A function is undefined at the x value of a vertical asymptote, thus restricting the domain of the function graphed. A function's range does not include the y value of a horizontal asymptote, since the whole point of an asymptote is that the function never actually takes on that value.

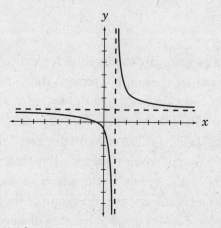

In this graph, there is a vertical asymptote at $x = 1$, and a horizontal asymptote at $y = 1$. Because of these asymptotes, the domain of the graphed function is the set of real numbers except 1 ($x \neq 1$), and the range of the function graphed is also the set of real numbers except 1 ($f(x) \neq 1$).

A hole is an isolated point at which a function is undefined. You'll recognize it in a graph as an open circle at the point where the hole occurs. Find it in the following figure:

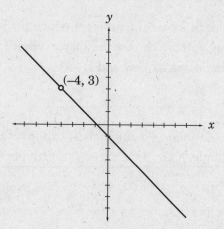

(–4, 3)

The hole in the graph above is the point (–4, 3). This means that the domain of the function is the set of real numbers except 4 ($x \neq -4$), and the range is the set of real numbers except 3 ($f(x) \neq 3$).

Identifying the Graphs of Polynomial Functions

Many of the functions on the Math IIC are polynomial functions. Although they can be difficult to sketch and identify, there are a few tricks to make it easier. If you can find the roots of a function, identify the degree, or understand the end behavior of a polynomial function, you will usually be able to pick out the graph that matches the function, and vice versa.

Roots

The roots (or zeroes) of a function are the x values for which the function equals zero, or, graphically, the values where the graph intersects the x-axis ($x = 0$). To solve for the roots of a function, set the function equal to 0 and solve for x.

A question on the Math IIC that tests your knowledge of roots and graphs will give you a function such as $f(x) = x^2 + x - 12$ along with five graphs and ask you to determine which graph is that of $f(x)$. To approach a question like this, you should start by identifying the general shape of the graph of the function. For the example function, $f(x) = x^2 + x - 12$, you should recognize that the graph of the function in the paragraph above is a parabola, and that it opens upward because of a positive leading coefficient.

This basic analysis should immediately eliminate several possibilities, but might still leave two or three choices. Solving for the roots of the function will usually get you to the one right answer. To solve for the roots, factor the function:

$$f(x) = x^2 + x - 12$$
$$= (x + 4)(x - 3)$$

The roots are –4 and 3, since those are the values at which the function equals 0. Given this additional information, you can choose the answer choice with the upward-opening parabola that intersects the x-axis at –4 and 3.

Degree

The degree of a polynomial function is the highest exponent to which the dependent variable is raised. For example, $f(x) = 4x^5 - x^2 + 5$ is a fifth degree polynomial, because its highest exponent is 5.

A function's degree can give you a good idea of its shape. The graph produced by an *n*-degree function can have as many as *n* – 1 "bumps" or "turns." These "bumps" or "turns" are technically called "extreme points."

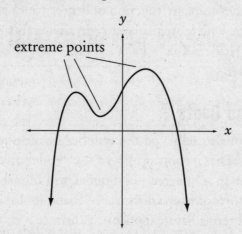

extreme points

Once you know the degree of a function, you also know the greatest number of extreme points a function can have. A fourth degree function can have at most three extreme points; a tenth degree function can have at most nine extreme points.

If you are given the graph of a function, you can simply count the number of extreme points. Once you've counted the extreme points, you can figure out the smallest degree that the function can be. For example, if a graph has five extreme points, the function that defines the graph must have at least degree six. If the function has two extreme points, you know that it must be at least third degree. The Math IIC will ask you questions about degrees and graphs that may look like this:

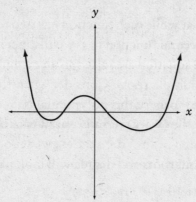

If the graph above represents a portion of the function $g(x)$, then which of the following could be $g(x)$?

(A) a
(B) $ax + b$
(C) $ax^2 + bx + c$
(D) $ax^3 + bx^2 + cx + d$
(E) $ax^4 + bx^3 + cx^2 + dx + e$

To answer this question, you need to use the graph to learn something about the degree of the function. Since the graph has three extreme points, you know the function must be at least of the fourth degree. The only function that fits that description is (E). Note that the answer could have been any function of degree four or higher; the Math IIC test will never present you with more than one right answer, but you should know that even if answer choice (E) had read $ax^7 + bx^6 + cx^5 + dx^4 + ex^3 + fx^2 + gx + h$ it still would have been the right answer.

Function Degree and Roots

The degree of a function also tells you the number of roots a function has. An nth degree polynomial always has n roots. $f(x) = 4x^5 - x^2 + 5$ has five roots. However, this rule does not mean that an nth degree polynomial will intersect the x-axis n times. There are actually two sorts of roots: distinct roots and multiple roots. In a function factored so that none of terms have exponents, a distinct root will appear only once while a multiple root will appear more than once. As an example, take a look at the quadratic equations

$$x^2 + 4x + 4$$
$$x^2 + 3x + 2$$

The two equations factor into:

$$x^2 + 4x + 4 = (x + 2)(x + 2)$$
$$x^2 + 3x + 2 = (x + 2)(x + 1)$$

Now it is quite easy to see that while each function has two roots, the first function has one double root, while the second function has two distinct roots.

If any of the terms in the equation are raised to an exponent, then the roots associated with those terms are multiple roots. Consider again the second-degree polynomial $x^2 + 4x + 4$. The factored form of this polynomial is $(x + 2)(x + 2)$, which can also be written as $(x + 2)^2$. Since the $(x + 2)$ term is raised to an exponent, the root that it defines, –2, is a multiple root.

A Math IIC question about roots and degree will look like this:

What is the distinct root of polynomial $f(x) = x(x - 3)^2(x + 6)^3$?

To answer this question, you simply need to know how to read the formula. Setting the equation to zero, you see that it has roots $\{x = 0, 3, -6\}$. Looking at the exponents of the respective terms, you know can see that root 0 is distinct, root 3 is a double root, and root –6 is a triple root. The distinct root of the polynomial is 0.

You can also use a graph to tell whether a root is distinct or multiple. If the graph of a function completely crosses the x-axis at a particular point, that root is distinct. If the graph of the function "bounces" off the x-axis and therefore only intersects at one point, then that point of intersection represents a multiple root.

End Behavior

The end behavior of a function is a description of what happens to the value of $f(x)$ as x approaches infinity and negative infinity. Think about what happens to a polynomial containing x if you let x equal a huge number, like 1,000,000,000. The polynomial is going to end up being an enormous positive or negative number.

The point is that *every* polynomial function either approaches infinity or negative infinity as x approaches positive and negative infinity. Whether a function will approach positive or negative infinity in relation to x is called the function's end behavior.

There are rules of end behavior that can allow you to use a function's end behavior to figure out its algebraic characteristics, or to figure out its end behavior based on its definition:

- If the degree of the polynomial is even, the function behaves the same way as x approaches both positive and negative infinity. If the coefficient of the term with the greatest exponent is positive, $f(x)$ approaches positive infinity at both ends. If the leading coefficient is negative, $f(x)$ approaches negative infinity at both ends.

- If the degree of the polynomial function is odd, the function exhibits opposite behavior as x approaches positive and negative infinity. If the leading coefficient is positive, the function increases as x increases, and decreases as x decreases. If the leading coefficient is negative, the function decreases as x increases and increases as x decreases.

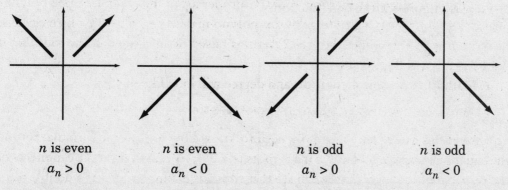

| n is even | n is even | n is odd | n is odd |
| $a_n > 0$ | $a_n < 0$ | $a_n > 0$ | $a_n < 0$ |

For the Math IIC, you should be able to determine a function's end behavior by simply looking at either its graph or definition.

Function Symmetry

One additional type of question you might see on the Math IIC involves identifying a function's symmetry. Some functions have no symmetry whatsoever. Others exhibit one of two types of symmetry and are classified as either even functions or odd functions.

Even Functions

An even function is a function for which $f(x) = f(-x)$. Even functions are symmetrical with respect to the y-axis. This means that a line segment connecting $f(x)$ and $f(-x)$ is a horizontal line. Some examples of even functions are $f(x) = \cos x$, $f(x) = x^2$, and $f(x) = |x|$. Here is a figure with an even function:

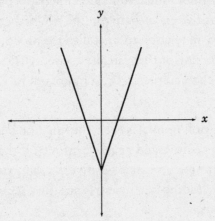

Odd Functions

An odd function is a function for which $f(x) = -f(-x)$. Odd functions are symmetrical with respect to the origin. This means that a line segment connecting $f(x)$ and $f(-x)$ contains the origin. Some examples of odd functions are $f(x) = \sin x$, and $f(x) = x$.

Here is a figure with an odd function:

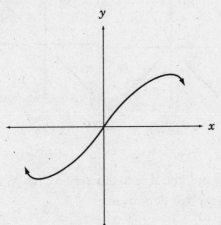

Symmetry Across the *x*-axis

No function can have symmetry across the *x*-axis, but the Math IIC will occasionally include a graph that is symmetrical across the *x*-axis to fool you. A quick check with the vertical line test proves that the equations that produce such lines are not functions:

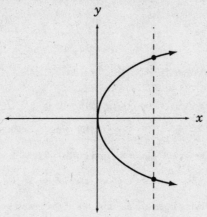

Review Questions

1. $f(x) = ax$, and $g(x) = bx$. If $f(g(x)) = 5x^2 + 2$, what is ab?

    (A) $ab = 5x$
    (B) $ab = 5x + \dfrac{2}{x}$
    (C) $ab = x^2$
    (D) $ab = 7x$
    (E) Impossible to tell

2. If $f(x) = 2x$ and $g(x) = \dfrac{x^2}{2}$, what is $f^{-1}(g^{-1}(2))$?

    (A) 0   (B) $\dfrac{\sqrt{2}}{2}$ (C) 1   (D) $\sqrt{2}$ (E) 2

3. If $f(x) = 2x - 3$, $g(x) = x + 1$, $h(x) = 3x$, and $g(f(3)) - h(x) = 1$, what is x?

    (A) 0   (B) .5   (C) 1   (D) 1.5   (E) 2

4. Which of the following lines are asymptotes of the graph $y = 2\dfrac{x+3}{x-2}$?

    I. $x = 2$
    II. $y = 2$
    III. $y = 0$

    (A) I only
    (B) II only
    (C) I and II only
    (D) I and III only
    (E) I, II, and III

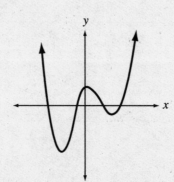

5. A portion of the graph of $y = f(x)$ is shown in the figure above. Which of the following could be $f(x)$?

    (A) $x^4 + ax^3 + bx^2 + cx$
    (B) $x^4 + ax^2 + b$
    (C) $-x^4 + ax^3 + bx^2 + cx + d$
    (D) $x^3 + ax^2 + bx + c$
    (E) $x^4 + b^2x^2 + c^2$

6.   Suppose $f(x) = -f(-x)$. Which of the following could be the graph of $y = f(x)$?

(A)
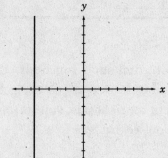

(B)
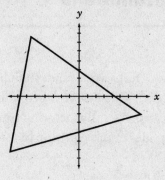

(C)
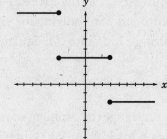

(D)
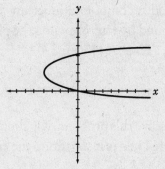

(E)
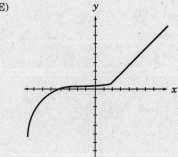

7.   What is the maximum value of the function $f(x) = 10 - 2(x - 3)(x + 3)$?

(A)   −28
(B)   −8
(C)   0
(D)   8
(E)   28

8.   If $f:(x, y) \to (x - y, x + y)$ for every pair (x, y) in the plane, for what points (x, y) is it true that $(x, y) \to (x, y)$?

(A) $(0, 0)$ only
(B)   The set of points (x, y) such that $x = 0$
(C)   The set of points (x, y) such that $y = 0$
(D)   The set of points (x, y) such that $x = y$
(E)   The set of points (x, y) such that $2x = y$

Explanations

1.   **(B)**

This question tests your understanding of compound functions. If $f(x) = ax$ and $g(x) = bx$, $f(g(x)) = f(bx) = abx$. From this point, the question is all algebra to solve the equation $abx = 5x^2 + 2$. By factoring an x out of the right side, you get $(ab)x = x(5x + 2/x)$. Divide both sides of this equation by x and you see that $ab = 5x + 2/x$.

2.   **(C)**

To evaluate this compound function, you must first find the inverses of f and g. The inverse is found by interchanging the places of x and y and solving for y: $f^{-1}(x) = x/2$, and $g^{-1}(x) = \sqrt{2x}$. Thus, $f^{-1}(g^{-1}(x)) = \sqrt{2x}/2$. Substituting 2 for x into this equation, the result is $\sqrt{4}/2 = 2/2 = 1$.

3.   **(C)**

In order to solve this problem, it is simpler to rearrange the problem so it looks like $h(x) = (g(f(3)) - 1$. Then just substitute the expression for $h(x)$ into the equation:

$$
\begin{aligned}
h(x) &= g(f(3)) - 1 \\
&= g(2 \times 3 - 3) - 1 \\
&= g(3) - 1 \\
&= 3 + 1 - 1 \\
&= 3
\end{aligned}
$$

Remember that you were given $h(x) = 3x$, and now you know that $h(x) = 3$. Equate the two and you get $3x = 3$ and $x = 1$.

4.   **(C)**

By graphing the function on your calculator, you should be able to see that statements I and II must be true, and statement III is false, making (C) the correct answer choice. Even without a calculator, though, you can calculate the asymptotes of this graph.

A vertical asymptote occurs in this graph where the function is undefined. The function is undefined at $x = 2$, so this is a vertical asymptote. By plugging in a series of numbers, you find that values of the function approach 2, but are never equal to 2. So there is a horizontal asymptote, the line $y = 2$.

One easy way to check your asymptotes is to plug the corresponding x and y values into the function. For example, when you plug in $x = 2$, the function should be undefined. To be sure that $x = 2$ is indeed an asymptote, and not a hole, plug in values on both sides of $x = 2$, like $x = \pm 2.01$, and make sure that one is very large and one is very small. This indicates that on one side of $x = 2$, the function approaches infinity, and on the other side the function approaches negative infinity.

5.　(B)

All of the answer choices are polynomials. You can analyze the polynomial's end behavior to narrow the choices. By observing the end behavior of f, you can determine whether the leading coefficient is positive or negative, and you can tell whether the degree of f is odd or even. From the graph, you can see that $f(x)$ increases without bound as x increases, and as x decreases. This means that the degree of f is even, and the leading coefficient is positive. This eliminates (C) and (D) as possible answers.

To choose between the remaining three possible answers requires closer analysis. First, note from the figure that $x = 0$ is not a root of the function, but $x = 0$ is a root of the function in (A). Therefore, this choice can be eliminated. Second, in the graph, f takes on positive and negative values. The function in (E) is positive for *all* values of x, because an even power of x is always positive, and c^2 is always positive. So, (E) can be eliminated from the answer choices, making (B) the only remaining possibility.

This is a difficult question, and the answer probably didn't jump out at you right away. Remember that when you have to analyze the graph of a function, or a function itself, you can use end behavior, roots, and which portions of the graph have positive and negative values of f as tools for your analysis.

6.　(E)

The condition that $f(x) = -f(-x)$ means that f is an odd function, which means that it is symmetrical with respect to the origin. The easiest way to answer this question is to choose which of the functions graphed are symmetrical with respect to the origin. The only graphs that satisfy this condition are the graphs in (D) and (E). Note, however, that the graph in (D) is actually not even the graph of a function, because it doesn't pass the vertical line test. The correct answer must be (E).

7.　(E)

To find the maximum value of the function, first multiply it out.

$$f(x) = 10 - 2(x - 3)(x + 3)$$
$$= 10 - 2(x^2 - 9)$$
$$= 10 - 2x^2 + 18$$
$$= -2x^2 + 28$$

The graph of the function $f(x) = -2x^2 + 28$ is a parabola opening downward, since the coefficient of x^2 is negative. This means the maximum value of the function will be the y-value of the vertex. To find the vertex of the parabola, set $x = 0$ and solve for $f(x)$. For this function, $f(0) = -2(0)^2 + 28 = 0 + 28 = 28$, so the vertex of the parabola is the point (0, 28), and the maximum value of f is 28.

8.   **(D)**

In order for $(x, y) \rightarrow (x, y)$, x must equal $x - y$ and y must equal $x + y$. These equations can be solved simultaneously:

$$x = x - y$$
$$+y = x + y$$
$$x + y = 2x$$
$$y = x$$

When $x = y$, the requirement that $(x, y) \rightarrow (x, y)$ is fulfilled for this function.

Statistics

STATISTICS QUESTIONS ON THE MATH IIC test your ability to manipulate and understand data. Only a few questions on the Math IIC will be devoted to statistics, and these questions don't cover many different topics.

Statistical Analysis

On the Math IIC you will occasionally be presented with a data set—a collection of measurements or quantities. An example of a data set is the set of test scores for the 20 students in Ms. McCarthy's math class.

71, 83, 57, 66, 95, 96, 68, 71, 84, 85, 87, 90, 88, 90, 84, 90, 90, 93, 97, 99

A question accompanying the data set will ask you a question that tests your ability to use the basic tools of statistics. Given a data set, you should be able to derive the four following values:

1. Arithmetic Mean

2. Median

3. Mode

4. Range

Arithmetic Mean

The arithmetic mean is the value of the sum of the elements contained in a data set divided by the number of elements found in the set.

$$\text{Arithmetic Mean} = \frac{\text{the sum of the elements of a set}}{\text{the number of elements in the set}}$$

On the Math IIC and in many high school math classes, the arithmetic mean often goes by "average." Sometimes it's just referred to as the mean.

To make our definition of the arithmetic mean more concrete, let's take a look at the test scores of the 20 students in Ms. McCarthy's math class. We've sorted the scores in her class in order from lowest to highest:

57, 66, 68, 71, 71, 83, 84, 84, 85, 87, 88, 90, 90, 90, 90, 93, 95, 96, 97, 99

To find the arithmetic mean of this data set, we must sum the scores, and then divide by 20, since that is the number of scores in the set. The mean of the math test scores in Ms. McCarthy's class is:

$$\text{mean} = \frac{57 + 66 + 68 + \cdots + 96 + 97 + 99}{20}$$
$$\text{mean} = \frac{1600}{20}$$
$$\text{mean} = 80$$

While some Math IIC questions might cover arithmetic mean in the straightforward manner shown in this example, it is more likely the test will cover mean in a more complicated way.

The Math IIC might give you $n - 1$ numbers of an n number set and the average of that set, and ask you to find the last number:

> If the average of four numbers is 22, and three of the numbers are 7, 11, and 18, then what is the fourth number?

Remember that the mean of a set of numbers is intimately related to the number of terms in the set and the sum of those terms. In the question above, you know that the average of the 4 numbers is 22. This means that the four numbers, when added together, must equal 4×22, or 88. Based on the sum of the three terms you are given, you can easily determine the fourth number by subtraction:

$$7 + 11 + 18 + \text{unknown number} = 88$$

Solving for the unknown number is easy: all you have to do is subtract 7, 11, and 18, from 88 to get 52, which is the answer.

The test might also present you with what we call an "adjusted mean" question. For example:

> The mean age of the 14 members of a ballroom dance class is 34. When a new student enrolled, the mean age increased to 35. How old is the new student?

This question is really just a rephrasing of the previous example. Here you know the original number of students in the class and the original mean of the students' ages, and you are asked to determine the mean after an additional term is introduced. To figure out the age of the new student, you simply need to find the sum of the ages in the adjusted class (with one extra student) and subtract from that the sum of the ages of the original class. To calculate the sum of the ages of the adjusted class:

$$\text{New Mean} = \frac{\text{The new sum of the students' ages}}{\text{The new class enrollment}}$$

$$15 = \frac{\text{The new sum of the students' ages}}{\text{The old class enrollment} + 1 \text{ new student}}$$

$$15 = \frac{\text{The new sum of the students' ages}}{34 + 1}$$

$$\text{The new sum of the students' ages} = 15 \times 25$$

$$\text{The new sum of the students' ages} = 525$$

By the same calculations, the sum of the students' ages in the original class is $14 \times 34 = 476$. So the new student added an age of $525 - 476 = 49$ years.

Median

The Math IIC might also ask you about the median of a set of numbers. The median is the number whose value is in the middle of the numbers in a particular set. Take the set: 6, 19, 3, 11, 7. Arranging the numbers in order of value results in the list below:

$$3, 6, 7, 11, 19$$

Once the numbers are listed in this ordered way, it becomes clear that the middle number in this group is 7, making 7 the median.

The set 3, 6, 7, 11, 19 contains an odd number of items, but in a set with an even number of items it's impossible to isolate a single number as the median, so calculating the median requires an extra step. Let's add one number to the set from the previous example:

$$3, 6, 7, 11, 15, 19$$

When the set contains an even number of elements, the median is found by taking the mean of the two middle numbers. The two middle numbers in this set are 7 and 11, so the median of the set is $\frac{7+11}{2} = 9$.

Mode

The mode is the element of a set that appears most frequently. In the set 10, 11, 13, 11, 20, the mode is 11 since it appears twice and all the other numbers appear just once. In a set where more than one number appears with the same highest frequency, there is more than one mode: the set 2, 2, 3, 4, 4 has modes of 2 and 4. In a set where all of the elements appear an equal number of times there is no mode.

The good news is that mode questions are easy. The bad news is that mode questions don't appear all that much on the Math IIC.

Range

The range measures the spread of a data set, or the difference between the smallest element and the largest. For the set of test scores in Ms. McCarthy's class:

57, 66, 68, 71, 71, 83, 84, 84, 85, 87, 88, 90, 90, 90, 90, 93, 95, 96, 97, 99

The range is $99 - 57 = 42$.

Probability

Probability is another related topic you might see on the Math IIC. You should be familiar with the probability formula and with applying the probability formula to calculate the likely outcome of independent events.

The Probability Formula

The probability of an event is a number between 0 and 1 that represents the likelihood of that event occurring. You can calculate the probability of an event by dividing the number of desired outcomes by the total number of possible outcomes.

$$\text{Probability} = \frac{\text{number of times a certain event might occur}}{\text{total number of events that might occur}}$$

For example, in a deck of 52 cards, the probability of pulling one of the 13 hearts from the deck is much higher than the likelihood of pulling out the ace of spades. To calculate an exact value for the probability of drawing a heart from the deck, divide the number of hearts you could possibly draw by the total number of cards in the deck.

$$P = \frac{\text{number of hearts in the deck}}{\text{total number of cards in the deck}}$$

$$P = \frac{13}{52}$$

$$P = \frac{1}{4}$$

In contrast, the possibility of drawing the single ace of spades from the deck is:

$$P = \frac{\text{number of aces of spades in the deck}}{\text{total number of cards in the deck}}$$

$$P = \frac{1}{52}$$

After looking at these examples, you should be able to understand the general formula for calculating probability. Here's another example:

> Joe has 3 green marbles, 2 red marbles, and 5 blue marbles. If all the marbles are dropped into a dark bag, what is the probability that Joe will pick out a green marble?

There are 3 ways for Joe to pick a green marble (since there are 3 different green marbles), but there are 10 total possible outcomes (one for each marble in the bag). Therefore you can simply calculate the probability of picking a green marble:

$$\begin{aligned} \text{Probability} &= \frac{\text{particular outcome}}{\text{total outcomes}} \\ &= \frac{\text{green marbles}}{\text{total marbles}} \\ &= \frac{3}{10} \end{aligned}$$

When calculating probabilities, always be careful to count all of the possible favorable outcomes among the total of possible outcomes. In the last example, you may have been tempted to leave out the three chances of picking a green marble from the total possibilities, yielding the equation $P = \frac{3}{7}$. If you did that, you'd be wrong.

The Range of Probability

The probability, P, of any event occurring will always be $0 \leq P \leq 1$. A probability of 0 for an event means that the event will *never* happen. A probability of 1 means the event will always occur. For example, drawing a green card from a standard deck of cards has probability 0; getting a number less than seven on a single roll of one die has probability 1.

If you are ever asked a probability question on the Math IIC, you can automatically eliminate any answer choices that are less than 0 or greater than 1.

Statistics

The Probability that an Event will *not* Occur

Some Math IIC questions ask you to determine the probability that an event will not occur. In that case, just figure out the probability of the event occurring, and subtract that number from 1.

Probability an event will not occur = 1 − probability of the event occurring

Probability and Multiple Events

The most difficult Math IIC probability questions deal with the probability of multiple events occurring. Such questions will always deal with independent events, that is, events whose probability is not dependent on the outcome of any other event. For these questions, the probability of both events occurring is the product of the outcomes of each event: $P(A) \times P(B)$, where $P(A)$ is the probability of the first event and $P(B)$ is the probability of the second event.

For example, the probability of drawing a spade from a full deck of cards *and* rolling a one with a six-sided die is the product of the probability of each event.

$$P = \frac{13}{52} \times \frac{1}{6}$$
$$= \frac{1}{4} \times \frac{1}{6}$$
$$= \frac{1}{24}$$

The same principle can be applied to finding the probability of a series of events. Take a look at the following problem:

> A teacher keeps a jar full of different flavored jelly beans on her desk and hands them out randomly to her class. But one particularly picky student likes only the licorice-flavored ones. If the jar has 50 beans in all: 15 licorice, 10 cherry, 20 watermelon, and 5 blueberry, and no other students are given jelly beans, what is the probability that the first three jelly beans the picky student is given are licorice-flavored?

In order to find the probability of three consecutive events, you should first find the probability of each event separately. The first jellybean the student is given has a $^{15}/_{50}$ chance of being licorice-flavored. The second jellybean, however, is a different story. There are now only 49 jelly beans left in the jar, so the probability of getting another licorice-flavored one is $^{14}/_{49}$. The third jelly bean has a probability of $^{13}/_{48}$. The odds of all three happening is:

$$P = \frac{15}{50} \times \frac{14}{49} \times \frac{13}{48}$$
$$= \frac{3}{10} \times \frac{2}{7} \times \frac{13}{48}$$
$$= \frac{1}{10} \times \frac{1}{7} \times \frac{13}{8}$$
$$= \frac{13}{560}$$

Permutations and Combinations

Permutations and combinations are counting tools. They have vast applications in probability, especially in determining the number of successful outcomes and the number of total outcomes in a given scenario. Questions about permutations and combinations on the Math IIC will not be complex, nor will they require advanced math. But you will need to understand how they work and how to work with them. Important to both of these undertakings is a familiarity with factorials.

Factorials

The factorial of a number, $n!$, is the product of the natural numbers up to and including n:

$$n! = n \times (n-1) \times (n-2) \times \cdots \times 3 \times 2 \times 1$$

If you are ever asked to find the number of ways that the n elements of a group can be ordered, you simply need to calculate $n!$. For example, if you are asked how many different ways 6 people can sit a table with six chairs, you could either list all of the possible seating arrangements or just answer $6! = 6 \times 5 \times 4 \times 3 \times 2 \times 1 = 720$.

Permutations

A permutation is an ordering of elements. For example, say you're running for student council. There are four different offices to be filled—president, vice-president, secretary, and treasurer—and there are four candidates running. Assuming the candidates don't care which office they're elected to, how many different ways can the student council be comprised?

The answer is $4!$ because there are 4 students running for office, and thus, 4 elements in the set.

Now say that due to budgetary costs, there are now only the three offices of president, vice-president, and treasurer to be filled. The same four candidates are still running. To handle this situation, we will now have to slightly change our method of calculating the number of permutations.

In general, the permutation, $_nP_r$, is the number of subgroups of size r that can be taken from a set with n elements:

$$_nP_r = \frac{n!}{(n-r)!}$$

For our example, we need to find $_6P_3$:

$$_6P_3 = \frac{6!}{6-3!} = \frac{6!}{3!} = \frac{6 \times 5 \times 4 \times 3 \times 2 \times 1}{3 \times 2 \times 1} = \frac{720}{6} = 120$$

Consider the following problem:

> At a dog show, three awards are given: best in show, first runner up, and second runner up. A group of ten dogs are competing in the competition. In how many ways can the awards be distributed?

This problem is a permutation, since the question asks us to order the top three finishers among 10 contestants in a dog show. There is more than one way that the same three dogs could get first place, second place, and third place and each arrangement is a different outcome. So, the answer is $_{10}P_3 = {}^{10!}/_{(10-3)!} = {}^{10!}/_{7!} = 720$.

Permutations and Calculators

Graphing calculators and most scientific calculators have a permutation function, labeled $_nP_r$. In most cases, you must enter n, then press the button for permutation, and then enter r. This will calculate a permutation for you, but often if n is a large number, the calculator cannot calculate $n!$. If this happens to you, don't give up! In cases like this, your knowledge of how the permutation function will save you. Since you know that $_{100}P_3$ is ${}^{100!}/_{(100-3)!}$ you can simplify it to ${}^{100!}/_{97!}$, or $100 \times 99 \times 98 = 970,200$.

Combinations

A combination is an unordered grouping of a set. An example of a scenario in which order doesn't matter is a hand of cards: a king, ace, and five is the same as an ace, five, and king.

Combinations are represented as $_nC_r$, or $\binom{n}{r}$, where unordered subgroups of size r are selected from a set of size n. Because the order of the elements in a given subgroup doesn't matter, this means that $\binom{n}{r}$ will be less than $_nP_r$. Any one combination can be turned into more than one permutation. $_nC_r$ is calculated as follows:

$$\binom{n}{r} = \frac{_nP_r}{r!} = \frac{n!}{(n-r)!r!}$$

Here's an example:

> Suppose that a committee of ten people must elect three leaders, whose duties are all the same. In how many ways can this be done?

In this example, the order in which the leaders are assigned to positions doesn't matter—the leaders aren't distinguished from each other in any way, as they were in the student council example. This distinction means that the question can be answered with a combination rather than a permutation. We are looking for how many different groups of three can be taken from a group of ten:

$$\binom{10}{3} = \frac{10!}{(10-3)!3!} = \frac{10!}{7!3!} = 120$$

There are only 120 different ways to elect 3 leaders, as opposed to 720 ways when their roles were differentiated.

Combinations and Calculators

There should be a combination function on your graphing or scientific calculator labeled $_nC_r$. Use it the same way as you use the permutation key.

Group Questions

Occasional Math IIC questions will pose questions about groups with overlapping members. For example:

> In a particular school, the school band has 42 members, the school orchestra has 35 members. 7 students play in both the band and the orchestra, and 231 students play in neither the band nor the orchestra. How many students are in this particular school?

To answer this question, carefully count the students. $231 + 42 + 35 = 308$ is a tempting answer, but in this solution, we are counting the students who play in both the band and orchestra twice. We must subtract 7 from this total to get the right answer: $308 - 7 = 301$.

Statistics

This question illustrates the formula for answering such questions. If two subgroups of a population share members, the equation that governs the total number of people in the population is:

Total Population =   Group Population
                    + Group A Population
                    + Group B Population
                    + Neither Group A nor B Population
                    − Group A and B Population

The last term of this formula subtracts the elements that were double-counted earlier.

Try another example:

A room contains 80 people. 30 have curly hair, 24 have blond hair, and 40 have hair that is neither curly nor blond. How many people in the room have curly, blond hair?

Use the formula: $80 = 30 + 24 + 40 − x$. Thus, $x = 14$ (14 people in the room have curly and blond hair). This formula works for all group problems in which there are only two groups involved.

Sets

Already in this chapter we've covered how to analyze the data in a set, and how to deal with two sets that have overlapping members. For the Math IIC, there are two more concepts concerning sets that you need to understand: union and intersection.

Union

The union of two or more sets is the set that contains all of the elements of the two original sets. The union of two sets, A and B, is symbolized this way: $A \cup B$.

For example, the union of the sets $A = \{1, 2, 3, 4, 5\}$ and $B = \{4, 5, 6, 7, 8\}$ is

$$A \cup B = \{1, 2, 3, 4, 5, 6, 7, 8\}$$

This set contains every element that is in either set. If x is an element of $A \cup B$, then it must be an element of A, or of B, or of both.

Intersection

The intersection of two sets is the set of their overlapping elements. The intersection of the two sets A and B is symbolized as $A \cap B$.

The intersection of the sets $A = \{1, 2, 3, 4, 5\}$ and $B = \{4, 5, 6, 7, 8\}$, for example, is $A \cap B = \{4, 5\}$. If x is an element of $A \cap B$, then x must be an element of both A and B.

Key Formulas

Arithmetic Mean

$$\text{Mean} = \frac{\text{The sum of the elements of a set}}{\text{The number of elements in the set}}$$

Permutation

$_nP_r = \frac{n!}{(n-r)!}$, where r is the size of the subgroup taken from a set with n elements.

Combination

$\binom{n}{r} = \frac{n!}{(n-r)!r!}$, $_nP_r/r!$, where r is the size of the subgroup taken from a set with n elements.

Probability

$$\text{Probability} = \frac{\text{number of times a certain event might occur}}{\text{total number of events that might occur}}$$

Total Elements of Overlapping Sets

If two subsets of a set share elements, the equation that governs the total number of elements in the set is:

$$\text{Total Elements} = \text{Group A Elements} + \text{Group B Elements}$$
$$+ \text{Neither Group A nor B Elements}$$
$$- \text{Group A and B Elements}$$

Review Questions

1. A figure skater competing at a local competition needs a mean of 5.8 (out of a total 6.0) to win the first place medal. If there are three judges, and one of them gives her a 5.5, what is the lowest score she can get from the remaining two judges if she still wants to finish first?

   (A)   4.8
   (B)   5.2
   (C)   5.5
   (D)   5.9
   (E)   6.0

2. Suppose events A, B, and C are independent. If $P(A \cap B) = 0.5$ and $P(A \cap B \cap C) = 0.25$, what is $P(C)$?

   (A) .05   (B) .2   (C) .25   (D) .5   (E) 2

3. Johnny has a 1% chance of getting a perfect score on the Math IIC SAT II. If he has a 5% chance of getting a perfect score on the Writing SAT II, what is the probability that he *won't* get a perfect score on either test?

   (A) .05   (B) .15   (C) .50   (D) .94   (E) .99

4. Joey wants to buy a three-scoop ice cream cone. There are 15 flavors to choose from. How many different three-scoop combinations can Joey get?

   (A)   5
   (B)   15
   (C)   150
   (D)   450
   (E)   455

5. A casting agent for a movie is looking to fill three female roles: the beautiful blonde, the beautiful brunette, and the beautiful redhead. If there are 40 actresses vying for one of the roles, how many different castings can there be? (Note: it matters which role each actress gets.)

   (A)   2,032
   (B)   15,984
   (C)   21,320
   (D)   59,280
   (E)   120,000

6. Suppose set A has 9 elements and set B has 4 elements. If C is the number of elements in $A \cup B$ and D is the number of elements in $A \cap B$, what is the minimum value of $C - D$?

   (A)   1
   (B)   4
   (C)   5
   (D)   9
   (E)   13

Explanations

1. **(D)**

In order for the mean of her scores to be 5.8, the sum of the three judges' scores, S, divided by three, must equal 5.8. The sum of the scores she needs to win is:

$$S = 3 \times 5.8 = 17.4$$

If one of the judges gives her a 5.5, then the sum of the other two judges' scores must be $17.4 - 5.5 = 11.9$. The lowest score she could receive would have to be averaged out by the highest scores she could receive, which would be a 6. Therefore, the lowest score would be $11.9 - 6.0 = 5.9$.

2. **(D)**

Immediately you can eliminate the last answer choice as a possibility, because the probability of an event is always between 0 and 1. Because the events are independent, the probability of any series of events happening is the product of their respective probabilities: $P(C \cap (A \cap B)) = P(C) \times P(A \cap B)$. From this equation you can see that

$$P(C) = P(C \cap (A \cap B)) \div P(A \cap B) = .25 \div .5 = .5$$

3. **(D)**

Because the two tests are independent of each other, the probability of any series of events happening is the product of their respective probabilities. Also, if P is the probability of an event happening, the probability of that event *not* happening is $1 - P$. Therefore, the probability of not scoring a perfect score on the Math IIC test is $1 - .01 = .99$ and for the Writing SAT II is $1 - .05 = .95$. The answer is the product of these two probabilities:

$$.99 \times .95 = .94$$

4. **(E)**

Since the order of the scoops doesn't matter, this is a combination question. To find the number of subgroups of size r that can be formed from a larger set n, use the following formula:

$$\binom{n}{r} = \frac{nP_r}{r!} = \frac{n!}{(n-r)!r!}$$

This problem asks you to take groups of 3 from a larger group of 15:

$$\frac{15!}{(15-3)!3!} = \frac{15!}{12!3!} = \frac{15 \times 14 \times 13}{3 \times 2 \times 1} = 455$$

5. **(D)**

Since it matters which role an actress gets, this is a permutation question. In order to find the number of permutations of size r that can be taken from a set with n elements, use the following formula:

$$_nP_r = \frac{n!}{(n-r)!}$$

This problem asks you to take groups of 3 from a larger group of 40:

$$\frac{40!}{40-3!} = \frac{40!}{37!} = 40 \times 39 \times 38 = 59280$$

6. **(C)**

To minimize C − D, minimize C and maximize D. The fewest possible elements in the union of a and b is 9, if b is a subset of a (i.e. all of the elements in b are also in a). This arrangement also maximizes the intersection of the sets: they must share 4 elements (all the elements in b). Therefore, C − D = 9 − 4 = 5. Any other situation results in a greater value for C − D.

Statistics

Miscellaneous Math

$\mathbf{W}$E'VE REVIEWED THE SEVEN MAJOR TOPICS tested by the Math IIC: algebra, plane geometry, solid geometry, coordinate geometry, trigonometry, functions, and statistics. But not all of the fifty questions on the test fall into these seven categories. This chapter on Special Math is devoted to those odds-and-ends topics that would otherwise fall through the cracks.

Logic

Logic questions don't look like math questions at all. Logic questions contain no numbers, no formulas, and no variables. Instead, logic questions contain a verbal statement, and a question that asks you to interpret the validity of the statement, or the effect of the given statement on another statement. For example:

> The statement "If Jill misses the bus, she will be late" is true. Which other statement must be true?
>
> (A)   If Jill does not miss the bus, she will not be late
> (B)   If Jill is not late, she missed the bus
> (C)   If a student misses the bus, he or she will be late
> (D)   Jill is late because she missed the bus
> (E)   If Jill is not late, she did not miss the bus

Even though it is stated in words, logic questions require a similar type of mathematical thinking, and there are methods for solving logic problems. Fortunately, on the Math IIC, there's really only one rule you need to know.

A logic statement is written in the form "If p, then q," where p and q are events. "If p, then q" can also be written as $p \leftrightarrow q$, and it states that if event p occurs, then event q will also occur.

Every "If p, then q" statement has an equivalent statement; this second statement is known as the contrapositive, which is always true. The contrapositive of "If p, then q" is "If not q, then not p." In symbols, the contrapositive of $p \leftrightarrow q$ is $\sim q \leftrightarrow \sim p$ (here, the symbol $\sim$ means "not"). To formulate the contrapositive of any logic statement, you must change the original statement in two ways.

1. Switch the order of the two parts of the statement. For example, "If p, then q" becomes "If q, then p."

2. Negate each part of the statement. "If q, then p" becomes "If not q, then not p."

When faced with a logic problem on the Math IIC, remember that if a given statement is true, then that statement's contrapositive is also true. Likewise, if a given statement is false, then that statement's contrapositive is also false.

Returning to the example problem, we are told that the given statement is true, so we should look for the contrapositive among the answer choices. (E) is the contrapositive of the original statement, so we know that it is true. Here's some more practice:

What is the contrapositive of "Every book on the shelf is old"?

You need to first rewrite this statement so that it is in the "If p, then q" form. So the given statement becomes "If a book is on the shelf, then it is old." The contrapositive of the statement is now easy to see: "If a book is not old, then it is not on the shelf."

Sequences

You might see one or two sequence questions on the Math IIC. The two types of sequences tested are arithmetic and geometric sequences.

Arithmetic Sequences

An arithmetic sequence is an ordered list of terms in which the difference between consecutive terms is constant. In other words, the same value or variable is added to each term in order to create the next term: if you subtract any two consecutive terms of the sequence, you will get the same difference. An example is $\{a_n\} = 1, 4, 7, 10, 13, \ldots$, where 3 is the constant increment between values.

The notation of an arithmetic sequence is

$$a_n = a_1 + (n-1)d$$

where a_n is the nth term of the sequence and d is the difference between consecutive terms. For the Math IIC, you must first be able to determine that a given sequence is an arithmetic sequence. To figure out if a sequence is arithmetic, take two sets of consecutive terms, and subtract the smaller term from the larger. If the difference between the terms in the two sets is equal, you've got yourself an arithmetic sequence. To figure out if the sequence $\{a_n\} = 1, 4, 7, 10, 13, \ldots$ is arithmetic, take two sets of consecutive terms $\{1, 4\}$ and $\{10, 13\}$, and subtract the first from the second:

$$4 - 1 = 3$$
$$13 - 10 = 3$$

Since the difference is equal, you know this sequence is arithmetic. You should be able to do three things with an arithmetic sequence:

1. Find d

2. Find the nth term

3. Calculate the sum of the first n terms

Finding *d*

To find the difference, d, between the terms of an arithmetic sequence, just subtract one term from the next term. The difference is d. For the arithmetic sequence $a_n = 1, 4, 7, 10, 13, \ldots, d = 4 - 1 = 3$. Here's a slightly more complicated form of this question:

If $a_4 = 4$ and $a_7 = 10$, find d.

This question gives you the fourth and seventh terms of a sequence:

$$a_n = a_1, a_2, a_3, 4, a_5, a_6, 10 \ldots$$

Since in arithmetic sequences d is constant between every term, you know that $d + 4 = a_5$, $a_5 + d = a + 6$, and $a_6 + d = 10$. In other words, the difference between the seventh term, 10, and the fourth term, 4, is $3d$. Stated as an equation:

$$10 = 4 + 3d$$

Solving this equation is a process of simple algebra.

$$3d = 6$$
$$d = 2$$

Finding the nth Term

To find the nth term in an arithmetic sequence, use the following formula:

$$a_n = a_1 + (n-1)d$$

In the example above, to find the 55th term we would have to find the value of a_1 first. Plug the values of $a_4 = 4$, $n = 4$ and $d = 2$ into the formula $a_n = a_1 + (n-1)d$ to find a_1. So, $a_{55} = -2 + (55-1)2 = -2 + (54)2 = -2 + 108 = 106$.

Finding the Sum of the First n Terms

In order to find the sum of the first n terms, simply find the value of the average term and then multiply that average by the number of terms you are summing.

$$\text{Sum of the first } n \text{ terms} = n\frac{a_1 + a_n}{2}$$

As you can see, this is simply n times the average of the first n terms. The sum of the first 55 terms of the above sequence would be $55(-2 + 106)/2 = 2,860$.

Geometric Sequences

A geometric sequence is a sequence in which the ratio of any term and the next term is constant. Whereas in an arithmetic sequence the *difference* between consecutive terms is always constant, in a geometric sequence the *quotient* of consecutive terms is always constant. The constant factor by which the terms of a geometric function differ is called the common ratio of the geometric sequence. The common ratio is usually represented by the variable r. Here is an example of a geometric sequence in which $r = 3$.

$$b_x = \frac{1}{3}, 1, 3, 9, 27, 81, \ldots$$

The general form of a geometric sequence is:

$$b_x = b_1, b_1r, b_1r^2, b_1r^3, \ldots$$

You should be able to identify a geometric sequence from its terms, and you should be able to perform three tasks on geometric sequences:

1. Find r
2. Find the nth term
3. Calculate the sum of the first n terms

Finding r

To find the common ratio of a geometric sequence, all you have to do is divide one term by the preceding term.

For example, the value of r for the sequence 3, 6, 12, 24, . . . is $\frac{6}{3} = 2$.

Finding the nth Term

To find the nth term of a geometric sequence, use the following formula:

$$b_n = b_1 r^{n-1}$$

For example, the 11th term of the sequence above is:

$$b_{11} = 3(2^{10}) = 3072$$

Finding the Sum of the First n Terms

To find the sum of the first n terms of a geometric sequence, use the following formula:

$$\text{Sum of the first } n \text{ terms} = b_1 \frac{1 - r^n}{1 - r}$$

So, the sum of the first 10 terms of the same sequence is:

$$3 \frac{1 - 2^{10}}{1 - 2} = 3069$$

The Sum of an Infinite Geometric Sequence

If the common ratio r of a geometric sequence is greater or equal to 1 (or less than or equal to –1), then each term is greater than or equal to the previous term, and the sequence does not converge. For these sequences, we cannot find a sum.

But if $-1 < r < 1$, then the terms of the sequence will converge toward zero. This convergence toward zero means that the sum of the entire geometric sequence can be approximated quite closely with the following formula:

$$\text{Sum of an infinite geometric sequence} = \frac{b_1}{1 - r}$$

where $-1 < r < 1$. For example:

What is the sum of the sequence 4, 2, 1, $\frac{1}{2}$, $\frac{1}{4}$ . . . ?

As a first step, make sure that the sum can be calculated by determining r. For this sequence, $r = \frac{1}{2}$, which is between -1 and 1, so the sum of the sequence is finite. Now, using the formula, the sum is $\frac{4}{(1 - \frac{1}{2})} = 8$.

Limits

For a function $f(x)$, the limit of the function is the value that the function approaches as x approaches a certain number. Here's an example:

What is the limit of $f(x) = \dfrac{x + 2}{x^2 - 2x - 8}$ as x approaches -2?

Normally, finding the limit should be easy. You would simply plug the value x approaches, in this case -2, into the function and produce the limit. But the Math IIC really only asks one type of question about limits—the test likes to ask you to determine the limit of a function at a point at which the function is not defined. But try and plug -2 into the function.

$$\begin{aligned}
f(x) &= \frac{x + 2}{x^2 - 2x - 8} \\
&= \frac{-2 + 2}{(-2)^2 - 2(-2) - 8} \\
&= \frac{0}{4 + 4 - 8} \\
&= \frac{0}{0}
\end{aligned}$$

It seems the function is not defined at $x = -2$, because division by zero is not allowed. This is precisely what the test *wants* you to think. But the assumption that this function is undefined at -2 is incorrect. And, luckily, there is an easy way to solve for the limit.

First, you need to factor the function so that it is in its most simplified state. For our example, the denominator can be factored:

$$x^2 - 2x - 8 = (x + 2)(x - 4)$$

Once the denominator has been factored, its easy to see that the function $\frac{x+2}{(x+2)(x-4)}$ simplifies to $\frac{1}{x-4}$. This simplified fraction *can* be evaluated at $x = -2$:

$$f(-2) = \frac{1}{-6}$$

$\frac{1}{-6}$ is the limit of f at $x = -2$.

Only if a function is undefined at a point at which you wish to find a limit, and the function cannot be factored any further, should you choose "the limit does not exist at this point" answer choice.

Imaginary and Complex Numbers

For most of the Math IIC test, we deal with real numbers. But every so often, a question will spring up that takes place outside the set of real numbers. These questions deal with imaginary and complex numbers.

Imaginary Numbers

Imaginary numbers are used to represent the even roots of negative numbers. They use the quantity i, where $i = \sqrt{-1}$. For example:

$$\sqrt{-16} = \sqrt{16}\sqrt{-1} = 4i$$

Numbers are called imaginary because they do not exist on their own according to the conventional rules of math.

Complex Numbers

A complex number is the sum of a real number and imaginary number. A complex number is written in the form of $a + bi$, where a and b are real numbers, and $i = \sqrt{-1}$.

There are three things you need to be able to do with complex numbers:

1. Know the powers of i

2. Know how to do operations on complex numbers, like addition, subtraction, and multiplication

3. Know how to graph a complex number in the complex plane, and how to find its absolute value

The Powers of *i*

The powers of *i* are easy to work with. For example:

Evaluate $i^2 \times i^9$.

The trick is to remember that the powers of *i* work in cycles of four:

- $i^1 = i$

- $i^2 = \sqrt{-1} \times \sqrt{-1} = (\sqrt{-1})^2 = -1$

- $i^3 = \sqrt{-1} \times \sqrt{-1} \times \sqrt{-1} = \sqrt{-1} \times (\sqrt{-1})^2 = -i$

- $i^4 = \sqrt{-1} \times \sqrt{-1} \times \sqrt{-1} \times \sqrt{-1} = (\sqrt{-1})^4 = 1$.

- This way, the expression $i^2 \times i^9$ becomes $(-1)(i) = -i$.

If you know these cycles, you can reduce any exponent of *i* to a much more manageable size. The expression $i^2 \times i^9$ becomes $(-1)(i) = -i$.

Operations on Complex Numbers

Algebraic manipulation of complex numbers is exactly like dealing with real numbers. See for yourself:

Simplify the expression $(3x + i)(x - 2i)$.

$$(3x + i)(x - 2i) =$$
$$3x^2 - 6xi + xi - 2i^2 =$$
$$3x^2 - 5xi - 2(-1) = 3x^2 - 5xi + 2$$

The Complex Plane

The complex plane is a plane similar to the coordinate plane, except that instead of having an *x*-axis and a *y*-axis, it has axes that allow you to plot complex numbers as well as real numbers.

The horizontal axis of a complex plane is called the real axis, and the vertical axis is called the imaginary axis. The complex number $a + bi$ is plotted in the complex plane exactly where the point (a, b) would be plotted in the standard coordinate plane. Take a look at the picture of the complex plane at the top of the opposite page, with various complex numbers plotted on it.

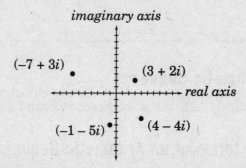

The magnitude of a complex number is the distance from the origin to that number in the complex plane. You can use the Pythagorean Theorem to calculate the magnitude of the complex number.

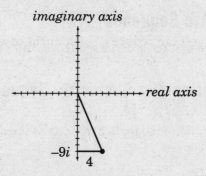

The magnitude of $a + bi$ is $\sqrt{a^2 + b^2}$. Try the following example:

What is the magnitude of the complex number $4 - 9i$?

The complex number $4 - 9i$ would be graphed on the plane as the point $(4, -9i)$. Using the Pythagorean theorem to calculate its magnitude: $\sqrt{4^2 + (-9)^2} = \sqrt{16 + 81} = \sqrt{97} \approx 9.85$.

Miscellaneous Math

Key Terms

n^{th} Term of an Arithmetic Sequence

$a_n = a_1 + (n-1)d$, where a_1 is the first term of the sequence and d its common difference.

Sum of the First n terms of an Arithmetic Sequence

$$\text{Sum} = n\frac{a_1 + a_n}{2}$$

n^{th} Term of a Geometric Sequence

$b_n = b_1 r^{n-1}$, where b_1 is the first term of the sequence, and r is the common ratio.

Sum of the First n Terms of a Geometric Sequence

$$\text{Sum} = b_1\frac{1 - r^n}{1 - r}$$

Review Questions

1. If the statement, "If a student studies hard, then that student will do well on the SAT IIs" is true, which of the following statements is also true?

   (A) If a student doesn't do well on the SAT IIs, then that student didn't study hard.
   (B) If a student studies hard, then that student won't do well on the SAT IIs.
   (C) If a student doesn't study hard, then that student will do well on the SAT IIs.
   (D) If a student does well on the SAT IIs, then that student didn't study hard.
   (E) If a student takes the SAT IIs, then that student will do well.

2. In the geometric series g_n, where $g_1 = 3$ and $g_3 = \frac{3}{4}$, what is g_{10}?

   (A) $\frac{3}{1024}$ (B) $\frac{3}{512}$ (C) $\frac{3}{16}$ (D) $\frac{3}{8}$ (E) $\frac{3}{2}$

3. What is the sum of the infinite geometric series x_n, given by $x_n = 4, 2, 1, \frac{1}{2}, \frac{1}{4}, ...$?

   (A) 6
   (B) 8
   (C) 9
   (D) 12
   (E) 16

4. What is $\lim\limits_{x \to 3} \dfrac{2x^3 - 5x^2 - 3x}{x - 3}$?

   (A) $\dfrac{2}{5}$

   (B) 3

   (C) 16

   (D) 21

   (E) Undefined

5. What is the product of $(2 + 3i)$ and $(\frac{1}{2} - i)$?

   (A) $4 - \dfrac{1}{2}i$

   (B) $4 + \dfrac{1}{2}i$

   (C) $-2 - \dfrac{1}{2}i$

   (D) $4 + \dfrac{7}{2}i$

   (E) $4 - \sqrt{2}$

6. What is the distance of $3 - 7i$ from the origin?

   (A) .398

   (B) 4

   (C) 7.62

   (D) 11.4

   (E) 16.6

Explanations

1. **(A)**

If a statement is true, the contrapositive of the statement will also be true false. To find the contrapositive, you need to take the opposite of both parts of the statement and then also switch the order. The contrapositive of the original sentence is "If a student doesn't do well on the SAT IIs, then that student didn't study hard."

2. **(B)**

Given two terms of a geometric sequence, it is possible to find the common ratio between consecutive terms. In any geometric series, $g_3 = g_1 \times r^{3-1} = g_1 \times r^2$. (More generally, $g_a = g_b \times r^{a-b}$.) In this problem, $\frac{3}{4} = 3r^2$. So, $r^2 = \frac{1}{4}$, and therefore $r = \frac{1}{2}$. Now that you know the value of r and the value of at least one term in the geometric sequence, you can find any term. In this case, $g_{10} = g_1 \times r^{10-1} = 3 \times (\frac{1}{2})^9 = \frac{3}{512}$.

3.   **(B)**

The sum of an infinite geometric series is finite if $|r| < 1$, and infinite if $|r| > 1$. The formula for x_n is $8 \times (½)^n$, where $r = ½$ is the common ratio between consecutive terms. The sum of this series is therefore finite. The formula for the sum of an infinite series is $x_1/1-r$, where r is the common ratio. In this problem, the sum is $4/1-.5 = 8$.

4.   **(D)**

In order to find the limit as it approaches a value, plug the value into the expression for x. For this problem you immediately run into a problem, because plugging 3 into the expression produces a 0 in the denominator, and you cannot divide by 0. If this happens, see if the expression can be factored:

$$\frac{2x^3 - 5x^2 - 3x}{x - 3} = \frac{x(2x^2 - 5x - 3)}{x - 3}$$
$$= \frac{x(2x + 1)(x - 3)}{x - 3}$$
$$= x(2x + 1)$$

Now you can plug 3 into the simplified expression:

$$3(2(3) + 1) = 3(6 + 1) = 3(7) = 21$$

5.   **(A)**

The algebra for complex numbers is the same as for real numbers. For this problem, use FOIL and keep in mind that $i^2 = -1$.

$$(2 + 3i)(\frac{1}{2} - i) = = 1 - 2i + \frac{3i}{2} - 3i^2$$
$$= 1 - \frac{1}{2}i + 3$$
$$= 4 - \frac{1}{2}i$$

6.   **(C)**

The magnitude of a complex number is the distance from the origin to that number in the complex plane. Using the Pythagorean Theorem, the magnitude of the complex number $a + bi$ is $\sqrt{a^2 + b^2}$. In this problem the complex number is $3 - 7i$, so its magnitude is $\sqrt{3^2 + (-7)^2} = \sqrt{9 + 49} = \sqrt{58} \approx 7.62$.

PRACTICE TESTS

Practice Tests Are Your Best Friends

In this crazy world of ours, there is one thing that you can always take for granted: the SAT II Math IIC will stay the same. From year to year and test to test, of the 50 Math IIC questions, seven or eight questions will cover equation solving, four to five will cover graphing functions, two to three will cover conic sections, etc. Obviously, different versions of the SAT II Math IIC aren't *exactly* the same. Individual questions will never repeat from test to test. But the subjects that the questions test, and the way in which the questions test those subjects, *will* stay constant.

This constancy can be a great benefit to you as you study for the test. To show how you can use the similarity between different versions of the SAT II Math IIC test to your advantage, we provide a case study.

Practice Tests

Using the Predictability of the SAT II Math IIC for Personal Gain

One day, an eleventh grader named Molly Bloom sits down at the desk in her room and takes a practice test for the SAT II Math IIC. Because it makes this example much simpler, let's say she takes the entire test and gets only one question wrong. Molly checks her answers and then jumps from her chair and does a little dance, shimmying to the tune of her own success. After her euphoria passes, she begins to wonder which question she got wrong and returns to her chair. She discovers that the question dealt with parabolas. Looking over the question, Molly at first thinks the test writers made a mistake and that she was right. But at second glance, she realizes that she had misidentified the vertex of the parabola. Molly saw she didn't have a good grasp on how to graph a parabola given its equation and studies up on her coordinate geometry. She learns the basics of conic sections and *what* causes a parabola's vertex to shift from the origin. All this takes her about ten minutes, after which she vows never to make a mistake on a question involving parabolas.

Analyzing Molly Bloom

Molly's actions seem minor. All she did was study a question she got wrong until she understood why she got it wrong and what she should have done to get it right. But the implications loom large. Molly answered the question incorrectly because she didn't understand the topic it was testing, and the practice test pointed out her shortcoming in the most noticeable way possible: she got the question wrong. After doing her goofy little dance, Molly wasn't content to simply see what the correct answer was and get on with her day. She wanted to see *how* and *why* she got the question wrong and what she should have done or needed to know to get it right. So, with a look of determination and a self-given pep talk, she spent time studying the question, discovered her misunderstanding of parabola graphs, and nailed down the ideas behind the material. If Molly were to take that same test again, she definitely would not get that question wrong.

"But she never will take that same test again, so she's never going to see that particular question again," some poor sap who hasn't read this guide might exclaim. "She wasted her time. Wow, Molly Bloom is dumb!"

Why That Poor Sap Really Is a Poor Sap

In some sense, that poor sap is correct: Molly never will take that exact practice test again. But the poor sap is wrong to call Molly derogatory names, because, as we know, the SAT II Math IIC is remarkably similar from year to year—both in the topics it covers and in the way it poses questions about those topics. Therefore, when Molly taught herself about conic sections and their graphs, she learned how to answer the similar questions dealing with parabolas and circles that will *undoubtedly* appear on every future practice test and on the real Math IIC.

By studying the results of her practice test and figuring out why she got her one question wrong and what she should have known and done to get it right, Molly has targeted a weakness and overcome it.

Molly and You

Molly has it easy. She took a practice test and got only one question wrong. Less than one percent of all people who take the SAT II Math IIC will be so lucky. Of course, the only reason Molly got that many right was so that we could use her as an easy example.

So, what if you take a practice test and get 15 questions wrong, and your errors span a number of different math topics? You should do exactly what Molly did. Take your test and *study it*. Identify every question you got wrong, figure out why you got it wrong, and then teach yourself what you should have done to get the question right. If you can't figure out your error, find someone who can.

Think about it. What does an incorrect answer mean? That wrong answer identifies a weakness in your test-taking, whether that weakness is an unfamiliarity with a particular math topic or a tendency to be careless. If you got 15 questions wrong on a practice test, then each of those 15 questions identifies a weakness in your ability to take the SAT II Math IIC or your knowledge about the topics tested by the SAT II Math IIC. But as you study each question and figure out why you got that question wrong, you are learning how to answer the questions that will appear on the real test. You are discovering your exact math weaknesses and addressing them, and you are learning to understand not just the knowledge behind the question, but the way that ETS asks its questions as well.

If you got 15 questions wrong, it will take a bit more time to study your mistakes. But if you invest that time and study your practice test properly, you will be avoiding future mistakes. Each successive practice test you take should have fewer errors, meaning less time spent studying those errors. More important, you'll be pinpointing what you need to study for the real SAT II Math IIC, identifying and overcoming your weaknesses, and learning to answer an increasing variety of questions on the specific topics covered by the test. Taking practice tests and studying them will allow you to teach yourself how to recognize and handle whatever the SAT II Math IIC throws at you.

Taking a Practice Test

The example of Miss Molly Bloom shows why studying practice tests can be an extremely powerful study tool. Now we're going to explain how to use that tool.

Controlling Your Environment

Although no one but you ever needs to see your practice-test scores, you should do everything in your power to make the practice test feel like the real SAT II Math IIC. The more your practice resembles the real thing, the more helpful it will be. When taking a practice test, follow these rules:

Take the tests timed. Don't give yourself any extra time. Be stricter with yourself than the meanest proctor you can think of. Also, don't give yourself time off for bathroom breaks. If you have to go to the bathroom, let the clock keep running; that's what'll happen on the real Math IIC.

Take the test in a single sitting. Training yourself to endure an hour of test-taking is part of your preparation.

Find a place to take the test without distractions. Don't take the practice test in a room with lots of people walking through it. Go to a library, your bedroom, an empty classroom—anywhere quiet.

By following these guidelines, you will be more focused while taking the practice test and you will achieve your target score more quickly. However, don't be too discouraged if you find these rules too strict; you can always bend them a little. Preparing for the SAT II Math IIC should not be so torturous that you don't study! Do whatever you have to do to make yourself study.

Ultimately, if you can follow all of the above rules to the letter, you will probably be better off. But if following those rules makes studying excruciating, find little ways to bend them so they don't interfere too much with your concentration.

Practice Test Strategy

You should take the test as if it were the real deal: go for the highest score you can get. This does not mean that you should be more daring than you would be on the actual test, guessing blindly even when you can't eliminate an answer. It doesn't mean that you should carelessly speed through the test. Follow the rules for guessing and for skipping questions that we outlined earlier. The more closely your attitude and strategies during the practice test reflect those you'll employ during the actual test, the more the practice test will accurately predict your strengths and weaknesses. You'll learn what areas you should study and how to pace yourself during the test.

Scoring Your Practice Test

After you take your practice test, you'll want to score it and see how you did. However, when you do your scoring, don't just tally up your raw score. As part of your scoring, you should also keep a list of every question you got wrong and every question you skipped. This list will be your guide when you study your test.

Studying Your ... No, Wait, Go Take a Break

You know how to have fun. Go do that for a while. Come back when you're refreshed.

Studying Your Practice Test

After grading your test, you should have a list of the questions you answered incorrectly or skipped. Studying your test involves using this list and examining each question you answered incorrectly, figuring out why you got the question wrong and understanding what you could have done to get the question right.

Why did you get the question wrong?

There are three reasons why you might have gotten an individual question wrong.

1. You thought you solved the answer correctly, but you actually didn't.

2. You managed to eliminate some answer choices and then guessed among the remaining answers; unfortunately, you guessed wrong.

3. You knew the answer but somehow made a careless mistake.

You should know which of these reasons applies to each question you got wrong.

What could you have done to get the question right?

The reasons you got a question wrong affect how you should think about it while studying your test.

If You Got a Question Wrong for Reason 1–Lack of Knowledge

A question answered incorrectly for Reason 1 identifies a weakness in your knowledge of the math tested on the Math IIC test. Discovering this wrong answer gives you an opportunity to target your weakness.

For example, if the question you got wrong refers to factoring quadratics, don't just memorize the roots of certain equations. Learn the fundamental techniques that make different quadratics result in different roots. Remember, you will *not* see a question exactly like the question you got wrong. But you probably *will* see a question that covers the same topic as the practice question. For that reason, when you get a question wrong, don't just figure out the right answer to the question. Study the broader topic that the question tests.

If You Got a Question Wrong for Reason 2–Guessing Wrong

If you guessed wrong, review your guessing strategy. Did you guess intelligently? Could you have eliminated more answers? If yes, why didn't you? By thinking in this critical way about the decisions you made while taking the practice test, you can train yourself to make quicker, more decisive, and better decisions.

If you took a guess and chose the incorrect answer, don't let that sour you on guessing. Even as you go over the question and figure out if there were any ways for you to have answered the question without having to guess, remind yourself that if you eliminated at least one answer, you followed the right strategy even if you got the question wrong.

If You Got a Question Wrong for Reason 3–Carelessness

If you discover you got a question wrong because you were careless, it might be tempting to say to yourself, "Oh, I made a careless error," and assure yourself you won't do that again. That is not enough. You made that careless mistake for a reason, and you should try to figure out why. Whereas getting a question wrong because you didn't know the answer constitutes a weakness in your knowledge about the test, making a careless mistake represents a weakness in your *method of taking the test*.

To overcome this weakness, you need to approach it in the same critical way you would approach a lack of knowledge. Study your mistake. Reenact your thought process on the problem and see where and how your carelessness came about: were you rushing? Did you jump at the first answer that seemed right instead of reading all the answers? Know your error and look it in the eye. If you learn precisely what your mistake was, you are much less likely to make that mistake again.

If You Left the Question Blank

It is also a good idea to study the questions you left blank on the test, since those questions constitute a reservoir of lost points. A blank answer is a result either of:

1. A total inability to answer a question

2. A lack of time

In the case of the first possibility, you should see if there was some way you might have been able to eliminate an answer choice or two and put yourself in a better position to guess. In the second case, look over the question and see whether you think you could have answered it. If you could have, then you know that you are throwing away points and probably working too slowly. If you couldn't, then carry out the steps above: study the relevant material and review your guessing strategy.

The Secret Weapon: Talking to Yourself

Yeah, it's embarrassing. Yeah, you'll look silly. But other than physical violence, talking to yourself is perhaps the best way to pound something into your brain. As you go through the steps of studying a question, you should talk them out. When you verbalize something to yourself, it makes it much harder to delude yourself into thinking that you're working if you're really not.

SAT II Math IIC
Practice Test I

MATHEMATICS LEVEL IIC TEST

REFERENCE INFORMATION

THE FOLLOWING INFORMATION IS FOR YOUR REFERENCE IN ANSWERING SOME OF THE QUESTIONS IN THIS TEST.

Volume of a right circular cone with radius r and height h: $V = \frac{1}{3}\pi r^2 h$

Lateral area of a right circular cone with circumference of the bace c and slant height ℓ: $S = \frac{1}{2}c\ell$

Volume of a sphere with radius r: $V = \frac{4}{3}\pi^3$

Surface area of a sphere with radius r: $S = 4\pi r^2$

Volume of a pyramid with base area B and height h: $V = \frac{1}{3}Bh$

GO ON TO THE NEXT PAGE ▶

MATHEMATICS LEVEL IIC TEST

For each of the following problems, decide which is the BEST of the choices given. If the exact numerical value is not one of the choices, select the choice that best approximates this value. Then fill in the corresponding oval on the answer sheet.

Notes: (1) A calculator will be necessary for answering some (but not all) of the questions in this test. For each question you will have to decide whether or not you should use a calcuator. The calculator you use must be at least a scientific calculator; programmable calculators and calculators that can display graphs are permitted.

(2) For some questions in this test you may need to decide whether your calculator should be in radian or degree mode.

(3) Figures that accompany problems in this test are intended to provide information useful in solving the problems. They are drawn as accurately as possible EXCEPT when it is stated in a specific problem that its figure is not drawn to scale. All figures lie in a plane unless otherwise indicated.

(4) Unless otherwise specified, the domain of any function f is assumed to be the set of all real numbers x for which $f(x)$ is a real number.

(5) Reference information that may be useful in answering the questions in this test can be found on the page preceding Question 1.

USE THIS SPACE FOR SCRATCHWORK.

1. If $x = t^3$ and $y = t^2 + 4$, what is y in terms of x?

    (A) $x + 4$

    (B) $x^2 + 4$

    (C) $\sqrt[3]{x} + 4$

    (D) $x\sqrt[3]{x} + 4$

    (E) $\sqrt[3]{x^2} + 4$

2. $\dfrac{x}{2y} - \dfrac{y}{2x} =$

    (A) $\dfrac{2x - 2y}{x - y}$

    (B) $\dfrac{x - y}{2y - 2x}$

    (C) $\dfrac{x^2 - y^2}{2xy}$

    (D) $\dfrac{x - y}{2xy}$

    (E) $\dfrac{x^2 + y^2}{2xy}$

GO ON TO THE NEXT PAGE

3. What is the range of $y = 3\sin\theta$?

    (A) $-3 < y < 3$

    (B) $0 \le y$

    (C) $-\dfrac{1}{3} \le y \le \dfrac{1}{3}$

    (D) $-1 \le y \le 1$

    (E) $-3 \le y \le 3$

4. What is the perimeter of a rectangle that has vertices $(1, \sqrt{2})$, $(1, 5)$, and $(3, 5)$?

    (A) 7.17
    (B) 9.23
    (C) 11.17
    (D) 15
    (E) 30

5. If $x, y,$ and z are nonzero real numbers and if $\dfrac{x - z^2}{y} = yz^2$
    then $x =$

    (A) y^2
    (B) $2z^2$
    (C) $y^2 - 2z^2$
    (D) $z^2(y^2 - 1)$
    (E) $z^2(y^2 + 1)$

6. In Figure 1, if $\sin\theta = 0.29$ then what is the value of $\dfrac{y}{x}$?

    (A) -0.34
    (B)   0.18
    (C)   0.29
    (D)   0.30
    (E)   0.96

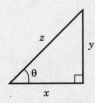

Figure 1

7. If $f(x) = x^2$ and $g(x) = \sqrt{x} + 2$, what is $g(f(2)) + f(1)$?

    (A) 3
    (B) 5
    (C) 6
    (D) 10
    (E) $\left(\sqrt{2} + 2\right)^2 + 1$

GO ON TO THE NEXT PAGE

8. If $\frac{2}{3}(x^3) = 3$ then what is the value of x?

    (A) 0.50
    (B) 1.04
    (C) 1.65
    (D) 2.08
    (E) 4.50

9. Under what conditions is the graph of $y = -bx + 1$ a vertical line?

    (A) if $b = 0$
    (B) if $0 \le b \le 1$
    (C) if $b = -1$
    (D) for all b
    (E) for no b

10. Where it is defined, $\dfrac{1 + \tan^2\theta}{\tan^2\theta} =$

    (A) 0
    (B) 1
    (C) $\csc^2\theta$
    (D) $\sin^2\theta$
    (E) $1 - \sin^2\theta$

11. A portion of the graph of $y = f(x)$ is shown in Figure 2. Assuming the graph continues in the pattern shown, what is the range of f?

    (A) Real numbers
    (B) Real numbers, such that $f(x) \ne 0$
    (C) Real numbers, excluding integers
    (D) Real numbers, such that $f(x) > 0$
    (E) Integers

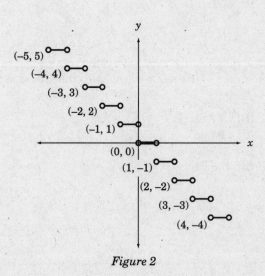

Figure 2

12. Which of the following is a zero of $f(x) = 3x^2 - x - 5$?

   (A) −2.14
   (B) −1.59
   (C)   0.62
   (D)   1.47
   (E)   3.33

13. If $\sin\theta = \dfrac{\sqrt{3}}{2}$ then $\dfrac{\cos\theta}{\csc\theta} =$

   (A) −3

   (B) $-\dfrac{\sqrt{3}}{4}$

   (C) $\dfrac{\sqrt{3}}{4}$

   (D) $\dfrac{\sqrt{3}}{2}$

   (E) $\sqrt{3}$

14. If $f(x) = x + 3$, which of the following equals $\dfrac{f(1) \times (f(7) + f(2))}{f(3)}$?

   (A) $f(5)$
   (B) $f(6)$
   (C) $f(7)$
   (D) $f(7) + 0.5$
   (E) $f(8)$

15. A sphere and a cone have equal volume and radii. If the radius of each of the solids is 3, what is the lateral area of the cone?

   (A)   58.29
   (B)   77.72
   (C)   96.38
   (D) 113.10
   (E) 116.58

GO ON TO THE NEXT PAGE

16. If the graph in Figure 3 is the graph of $y = |f(x)|$, then which of the following graphs could *not* be the graph of $f(x)$?

(A)

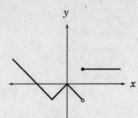

(B)

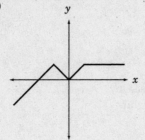

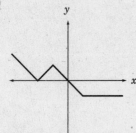

Figure 3

(C)

(D)

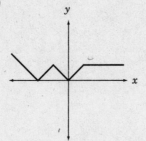

(E)

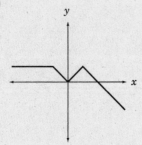

17. The median of a set of numbers is 7.4. If the greatest number in the set is removed, which of the following choices could *not* be the median of the new set?

(A) 6.4
(B) 7
(C) 7.4
(D) 9
(E) Not enough information to tell

GO ON TO THE NEXT PAGE

MATHEMATICS LEVEL IIC TEST—*Continued*

18. In Figure 4, if $\cot \theta = 0.25$ then what is the value of x?

    (A) 1 (B) 2 (C) 4 (D) 16 (E) 32

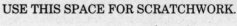

Figure 4

19. If the current value of a given object is $15, and it increases in value at a rate of 12.5% annually, what will the object's value be in 14 years?

    (A) $59
    (B) $67
    (C) $71
    (D) $78
    (E) $83

20. If $-2 \leq x \leq 4$, and $f(x) = \left| x^2 - 9 \right|$, then what is the range of f?

    (A) $y \geq 0$
    (B) $0 \leq y \leq 7$
    (C) $5 \leq y \leq 7$
    (D) $0 \leq y \leq 9$
    (E) $y \leq 9$

21. What number must be added to each of the numbers 0, 8, and 32 so that they form consecutive terms of a geometric sequence?

    (A) 2 (B) 3 (C) 4 (D) 5 (E) 6

22. If $f(x) = f^{-1}(x)$ for all real numbers x, what might $f(x)$ equal?

    (A) x
    (B) x^2
    (C) $x + 1$
    (D) $2x$
    (E) $2x^2$

GO ON TO THE NEXT PAGE ➡

23. For which of the following values of θ is $\tan\theta$ always greater than $\cos\theta$?

    (A) $0° < \theta < 45°$
    (B) $45° < \theta < 90°$
    (C) $90° < \theta < 135°$
    (D) $135° < \theta < 180°$
    (E) not possible

24. What is the domain of the function: $f(x) = \dfrac{1}{2x^3 + 2x^2 - 24x}$

    (A) $x < -4$ or $x > 3$
    (B) $-4 < x < 8$
    (C) $x \neq -4, 0, 3$
    (D) $x > 0$
    (E) $x \neq 0, 8$

25. For all θ, $(\pi^{\cos(-\theta)})(\pi^{-\cos\theta}) =$

    (A) 1
    (B) $\pi^{2\cos(-\theta)}$
    (C) $\pi^{-2\cos\theta}$
    (D) $\pi^{-2\cos(-\theta)}$
    (E) $\pi^{\cos 2\theta}$

26. The graph of $y = f(x)$ is shown in Figure 5. Which of the following statements must be true?

    I. $|f(x)| \geq 0$
    II. $f(x) = -f(-x)$
    III. If $x_1 > x_2$, then $f(x_1) < f(x_2)$

    (A) I only
    (B) I and II only
    (C) I and III only
    (D) II and III only
    (E) I, II, and III

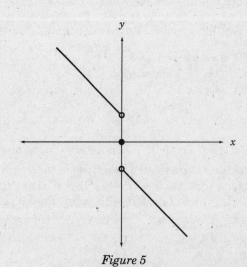

Figure 5

GO ON TO THE NEXT PAGE

27. If $36x^4 - 126x^2 + 108 = 0$, which of the following is *not* a valid value of x:

   (A) -1.41
   (B) -1.22
   (C) 0
   (D) 1.22
   (E) 1.41

28. f is a function. Suppose the following two statements are true of f:

   I. f has a root at $x = 2$.
   II. The graph of $y = f(x)$ has exactly two asymptotes, at $x = -1$ and $y = 1$.

   Which of the following functions could be f?

   (A) $f(x) = \dfrac{x-1}{x+1}$

   (B) $f(x) = (x-1)(x+2)$

   (C) $f(x) = (x-2)(x+1)$

   (D) $f(x) = \dfrac{x-2}{x+1}$

   (E) $f(x) = \dfrac{(x-2)(x-1)}{x+1}$

29. $f(x) = x^3 + 2x^2 - 8x$. For what values of x is $f(x) \ge 0$?

   (A) $x \ge 2$
   (B) $x \le 0$
   (C) $0 \le x \le 2$ and $x \ge 5$
   (D) $-4 \le x \le 0$ and $x \ge 2$
   (E) $-4 \le x \le 2$

30. Point $(-4, 3)$ is located on a circle in the coordinate plane given by the equation $(x + 1)^2 + (y + 1)^2 = r^2$. If r is the radius of the circle, which of the following points must also lie on the circle?

   (A) $(-6, -2.8)$
   (B) $(-3.9, 2)$
   (C) $(1, 2.7)$
   (D) $(-1, -4)$
   (E) $(2, 3)$

GO ON TO THE NEXT PAGE

31. $f(x) = \begin{cases} e^x + 1 & \text{if } x \geq 0 \\ -x^2 + 2 & \text{if } x < 0 \end{cases}$

What is the range of f?

(A) $y \geq 1$
(B) $y \geq 2$
(C) $y > 0$
(D) $y < 0$
(E) All real numbers

32. For what value(s) of x is the inverse of $f(x) = \dfrac{1}{x^3}$ *not* defined:

(A) $x \leq 0$
(B) $x < 0$
(C) $x = 0$ only
(D) $x > 0$
(E) $x \geq 0$

33. If a and b are nonzero real numbers and $(3.92)^a = (7.86)^b$, what is the value of $\left(\dfrac{b}{a}\right)^2$?

(A) 0.44
(B) 0.66
(C) 0.90
(D) 1.5
(E) 2.3

34. In an arithmetic sequence a_n, $a_8 = 5$ and $a_{11} = 20$. What is a_{100}?

(A) 430
(B) 435
(C) 465
(D) 470
(E) 535

GO ON TO THE NEXT PAGE

35. A monkey sits atop a tree and sees two birds. He can look at one of the birds by tilting his head up at an angle of θ_1 above the horizontal. He can look at the second bird by tilting his head down at an angle of θ_2 below the horizontal. If both birds are a horizontal distance of d meters from the tree (i.e., one is flying directly above the other), how far apart vertically are the two birds, in meters?

 (A) $\dfrac{d}{3}$

 (B) $d(\sin \theta_1 + \sin \theta_2)$
 (C) $d(\cos \theta_1 + \cos \theta_2)$
 (D) $d \tan(\theta_1 + \theta_2)$
 (E) $d(\tan \theta_1 + \tan \theta_2)$

36. Jim owns a small business. By Jim's estimate, he has a 40% chance of making a $5,000 profit in the next year, and a 60% chance of losing $2,000. If an "expected profit" is the product of a profit and the probability of making that profit, what is Jim's expected profit in the next year?

 (A) −$200
 (B) $800
 (C) $2,200
 (D) $3,000
 (E) $7,000

37. $\vec{u}$ has initial point $(-2, 2)$ and terminal point $(2, 5)$. $\vec{v}$ has initial point $(1, 5)$ and terminal point $(-2, 4)$. What is $\vec{u} - \vec{v}$?

 (A) $(4, 3)$
 (B) $(7, 2)$
 (C) $(2, 6)$
 (D) $(-1, 3)$
 (E) $(7, 4)$

38. If $f^{-1}(x) = 11x^2$ for $x > 0$, then $f(2) =$

 (A) 0.18
 (B) 0.43
 (C) 0.60
 (D) 22
 (E) 44

GO ON TO THE NEXT PAGE

39. $\sin^{-1}(\sin 45°) =$

    (A) .0123
    (B) .707
    (C) 15°
    (D) 45°
    (E) 90°

40. In a given geometric sequence g_n, $g_4 = 5$ and $g_6 = 11.25$. What is $g_{14} \div g_{17}$?

    (A) $\dfrac{8}{27}$ (B) $\dfrac{4}{9}$ (C) $\dfrac{2}{3}$ (D) $\dfrac{8}{9}$ (E) $\dfrac{9}{8}$

41. A right triangle in 3-dimensional space is formed by the points $(2,-2,1)$, $(2,-2,7)$, and $(5,2,1)$. What is the length of the hypotenuse of the triangle?

    (A) 5.00
    (B) 6.00
    (C) 6.71
    (D) 7.81
    (E) 10.63

42. Which of the following expresses the polar point $(3, \dfrac{5\pi}{6})$ in rectangular coordinates?

    (A) $(-1.7, -3.14)$
    (B) $(-0.87, 0.5)$
    (C) $(1.5, 3.14)$
    (D) $(-2.6, 1.5)$
    (E) $(0.78, 2.3)$

GO ON TO THE NEXT PAGE

43. $\dfrac{(n+1)! \times (n-1)!}{(n!)^2} =$

   (A) $(n+1)(n-1)$

   (B) $\dfrac{n+1}{n}$

   (C) $\dfrac{1}{n^2}$

   (D) $\dfrac{(n+1)(n-1)}{n}$

   (E) n

44. A circle with equation $(x-3)^2 + (y-3)^2 = 16$ is rotated around the line $y = x$. What is the volume of the solid that is created?

   (A) 256.29
   (B) 268.06
   (C) 301.97
   (D) 312.75
   (E) 316.33

45. Suppose the following statement is true: "If the watch costs less than forty dollars, Jim will buy it." Which of the following statements must also be true?

   I. If the watch costs more than forty dollars, Jim will not buy it.
   II. If Jim buys the watch, it costs less than forty dollars.
   III. If Jim doesn't buy the watch, the watch costs at least forty dollars.

   (A) I only
   (B) I and II only
   (C) III only
   (D) II and III only
   (E) None of the three statements must be true

GO ON TO THE NEXT PAGE

46. An ellipse has equation $100x^2 + 25y^2 = 175$. What is the length of the major axis of the ellipse?

    (A) 1.51
    (B) 2.65
    (C) 3.50
    (D) 5.29
    (E) 7.00

47. Let $f(a, b) = |a + b \times i|$ and $g(a, b) = |a| + |b \times i^2|$. What is $g(3, 4) - f(3, 4)$?

    (A) −2
    (B) −1
    (C) 0
    (D) 2
    (E) 18

48. For which of the following is $f(x)$ positive for all real values of x?

    I. $f(x) = \sqrt{x^2 + 4}$

    II. $f(x) = \sin\left(x - \dfrac{\pi}{2}\right)$

    III. $f(x) = 2^{x-1}$

    (A) None
    (B) I only
    (C) II only
    (D) I and II
    (E) I and III

GO ON TO THE NEXT PAGE

49. What is $\lim\limits_{x \to 2} \dfrac{1}{x-2}$?

    (A) 0

    (B) 1

    (C) ∞

    (D) $-\infty$

    (E) The limit does not exist.

50. If mn is an integer, which of the following must also be an integer?

    (A) $2mn$

    (B) m

    (C) n

    (D) $mn + 2n$

    (E) $\dfrac{3}{mn}$

S T O P

IF YOU FINISH BEFORE TIME IS CALLED, YOU MAY CHECK YOUR WORK ON THIS TEST ONLY.
DO NOT TURN TO ANY OTHER TEST IN THIS BOOK.

SAT II Math IIC Practice Test I Explanations

Calculating Your Score

Your raw score for the SAT II Math IIC test is calculated from the number of questions you answer correctly and incorrectly. Once you have determined your raw score, use the conversion table on page 17 of this book to calculate your scaled score.

To Calculate Your Raw Score

Count the number of questions you answered correctly: _____
A

Count the number of questions you answered incorrectly, and multiply that number by $\frac{1}{4}$:

_____ X $\frac{1}{4}$ = _____
B   C

Subtract the value in field C from value in field A: _____
D

Round the number in field D to the nearest whole number. This is your raw score: _____
E

Answers to SAT II Math IIC Practice Test I

Question Number	Correct Answer	Right	Wrong	Question Number	Correct Answer	Right	Wrong
1.	E	___	___	26.	E	___	___
2.	C	___	___	27.	C	___	___
3.	E	___	___	28.	D	___	___
4.	C	___	___	29.	D	___	___
5.	E	___	___	30.	E	___	___
6.	D	___	___	31.	E	___	___
7.	B	___	___	32.	C	___	___
8.	C	___	___	33.	A	___	___
9.	E	___	___	34.	C	___	___
10.	C	___	___	35.	E	___	___
11.	E	___	___	36.	B	___	___
12.	D	___	___	37.	E	___	___
13.	C	___	___	38.	B	___	___
14.	C	___	___	39.	D	___	___
15.	E	___	___	40.	A	___	___
16.	E	___	___	41.	D	___	___
17.	D	___	___	42.	D	___	___
18.	B	___	___	43.	B	___	___
19.	D	___	___	44.	B	___	___
20.	D	___	___	45.	C	___	___
21.	C	___	___	46.	D	___	___
22.	A	___	___	47.	D	___	___
23.	B	___	___	48.	E	___	___
24.	C	___	___	49.	E	___	___
25.	A	___	___	50.	A	___	___

Math IIC Test I Explanations

1. (E) Equation Solving

This question asks for y in terms of x, but y is given in terms of t. Fortunately, t can easily be described in terms of x by combining the two equations. First, solve for t in terms of x by taking the cube root of both sides of the first equation. Now $t = \sqrt[3]{x}$. Plugging in this for t in the second equation: $y = (\sqrt[3]{x})^2 + 4 = \sqrt[3]{x^2} + 4$.

2. (C) Fundamentals

To add or subtract fractions, you must first find the lowest common denominator. The denominators are $2x$ and $2y$, so the lowest common is $2xy$. Multiply the first fraction by $\frac{x}{x}$ and the second fraction by $\frac{y}{y}$. Since you're multiplying both fractions by 1, the expression does not change in value. It does, however, become easy to do the arithmetic. The expression is now:

$$\frac{x}{2y}\left(\frac{x}{x}\right) - \frac{y}{2x}\left(\frac{y}{y}\right) = \frac{x^2 - y^2}{2xy}$$

3. (E) Graphing in the Entire Coordinate Plane

This problem is simple if you know your trig functions and are familiar with their graphs. The range for $y = \sin\theta$ is $-1 \leq y \leq 1$. Remember, the graph of this function is a wave, and it never goes higher than 1 or lower than -1. So, since $y = 3 \sin\theta = 3 \times \sin \theta$, the values for y are multiplied by 3. The range for this function is therefore $-3 \leq y \leq 3$.

4. (C) Lines and Distance

Only three of the four vertices are given. The first step is to find the fourth. A quick drawing of the rectangle shows that the fourth vertex is located at $(3, \sqrt{2})$. A good, but quick, drawing is always helpful when dealing with figures and plotted points.

Finding the perimeter of this rectangle requires knowing its length and width. The distance from $(1, 5)$ to $(3,5)$ is the width and the distance from $(1, \sqrt{2})$ to $(1, 5)$ is the length. Since the sides of this rectangle are vertical and horizontal, their lengths can be calculated with a quick subtraction—it is unnecessary to use the distance formula. The distance from $(1, 5)$ to $(3, 5)$ is 2, and the distance from $(1, \sqrt{2})$ to $(1, 5)$ is $5 - \sqrt{2} = 3.586$. Thus the perimeter is $2(2) + 2(3.586) = 11.17$.

5. (E) Equation Solving

To solve for x, the first step is to cancel out the denominator. When solving for a variable, move all other terms to the opposite side of the equation. So, multiply both sides by y. The equation becomes $x - z^2 = y^2z^2$. Now to solve for x, add z^2 to both sides, which yields $x = y^2z^2 + z^2$. However, the correct answer is in a more simplified form. After factoring out the common term, z^2, the final answer is $x = z^2(y^2 + 1)$.

6. (D) Basic Functions and the Right Triangle

The key to this question is remembering to use your calculator. Since you are given the value for $\sin \theta$, use the inverse sine function to find θ: $\theta = \sin^{-1}(0.29) = 16.86°$. If your calculator is in radians mode (instead of degrees), it will display 0.294. Since the instructions say that all measures are in degrees, make sure your calculator is set to degrees before you start.

To solve for the ratio $\frac{y}{x}$, remember the definition of the tangent function: $\tan \theta = {}^{opposite}/_{adjacent}$. In this figure, the fraction ${}^{opposite}/_{adjacent}$ happens to be exactly the ratio we want, $\frac{y}{x}$. Since you have calculated θ above, simply plug it into the tangent function to obtain $\tan (16.86) = 0.30$. If you're in radians mode, your calculator should also display $\tan (0.294) = 0.30$.

7. (B) Evaluating Functions

To evaluate the compound function, $g(f(2))$, first calculate $f(2)$. Then substitute the answer to calculate g at $f(2)$.

$$
\begin{aligned}
g(f(2)) + f(1) &= g(f(2)) + f(1) \\
&= g(2^2) + 1^2 \\
&= g(4) + 1 \\
&= (\sqrt{4} + 2) + 1 \\
&= (2 + 2) + 1 \\
&= 5
\end{aligned}
$$

8. (C) Equation Solving

First, simplify the equation by multiplying both sides by 3, which eliminates the denominator. Now the equation is $2x^3 = 9$. Next, divide through by 2, giving $x^3 = 4.50$. Finally, take the cube root of both sides, which leaves $x = \sqrt[3]{4.50} = 1.65$.

9. (E) Lines and Distance

This question describes a line in slope-intercept form, $y = mx + b$. Recall that the coefficient in front of the x is the slope of the line, and the constant is the intercept on the y-axis. Do not be misled by the fact that the coefficient in the question is $-b$; in the equation given, $-b$ is the slope and 1 is the y-intercept.

A vertical line has a slope that is not defined. Therefore, it cannot be described in this form. A vertical line can only be described as $x = a$. Notice that for any value b, the slope of the given line would be defined and therefore the line would not be vertical. The answer, therefore, is that for no b is this line vertical.

10. (C) Trigonometric Identities

When approaching a complicated trigonometry expression, try to use an identity that will help reduce or simplify it. This problem in particular can be solved in a number of ways. The most direct requires knowledge of the Pythagorean identity: $1 + \tan^2\theta = \sec^2\theta$. Using this identity and the definitions $\sec^2\theta = {}^1/_{\cos^2\theta}$ and $\tan^2\theta = {}^{\sin^2\theta}/_{\cos^2\theta}$ the equation can be quickly reduced.

$$
\begin{aligned}
\frac{1 + \tan^2\theta}{\tan^2\theta} &= \frac{\sec^2\theta}{\tan^2\theta} \\
&= \frac{1}{\cos^2\theta}\,\frac{\cos^2\theta}{\sin^2\theta} \\
&= \frac{1}{\sin^2\theta} \\
&= \csc^2\theta
\end{aligned}
$$

11. (E) Graphing Functions

The range of a function is the set of all values of $f(x)$. In the figure given with the question, $y = f(x)$, so to find the range, observe what values of y are included in the graph. These values are all integers.

12. **(D)** Polynomials

The quickest way to solve this problem is to try each answer. Plugging 1.47 in for x is the only way to make $f(x) = 0$.

Alternatively, you should have noticed that this is a quadratic function. It cannot be factored, but it can be solved using the quadratic formula. For an equation in the form of $ax^2 + bx + c = 0$, the formula is:

$$x = \frac{-b \pm \sqrt{b^2 - 4ac}}{2a}$$

$$= \frac{-(-1) \pm \sqrt{(-1)^2 - 4(3)(-5)}}{2(3)}$$

$$= \frac{1 \pm \sqrt{1 - (-60)}}{6}$$

$$= \frac{1 \pm \sqrt{61}}{6}$$

The two roots are –1.14 and 1.47.

13. **(C)** Basic Functions and the Right Triangle

The expression $\frac{\cos\theta}{\csc\theta}$ can be simplified. Recall the definition of cosecant: $\csc\theta = \frac{1}{\sin\theta}$. Substituting simplifies the original expression:

$$\frac{\cos\theta}{\frac{1}{\sin\theta}}$$

Carrying out the division, the expression becomes: $\cos\theta\sin\theta$. It is given that $\sin\theta = \frac{\sqrt{3}}{2}$, therefore we know that the triangle is a 30-60-90 triangle, and $\cos\theta\sin\theta = (\frac{\sqrt{3}}{2})(\frac{1}{2}) = \frac{\sqrt{3}}{4}$.

14. **(C)** Evaluating Functions

f is given, so it only requires a simple substitution to calculate the expression.

$$\frac{f(1) \times (f(7) + f(2))}{f(3)} = \frac{(1+3)((7+3)+(2+3))}{(3+3)}$$

$$= \frac{4 \times 15}{6}$$

$$= \frac{60}{6}$$

$$= 10$$

The final step is recognizing which possible answer choice is equal to 10. Since the function f simply adds 3 to x, $f(7) = 10$.

15. **(E)** Prisms, Solids That Aren't Prisms

Everything needed to calculate the volume of the sphere is given: $\frac{4}{3}\pi r^3 = \frac{4}{3}\pi(3^3) = 36\pi$, which we know is also the volume of the cone. This is why the sphere was mentioned in the problem. Knowing the volume of the cone allows the calculation of the rest.

The cone's radius is known, but neither its height, h, nor its lateral length, l, are known. Since its volume is now known, however, working backwards is possible. The formula is:

$$\text{volume of a cone} = \frac{1}{3}\pi r^2 h$$

$$\frac{1}{3}\pi 3^2 h = 36\pi$$

$$3h = 36$$

$$h = 12$$

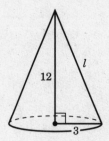

The radius, height, and lateral side of the cone form a right triangle, so l can be calculated with the Pythagorean theorem.

$$3^2 + 12^2 = l^2$$

$$153 = l^2$$

$$l = \sqrt{153}$$

The lateral area of the cone is $\pi(3)(\sqrt{153}) = 116.58$.

16. (E) Graphing Functions

By reflecting any portion of the graph of $y = |f(x)|$ across the x-axis, you create the graph of a possible $f(x)$ (because the absolute value function takes negative values of f and makes them positive, which is represented graphically by a reflection over the x-axis). The first four answer choices are all the same as the graph of $y = |f(x)|$, with some portion of the graph reflected across the x-axis—thus, they are possible graphs of f. The last choice, (E), however, is the graph of of $y = |f(x)|$ reflected over the y-axis (with a portion also reflected over the x-axis. It, therefore, cannot possible be the graph of f. Consider the point of the graph in (E), for example, where $f(x) = 0$ for some $x > 0$. If this were true, then the graph of $y = |f(x)|$ would be equal to zero for some $x > 0$, but it is clearly not (look at Figure 3). Thus, the correct answer choice is (E).

17. (D) Statistical Analysis

Recall the definition of median: 1) The median of an ordered set with n elements, where n is odd, is the value of the $\frac{n+1}{2}$th element, and 2) the median of an ordered set of n elements, where n is even, is the average of the $\frac{n}{2}$th element and the $\frac{n+1}{2}$th element.

If the greatest number in a set is removed, the median of the new set must be less than or equal to the median of the original set. The only such number among the answer choices that disobeys this rule is 9.

You can also look at this problem in a more intuitive way. The median is in middle of the list of numbers in the set, from the smallest to greatest. Removing the greatest number shifts the "middle" to a lower value, or does not change it. It cannot increase the median.

18. (B) Basic Functions and the Right Triangle

Recall the definition of the cotangent: $\cot\theta = \frac{adjacent}{opposite}$. The opposite and adjacent sides to θ are given, as well as the value of $\cot\theta$. Applying the definition above, it follows that $\cot\theta = \frac{x}{8} = 0.25$. Multiplying both sides by 8 solves the problem, giving $x = 8(0.25) = 2$.

19. **(D)** Equation Solving

Because the object increases at a rate of 12.5% per year, the object will be worth 112.5% of its original value after one year. However, if another year passes, that object will actually be worth 112.5% of 112.5% of the original value. After 14 years, the object will be worth its initial value times 112.5% 14 times. After 14 years, the object is worth $15(1.125)^{14} \approx 78$.

20. **(D)** Domain and Range

The absolute value of any number is never negative, so immediately eliminate (E). Because the domain of this function is restricted to $-2 \leq x \leq 4$, however, you can't assume that the range of the function is simply $y \geq 0$.

Consider the values of the function $f(x) = |x^2 - 9|$ over the given restricted domain of $-2 \leq x \leq 4$. First, for $x = -2$:

$$\begin{aligned} f(-2) &= |-2^2 - 9| \\ &= |4 - 9| \\ &= |-5| \\ &= 5 \end{aligned}$$

Next, for $x = 4$:

$$\begin{aligned} f(4) &= |4^2 - 9| \\ &= |16 - 9| \\ &= |7| \\ &= 7 \end{aligned}$$

Before selecting (C), check if there are any values of x within the given domain that could result in values greater than 7 and/or less than 5. Since this is a multiple-choice question, the easiest way to do this is to check out the other answer choices. Are there values of x between -2 and 4 that make $f(x) = 0$ or $f(x) = 9$? Setting $f(x) = 9$ gives $x = \sqrt{18}$ or $x = 0$. $x = \sqrt{18} = 4.24$ is not in the given domain, but $x = 0$ is. This means that when $x = 0$, $f(x) = 9$, so the range of f must include 5, 7, and 9. Since answer choice (E) was eliminated already, the only possible choice left is the correct one, $0 \leq y \leq 9$.

21. **(C)** Sequences

The ratio of consecutive terms of a geometric sequence is constant. Knowing this, a simple equation can be set up to find x, the number which must be added to 0, 8, and 32 to make them consecutive terms of a geometric sequence:

$$\begin{aligned} \frac{8 + x}{0 + x} &= \frac{32 + x}{8 + x} \\ (8 + x)^2 &= (32 + x)x \\ 64 + 16x + x^2 &= 32x + x^2 \\ 64 &= 16x \\ x &= 4 \end{aligned}$$

22. **(A)** Evaluating Functions

The usage of "might" in the question hints that there could be more than one possible answer. In fact, an effort to solve this problem directly would yield a variety of results. The best way to attack this question is to check each answer to see which one works. The definition of inverse states that for any function, f, $f(f^{-1}(x)) = x$. But if $f(x) = x$ (the first answer choice), then $f(f^{-1}(x)) = f(x)$. So $f^{-1}(x) = x = f(x)$. Some of the other choices may be true for select values of x, but only $f(x) = x$ holds true for all real numbers.

23. **(B)** Basic Functions and the Right Triangle

Remember that as θ increases from $0°$ to $90°$ the cosine function is always decreasing. Meanwhile, the tangent function is always increasing over the same range. Furthermore, from $0°$ to $45°$, the tangent function is not always greater than the cosine. At $45°$, the tangent function is greater than the cosine function; since cosine always decreases and tangent always increases between $0°$ to $90°$, and tangent is already greater than cosine at $45°$, then tangent will be greater than cosine for all values of θ between $45°$ and $90°$.

24. **(C)** Domain and Range

The domain of a function must exclude any numbers for which $f(x)$ is undefined. A fraction is undefined when its denominator is equal to 0. So, in order to find out what x–values make the function undefined, we set the denominator of the fraction equal to 0. That is, $2x^3 + 2x^2 - 24x = 0$. Solving for x, we get:

$$2x^3 + 2x^2 - 24x = 0$$
$$2x(x^2 + x - 12) = 0$$
$$2x(x + 4)(x - 3) = 0$$

Thus, the function is undefined (has denominator equal to zero) for $x = 0$, $x = -4$, and $x = 3$, and therefore these values of x cannot be in the domain of the function.

25. **(A)** Basic Functions and the Right Triangle

The trick to this question is remembering that the cosine function is even. In an even function, $f(-x) = f(x)$ for all values of x in the domain. Thus, if $\cos \theta$ is an even function, then $\cos(-\theta) = \cos \theta$ for all θ. Substitute $\cos \theta$ in for $\cos(-\theta)$ above. This gives $\pi^{\cos\theta} \pi^{-\cos\theta}$. The rest is algebra. When multiplying similar bases, add the exponents. This yields $\pi^{\cos\theta-\cos\theta} = \pi^0 = 1$.

26. **(E)** Graphing Functions

Check each statement. Clearly, statement I is true of all functions: the absolute value function returns the opposite of all negative values. Its range is nonnegative. The second statement is the equivalent of saying that the function is odd. In other words, the function is symmetrical with respect to the origin. Although this can't be rigorously verified from the sketch of the graph, you may assume that it is true (just like you can assume that a line which looks straight is indeed straight). The third statement says basically that as x gets larger, $f(x)$ decreases. The statement actually says that for any pair of x values, the larger $f(x)$ is associated with the smaller x. You can test this by simply looking at the graph of the function and seeing if this is untrue for any pair of x values. It is not. Thus, the third statement is true. All three statements are true.

27. **(C)** Equation Solving

A little intuition is the quickest way to solve this one. Notice that substituting 0 for x will clearly and quickly make the equation false. 0 is therefore the correct answer. A quick calculator check can also confirm that all the other answer choices satisfy the equation.

Alternatively, this problem can be solved with algebra. To figure out which choice is invalid, solve for all the values of x. First, to simplify, divide through by 9, giving $4x^4 - 14x^2 + 12 = 0$. Next, $4x^4 - 14x + 12$ can be factored into $(2x^2 - 3)(2x^2 - 4)$. Now, using the zero product property, $2x^2 - 3 = 0$, and $2x^2 - 4 = 0$. Solving these equations yields $x = -1.22, 1.22$ and $x = -1.41, 1.41$. Therefore, 0 is not a valid value of x.

28. **(D)** Graphing Functions

By graphing all five answer choices, you could find the correct answer, but in this problem, you could probably do it faster by analyzing the properties of f. The first condition to check is the condition that f has a root at $x = 2$. This means that $f(2) = 0$. This is not true of (A) and (B), so they can immediately be eliminated.

Now check the second condition, that f has asymptotes at $x = -1$ and $y = 1$. Note that the function $f(x) = (x-2)(x+1)$, in (C), is a parabola. Parabolas don't have asymptotes, so (C) can be eliminated.

This leaves (D) and (E). By multiplying the two binomials in the numerator of the function in (E), it becomes $f(x) = (x^2 - 3x + 2)/(x + 1)$. This function has a vertical asymptote at $x = -1$, where it is undefined, but it has no horizontal asymptote. This is because the degree of the polynomial in the numerator is one greater than the degree of the polynomial in the denominator, which means that the graph of this function will have a diagonal asymptote. Even if you didn't see this, you can solve the equation $(x-2)(x-1)/(x+1) = 1$, using the quadratic formula, to see that for $x = 2 + \sqrt{3}$, $y = 1$, meaning that $y = 1$ is not a horizontal asymptote of the function in (E). Thus, the answer is (D).

29. **(D)** Domain and Range

Begin by determining for which x–values the function $f(x)$ is equal to 0:

$$x^3 + 2x^2 - 8x = 0$$
$$x(x^2 + 2x - 8) = 0$$
$$x(x + 4)(x - 2) = 0$$
$$x = 0 \text{ or } x = -4 \text{ or } x = 2$$

This shows that the graph of $f(x)$ crosses the x–axis three times, at $x = -4$, 0, and 2. In other words, at each of these points, and only at these points, the graph of $f(x)$ goes from negative to positive or vice versa. Now, simply test values of x in order to see where the graph is positive. For example, values of x that are greater than or equal to 2, let's say $x = 3$, yields $f(3) = (3^3) + 2(3^2) - 8(3) = 21$. So, for the $x \le 2$ section of the graph, $f(x) \ge 0$. Thus, answer choices not including $x \ge 2$ can be eliminated, ruling out (B), (C), and (E).

So, if the graph of $f(x)$ is positive for $x > 2$, and it crosses the x–axis at $x = -4$, 0, and 2, then the graph must be negative for $0 < x < 2$, positive for $-4 < x < 0$, and negative again for $x < -4$.

30. **(E)** Other Important Graphs and Equations

Since the point $(-4, 3)$ lies on the circle, the distance from the center to this point will be the radius. The equation of a circle centered at (h, k) with radius r is:

$$(x - h)^2 + (y - k)^2 = r^2$$

So the center of the circle is $(-1, -1)$. The radius of the circle is the distance from $(-1, -1)$ to $(-4, 3)$. Using the distance formula to find r:

$$r = \sqrt{(-4 - (-1))^2 + (3 - (-1))^2}$$
$$= \sqrt{(-4 + 1)^2 + (3 + 1)^2}$$
$$= \sqrt{(-3)^2 + 4^2}$$
$$= \sqrt{9 + 16}$$
$$= \sqrt{25}$$
$$= 5$$

Thus, the equation of the circle is $(x + 1)^2 + (y + 1)^2 = 25$. To find the other point that lies on the circle, plug in the answer choices to find the one that works out:

(A), (−6, −2.8):
$(−6 + 1)^2 + (−2.8 + 1)^2 = 28.24 \neq 25$

(B), (−3.9, 2):
$(−3.9 + 1)^2 + (2 + 1)^2 = 17.41 \neq 25$

(C), (1, 2.7):
$(1.2 + 1)^2 + (2.7 + 1)^2 = 17.69 \neq 25$

(D), (−1, −4):
$(−1 + 1)^2 + (−4 + 1)^2 = 9 \neq 25$

(E), (2, 3):
$(2 + 1)^2 + (3 + 1)^2 = 25$

Thus, (E) is the correct answer.

31. **(E)** Domain and Range

Consider each part of the function over its given domain. First, for all $x < 0$, $f(x) = -x^2 + 2$. The graph of this function is a parabola opening downward, with vertex at (0, 2). However, the domain of this function is $x < 0$. So, the graph of the function will end at the point (0, 2), but will not include this point. Take a look at this part of the function graphed:

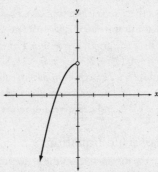

Now consider the second part of the function. $f(x) = e^x + 1$ for all $x \geq 0$. So, for $x = 0$, $f(0) = e^0 + 1 = 2$. So, the graph of this function will include the point (0, 2), and will increase exponentially as x increases. Here's the entire function graphed:

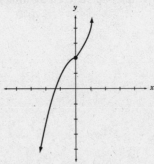

It should be clear from this graph that the range of the combined function includes all real numbers.

32. **(C)** Equation Solving

To find the inverse of a given function, set $f(x) = y$. Next, replace x with y and y with x and then solve the equation for y. This resultant equation for y is the inverse, $f^{-1}(x)$. Following these steps, set $y = f(x) = \frac{1}{x^3}$. Then, after swapping variables, it follows that $x = \frac{1}{y^3}$. Now, solve for y:

$$x = \frac{1}{y^3}$$

$$\frac{1}{x} = y^3$$

$$\sqrt[3]{\frac{1}{x}} = y$$

So, $f^{-1}(x) = \sqrt[3]{\frac{1}{x}}$, or $\frac{1}{\sqrt[3]{8}}$. Positive values of x do in fact yield values for the inverse function (e.g., $\frac{1}{\sqrt[3]{8}} = \frac{1}{2}$). Negative values of x are also defined (e.g., $\frac{1}{\sqrt[3]{-8}} = \frac{1}{-2} = -\frac{1}{2}$). However, when $x = 0$, the inverse function is not defined since $\frac{1}{\sqrt[3]{0}} = \frac{1}{0}$, and dividing by zero is undefined. Therefore, for $x = 0$ only, this inverse function is undefined.

33. **(A)** Equation Solving

Seeing a desired variable in the exponent of an expression is a good hint that logarithms are needed. In this case, the power rule is necessary: $\log_b a^n = n \log_b a$. Applying this above, take the logarithm of both sides (it does not matter what base, as long as both logarithms are of the same base; the default base for logarithms on calculators is 10). You should now have $a \log_{10} 3.92 = b \log_{10} 7.86$, and you can solve for $\frac{a}{b}$:

$$a \log_{10} 3.92 = b \log_{10} 7.86$$

$$\frac{a \log_{10} 3.92}{b} = \log_{10} 7.86$$

$$\frac{a}{b} = \frac{\log_{10} 7.86}{\log_{10} 3.92}$$

The question asks for:

$$\left(\frac{b}{a}\right)^2 = \left(\frac{\log_{10} 3.92}{\log_{10} 7.86}\right)^2 = 0.44$$

34. **(C)** Sequences

By definition of arithmetic sequence, the difference between any two consecutive terms is the same. Therefore, given two terms, it should be easy to find the difference. In general, $a_x = a_y + (x - y)d$, where d is the common difference between any two terms. In this case, $a_8 = a_{11} + (8 - 11)d$. Filling in the values that are given in the problem, you can write $5 = 20 + -3d$. This can be solved for d:

$$5 = 20 + -3d$$
$$-15 = -3d$$
$$d = 5$$

Given the common difference d and at least one term of the arithmetic sequence, you can find any other term of the sequence. In this problem, find a_{100}:

$$a_{100} = a_{11} + (100 - 11)d$$
$$= 20 + 89(5)$$
$$= 20 + 445$$
$$= 465$$

35. (E) Basic Functions and the Right Triangle

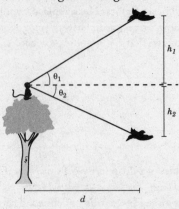

This problem requires a graph. The figure above depicts the situation in this problem. Since it is given the angle at which the monkey on the tree sees the first bird (θ_1), and the horizontal distance to this bird (d), the tangent function can calculate the vertical distance (h_1) from the first flying bird to the monkey. Remember: $\tan\theta = {}^{\text{opposite}}/_{\text{adjacent}}$. Thus, $\tan\theta_1 = {}^{h_1}/_d$. Multiplying through by d gives $h_1 = d\tan\theta_1$.

The same process can be used to find the vertical distance of the second bird from the monkey; again, the monkey looks down at an angle of θ_2, and so using the tangent function, $\tan\theta_2 = {}^{h_2}/_d$. Therefore, $h_2 = d\tan\theta_2$.

The two values added together give the total distance between the birds: $h_1 + h_2 = d\tan\theta_1 + d\tan\theta_2 = d(\tan\theta_1 + \tan\theta_2)$.

36. (B) Probability

Jim's expected profit for the next year is $(.4)(5000) + (.6)(-2000) = 2000 - 1200 = 800$.

37. (E) Other Important Graphs and Equations

Vector u, which begins at $(-2, 2)$ and ends at $(2, 5)$ can be written as $\vec{u} = (2-(-2), 5-2) = (4, 3)$. Similarly, vector v, which begins at $(1, 5)$ and ends at $(-2, 4)$ can be written as $\vec{v} = (-2-1, 4-5) = (-3, -1)$.

Then, to subtract vectors, just subtract their respective components. In this case, $\vec{u} = (4,3)$ and $\vec{v} = (-3, -1)$, so $\vec{u} - \vec{v} = (4-(-3), 3-(-1)) = (7, 4)$.

38. (B) Equation Solving

The most important part of this question is understanding how to obtain the original function, $f(x)$, from its inverse function: $f^{-1}(x)$. First, set $f^{-1}(x) = y$. Next, replace x with y and y with x and then solve the equation for y. This resultant equation for y is the original function, $f(x)$. Applying this to the above equation: $x = 11y^2$ by swapping variables. Then, to solve, divide both sides by 11 and take the square root of both sides, getting $y = \sqrt{\frac{x}{11}}$. Finally, plug in 2 for x: $f(2) = \sqrt{\frac{2}{11}} = 0.43$.

39. (D) Inverse Trigonometric Functions

The easiest way to solve this problem is to use your calculator. (If you do, make sure you're in degrees mode and not radians.) However, it is also quickly solvable by recalling the definitions of sine and arcsine. Arcsine is the inverse of the sine function over its first half cycle. Since 45° is in the first half cycle of the sine graph, $\sin^{-1}(\sin\theta) = \theta$ and the answer is 45°.

40. **(A)** Sequences

To solve this problem, find the common ratio r between consecutive terms of g_n. To find r, write the equation $g_6 = g_4 \times r^{6-4} = g_4 \times r^2 = 5r^2 = 11.25$. Thus $r^2 = {}^{11.25}/_5 = 2.25$ and $r = {}^3/_2$. Next, use the same principle to write $g_{17} = g_{14} \times r^{17-14} = g_{14} \times r^3$. So, $g_{17} \div g_{14} = r^3 = ({}^3/_2)^3 = {}^{3^3}/_{2^3} = {}^{27}/_8$. The question asks for the reciprocal of this value, $g_{14} \div g_{17}$, which equals ${}^8/_{27}$.

41. **(D)** Other Important Graphs and Equations

There are two ways to go about solving this problem. The first way is to notice that the right angle occurs at the point $(2,-2,1)$, since it shares a x–coordinate with $(5, 2, 1)$ and an x- and y-coordinate with $(2, -2, 7)$. So, the hypotenuse is the side opposite this angle, and therefore, the length of the hypotenuse is the distance between points $(2,-2,7)$ and $(5,2,1)$. Using the 3–dimensional distance formula, this is:

$$d = \sqrt{(5-2)^2 + (2-(-2))^2 + (1-7)^2}$$
$$= \sqrt{3^2 + 4^2 + (-6)^2}$$
$$= \sqrt{61}$$
$$\approx 7.81$$

Which gives us (D).

The other way to solve this problem requires using the 3–D distance formula three times, to find the lengths of each of the sides of the triangle. The longest side of a right triangle is always the hypotenuse, which is the answer we are looking for. This method may take a bit longer, but if you have trouble visualizing 3–dimensional figures, it may be easier.

42. **(D)** Other Important Graphs and Equations

To find the rectangular coordinates of a point (r, θ), use the conversion formulas $x = r \cos \theta$ and $y = r \sin \theta$. In this case, $x = 3 \cos {}^{5\pi}/_6 \approx -2.6$ and $y = 3 \sin {}^{5\pi}/_6 = 1.5$. This gives us the point $(-2.6, 1.5)$.

43. **(B)** Permutations and Combinations

Here's an example that should help illustrate this question. Consider $n = 3$. So $n! = 3 \times 2 \times 1$, $(n + 1)! = 4! = 4 \times 3 \times 2 \times 1$ and $(n - 1)! = 2! = 2 \times 1$. This means that $(n + 1)! = (n + 1) \times n!$ and $n! = n \times (n - 1)!$. Similarly, the given expression can be simplified, canceling out most terms:

$$\frac{(n + 1)! \times (n - 1)!}{(n!)^2} = \frac{(n + 1)(n)(n - 1)(\ldots) \times (n - 1)(\ldots)}{((n)(n - 1)(\ldots))^2}$$
$$= \frac{\{(n + 1)(n)\}\{(n - 1)(\ldots)\}^2}{n^2 \{(n - 1)(\ldots)\}^2}$$
$$= \frac{(n + 1)(n)}{(n)(n)}$$
$$= \frac{n + 1}{n}$$

44. (B) Prisms, Solids That Aren't Prisms

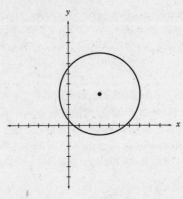

Either by graphing it or analyzing the equation, you should see that the circle has a center at (3, 3) and radius of 4. So, the line $y = x$ goes through the center of the circle, and a sphere of radius 4 is created when the circle is rotated about the line. Now, the volume of the sphere can be calculated:

$$\frac{4}{3}\pi r^3 = \frac{4}{3}\pi(4)^3 = 268.08$$

45. (C) Logic

An important thing to remember when dealing with logic statements is that a statement and its contrapositive (the opposite, reverse version of the statement) are equivalent. So, given that the statement about Jim and his watch–buying is true, the contrapositive of this statement, statement III, must also be true. It remains to investigate the other two statements, statements I and II. Statement I is the inverse of the original statement—it could be either true or false. Statement II is the converse of the original statement. It, too, could be either true or false. Thus, the correct choice is only III.

46. (D) Other Important Graphs and Equations

The equation of an ellipse centered at the origin and with axial intersections at ($\pm a$, 0) and (0, $\pm b$) is:

$$\frac{x^2}{a^2} + \frac{y^2}{b^2} = 1$$

To put $100x^2 + 25y^2 = 175$ into this form, divide through by 175 to get $\frac{4x^2}{7} + \frac{y^2}{7} = 1$. So, the ellipse intersects the y–axis at $\pm\sqrt{7}$. Therefore, the length of the major axis is $2\sqrt{7} = 5.29$.

47. (D) Imaginary and Complex Numbers

First, evaluate $g(3, 4)$:

$$
\begin{aligned}
g(3, 4) &= |3| + |4i^2| \\
&= |3| + |-4| \\
&= 3 + 4 \\
&= 7
\end{aligned}
$$

Now, to find $f(3, 4)$, use the distance formula on (3, 4).

$$
\begin{aligned}
f(3, 4) &= |3 + 4i| \\
&= \sqrt{3^2 + 4^2} \\
&= \sqrt{25} \\
&= 5
\end{aligned}
$$

So $g(3, 4) - f(3, 4) = 7 - 5 = 2$.

48. **(E)** Domain and Range

Consider $f(x) = \sqrt{x^2 + 4}$ first. The square root of any number is greater than or equal to 0. So this function will be positive (greater than 0) for all values of x, unless there is some x such that $f(x) = 0$. $\sqrt{x^2 + 4} = 0$ when $x^2 + 4 = 0$, which would mean that $x^2 = -4$, which is not possible with real numbers. Therefore, $\sqrt{x^2 + 4}$ can never equal 0, and $f(x) = \sqrt{x^2 + 4}$ is positive for all x. Thus, (A) and (C) can be eliminated.

Now consider $f(x) = \sin(x - \frac{\pi}{2})$. The range of a sine function is $-1 \le y \le 1$, so this function is not positive for all values of x. Therefore, (D) can be eliminated. Note that the function $f(x) = \sin(x - \frac{\pi}{2})$ has the same range as the function $f(x) = \sin x$. You can check this by graphing the function, but subtracting $\frac{\pi}{2}$ from the x does not change the range of the function—it merely shifts the graph of the function to the left.

Finally, consider $f(x) = 2^{x-1}$. A positive number raised to any power will always be positive, so this function is greater than 0 for all values of x. I and III are the correct choices.

49. **(E)** Limits

The expression is clearly not defined at $x = 2$, and this can be confirmed by plugging in $x = 2$: the denominator would be 0. However, a limit is still possible in this case, so it's important to continue. Either by graphing this expression over x, or simply by plugging in values, it should be apparent that as x approaches 2 from the left, the denominator becomes an extremely small negative number. This makes the whole expression approach negative infinity. For this reason, the graph has a vertical asymptote at $x = 2$, and from the left, the graph heads downward. Coming from the right of $x = 2$, the denominator approaches extremely small positive values, making the whole expression approach positive infinity. This can be seen on a graph; from the right the graph goes upward along the asymptote. Because the limits from the two sides of $x = 2$ are different, the limit does not exist.

50. **(A)** Fundamentals

Clearly, doubling any integer creates another integer. For this reason, the first choice, $2mn$ is correct. For peace of mind, the other choices can be canceled by use of counterexamples. To cancel an answer option, simply find values of m and n that make mn an integer, but make the option false.

For example, suppose $m = \frac{3}{2}$ and $n = \frac{4}{3}$. The product of these two fractions is indeed an integer: mn = $(\frac{3}{2})(\frac{4}{3}) = 2$. Plug these values into each of the answer choices to see which produces an integer. (A) results in $2mn = 2(2) = 4$, an integer. Choices (B) and (C) can be eliminated, since neither fraction m or n are integers. (D) also results in a fraction, since $2n = \frac{8}{3}$ is added to mn. Clearly, $2mn$ is the only choice that is always an integer.

SAT II Math IIC

Practice Test II

MATHEMATICS LEVEL IIC TEST

DO NOT DETACH FROM BOOK.

GO ON TO THE NEXT PAGE

MATHEMATICS LEVEL IIC TEST

For each of the following problems, decide which is the BEST of the choices given. If the exact numerical value is not one of the choices, select the choice that best approximates this value. Then fill in the corresponding oval on the answer sheet.

Notes: (1) A calculator will be necessary for answering some (but not all) of the questions in this test. For each question you will have to decide whether or not you should use a calcuator. The calculator you use must be at least a scientific calculator; programmable calculators and calculators that can display graphs are permitted.

(2) For some questions in this test you may need to decide whether your calculator should be in radian or degree mode.

(3) Figures that accompany problems in this test are intended to provide information useful in solving the problems. They are drawn as accurately as possible EXCEPT when it is stated in a specific problem that its figure is not drawn to scale. All figures lie in a plane unless otherwise indicated.

(4) Unless otherwise specified, the domain of any function f is assumed to be the set of all real numbers x for which $f(x)$ is a real number.

(5) Reference information that may be useful in answering the questions in this test can be found on the page preceding Question 1.

USE THIS SPACE FOR SCRATCHWORK.

1. If $a = 4$, $b = \frac{1}{2}$, and $c = -1$, then $(ab^2c^3)^2 =$

   (A) −4   (B) −1   (C) 1   (D) 2   (E) 4

2. What is the number of digits obtained by carrying out $11,111^3$?

   (A) 5   (B) 7   (C) 12   (D) 13   (E) 15

3. How many times does $y = \tan x$ cross the x-axis within the domain $0 \le x \le 2\pi$?

   (A) 0   (B) 1   (C) 2   (D) 3   (E) 4

GO ON TO THE NEXT PAGE

4. Which of the following could be an equation for l in Figure 1?

    (A) $y = 0$
    (B) $y = x$
    (C) $y = 3$
    (D) $x = 3$
    (E) It cannot be determined

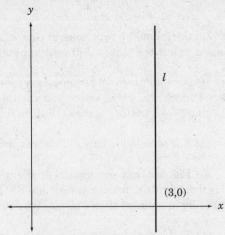

Note: Figure not drawn to scale.
Figure 1

5. If $\sqrt{-6x} = 2$, then $x =$

    (A) -1.50
    (B) -0.67
    (C) 0.67
    (D) 1.00
    (E) 1.50

6. If $\tan \theta = 1.73$ then $\sin^2 \theta =$

    (A) 0.22
    (B) 0.34
    (C) 0.75
    (D) 0.86
    (E) 1.73

7. If $f(x) = 3x + 3$ and $g(x) = 2x$, which of the following is equal to 18?

    (A) $f(g(2))$
    (B) $f(2) + g(2)$
    (C) $g(f(2))$
    (D) $f(2) - g(2)$
    (E) $f(2) \times g(2)$

8. If $(x + 3)^3 = 9$, then $x =$

    (A) -0.92
    (B) 0
    (C) 2.08
    (D) 3
    (E) 5.08

GO ON TO THE NEXT PAGE

9. The line $y = bx + 3$ lies in only two quadrants if and only if:

 (A) $b = 0$
 (B) $0 \le b \le 1$
 (C) $b = 1$
 (D) $b = -2$
 (E) $-3 \le b \le 3$

10. If $\cos x = \dfrac{1}{6}$, what is $\dfrac{\sin 2x}{\sin x}$?

 (A) 0

 (B) $\dfrac{1}{4}$

 (C) $\dfrac{1}{3}$

 (D) $\dfrac{1}{6}$

 (E) 1

11. Which of the functions graphed below has a range of $[-5, 5)$?

 (A)

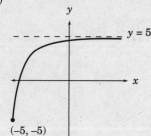

 (B)

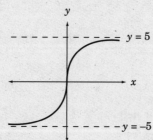

 (C)

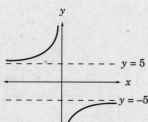

 (D)

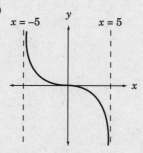

 (E)

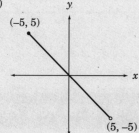

GO ON TO THE NEXT PAGE

12. If -4 and 2 are both zeros of the polynomial $g(x)$, then a factor of $g(x)$ is

   (A) $x^2 + 2x - 8$
   (B) $x^2 - 8$
   (C) $x^2 - 2x + 8$
   (D) $x^2 + 8$
   (E) $x^2 - 2x - 8$

13. If $\theta = 76°$, $\tan\theta \csc\theta =$

   (A) 0.24
   (B) 0.82
   (C) 1.03
   (D) 1.21
   (E) 4.13

14. If $f(x) = 3x$ and $g(x) = x^2$, what is $\dfrac{f(3) + g(4)}{g(5)}$?

   (A) 1   (B) 2   (C) 2.5 (D) 3   (E) 4

15. The height of the pyramid in Figure 2 is three times the height of the box. The area of the base of the pyramid is half the area of the base of the box. If the volume of the pyramid is V, what is the volume of the box in terms of V?

   (A) $\dfrac{1}{4} V$

   (B) $\dfrac{2}{3} V$

   (C) $2V$

   (D) $\dfrac{5}{2} V$

   (E) $4V$

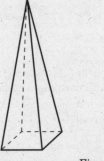

Figure 2

16. The graph of $y = f(x)$ is shown in Figure 3. Which of the following graphs could be the graph of $-f(x)$?

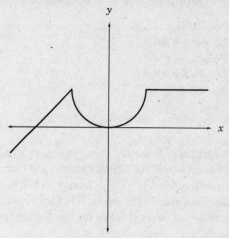

Figure 3

(A)

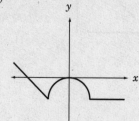

(B)

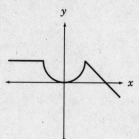

(C)

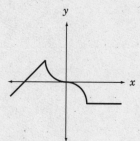

(D)

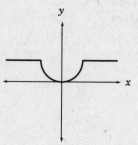

(E)

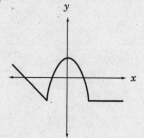

17. The mean weight of a group of students is 100 pounds. A new member who weighs 150 pounds joins the group, and the mean weight of the group increases to 110 pounds. How many students were in the group before the new member joined?

 (A) 4
 (B) 5
 (C) 10
 (D) 15
 (E) Not enough information to tell

GO ON TO THE NEXT PAGE

18. In Figure 4, what is $\dfrac{x-y}{r}$ in terms of θ?

   (A) 1
   (B) $\cos\theta - \sin\theta$
   (C) $\sin\theta - \cos\theta$
   (D) $\sin\theta + \cos\theta$
   (E) $\tan\theta$

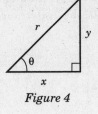

Figure 4

19. A certain radioactive element decays exponentially. A, the amount remaining at any given time t can be found using the equation $A = A_o e^{-t/300}$, where A_o is the initial amount and t is the time elapsed in years. What is this element's *half-life* (the number of years it takes for exactly half of the initial amount to decay)?

   (A) 92
   (B) 150
   (C) 158
   (D) 208
   (E) Not enough information is given.

20. In the geometric series where $g_1 = 2$ and $g_{n+1} = 3g_n$, what is $g_4 - g_2$?

   (A) 3
   (B) 12
   (C) 30
   (D) 44
   (E) 48

21. If $f(x) = 7x + 4$ and $f^{-1}(g(3)) = 7$, which of the following could be $g(x)$?

   (A) $10x + 2$
   (B) $20x + 5$
   (C) $5x^2 + 8$
   (D) $7x^2$
   (E) $\dfrac{x}{7}$

GO ON TO THE NEXT PAGE

22. If $f(x) = 2x$, what is $f^{-1}(3x + 6)$?

    (A) $\dfrac{3x}{2}$

    (B) $\dfrac{3x}{2} + 3$

    (C) $\dfrac{3x}{2} + 6$

    (D) $6x + 6$

    (E) $6x + 12$

23. Which of the following statements is TRUE?

    (A) For all θ, $\cos\theta > 0$
    (B) For all θ, $\cos\theta < 0$
    (C) For all θ, $\cos(-\theta) = -\cos\theta$
    (D) For all θ, $\cos(-\theta) = \cos\theta$
    (E) For all θ, $\cos(-\theta) < 0$

24. What is the maximum value of the function $f(x) = -3x^2 + 8$?

    (A) -4
    (B) 0
    (C) 2
    (D) 8
    (E) 15

25. A function f is an odd function if, for all values of x in the domain, $f(-x) = -f(x)$. Which of the following is an odd function?

    (A) $\cos(x)$
    (B) $\sin(x)\cos(x)$
    (C) $\cos^2(x)$
    (D) $\sin^2(x)$
    (E) $\sin^2(x)\cos(x)$

GO ON TO THE NEXT PAGE

26. The graph of $y = f(x)$ is shown in Figure 5. Which of the following statements must be true?

    I. The range and domain of $f(x)$ are equal.
    II. The graph of $y = f(x)$ contains a horizontal asymptote at $y = -1$.
    III. $f(x)$ is an even function.

(A) I only
(B) II only
(C) III only
(D) I and III only
(E) I, II, and III

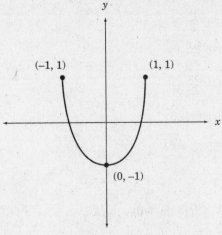

Figure 5

27. If a, b, and c are nonzero real numbers, under which of the following conditions is $\dfrac{a}{b} < \dfrac{c}{b}$ *always true*:

(A) $0 < a < c$
(B) $0 < a < c, b < 0$
(C) $0 < a < c, b < 0$
(D) $0 < c < a$
(E) $0 < c < a, b < 0$

28. Suppose the graph of $y = f(x)$ has a vertical asymptote at $x = 4$ and a horizontal asymptote at $y = -1$. If $g(x) = \dfrac{1}{2}f(x)$, which lines are the asymptotes of the graph of $g(x)$?

(A) $x = 2, y = -\dfrac{1}{2}$

(B) $x = 2, y = -1$

(C) $x = 4, y = -1$

(D) $x = 4, y = -\dfrac{1}{2}$

(E) Not enough information to tell

GO ON TO THE NEXT PAGE

USE THIS SPACE FOR SCRATCHWORK.

29. $f(x) = 3x^3 + 4x^2 + x$. What are all the values of x such that $f(x) \geq 0$?

    (A) $x \geq 0$

    (B) $x \leq -1$ or $-\dfrac{1}{3} \leq x \leq 0$

    (C) $x \leq -1$ or $x \geq 0$

    (D) $-1 \leq x \leq -\dfrac{1}{3}$ or $x \geq 0$

    (E) $-1 \leq x \leq 0$

30. A circle has center $(2, b)$ and radius 6. If the points $(-1, 3)$ and $(2, 3.8)$ lie on the circle, what is the value of b?

    (A) -2.2
    (B) -1
    (C) 3.3
    (D) 6.7
    (E) 8.2

31. $f(x) = \begin{cases} -x^2 & \text{if } x > -1 \\ 2x + 3 & \text{if } x \leq -1 \end{cases}$

What is the range of f?

    (A) $y \leq 1$
    (B) $y \leq 0$
    (C) $y < -1$
    (D) $y < 1$
    (E) All real numbers

32. If $x = \log_2 t$ and $y = t^2$, what is y in terms of x?

    (A) 2
    (B) x
    (C) 2^x
    (D) 2^{2x}
    (E) 2^{x^2}

GO ON TO THE NEXT PAGE

33. If m and n are nonzero real numbers and $\log_3 m = 1.50 - \log_3 n$, what is the value of mn?

(A) 1.84
(B) 3.38
(C) 5.20
(D) 7.32
(E) 7.59

34. What is the sum of the infinite geometric series g_n, given by

$g_n = \left(\dfrac{3}{2}\right)^n$?

(A) $\dfrac{3}{2}$

(B) $\dfrac{9}{4}$

(C) 3

(D) ∞

(E) Not enough information to tell

35. If $\tan\theta = \sqrt{\sec\theta - 1}$, which one of the following is a possible value for θ?

(A) $\dfrac{-\pi}{2}$ (B) $\dfrac{-\pi}{4}$ (C) 0   (D) $\dfrac{\pi}{2}$ (E) $\dfrac{\pi}{2}$

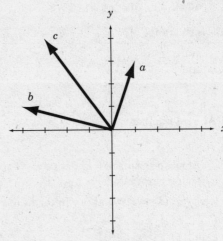

Figure 6

36. A two-sided coin is flipped four times. Given that the coin landed heads up more than twice, what is the probability that it landed heads up all four times?

(A) $\dfrac{1}{16}$ (B) $\dfrac{1}{6}$ (C) $\dfrac{1}{5}$ (D) $\dfrac{1}{4}$ (E) $\dfrac{1}{2}$

37. In Figure 6, if $\vec{c} = \vec{a} + \vec{b}$, then what is the magnitude of $\vec{c}$?

(A) 3   (B) 4   (C) 5   (D) 6   (E) 8

GO ON TO THE NEXT PAGE

38. If $f(x) = \log_7 3x$, then $f^{-1}(1.25) =$

    (A)   0.57
    (B)   0.68
    (C)   2.88
    (D)   3.80
    (E) 11.39

39. $\tan^{-1}(\sin 25°) =$

    (A) 0
    (B) 14.6°
    (C) 22.9°
    (D) 50°
    (E) 75°

40. In an arithmetic sequence, $a_5 = a_{10} - 3$ and $a_3 = -2$. Between which two consecutive terms does 0 lie?

    (A) a_4 and a_5
    (B) a_5 and a_6
    (C) a_6 and a_7
    (D) a_7 and a_8
    (E) a_9 and a_{10}

41. Sphere O has a radius of 5 and its center at the origin. Which of the following points lies inside of the sphere?

    (A) $(-1, 2, 4)$
    (B) $(-1, 3, 5)$
    (C) $(2, -2, 6)$
    (D) $(6, 2, 3)$
    (E) $(-5, 1, 2)$

GO ON TO THE NEXT PAGE

42. A target lies flat on the ground exactly d meters away from a building. Billy, who is on one of the floors of the building, looks down at the target at an angle of θ_2 with respect to the building. Bob, who is on a higher floor, looks down at the target at an angle of θ_1 with respect to the building. How much higher up than Billy is Bob, in meters?

(A) $d \cos(\theta_1 - \theta_2)$

(B) $d \tan(\theta_1 - \theta_2)$

(C) $d(\tan \theta_1 - \tan \theta_2)$

(D) $d(\dfrac{1}{\cos \theta_1} - \dfrac{1}{\cos \theta_2})$

(E) $d(\dfrac{1}{\tan \theta_1} - \dfrac{1}{\tan \theta_2})$

43. Let z be a complex solution to the equation $x^2 - 2x + 2 = 0$. What does $|z|$ equal?

(A) 1
(B) 1.41
(C) 2.45
(D) 3
(E) 3.73

44. Figure 7 shows a pyramid inscribed in a cube. If points A, B, C, and D are midpoints of the edges of the cube, what is the ratio of the volume of the pyramid to the volume of the cube?

(A) 1:3
(B) 2:5
(C) 3:5
(D) 1:6
(E) 2:9

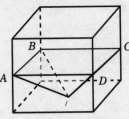

Figure 7

GO ON TO THE NEXT PAGE

45. Suppose you set out to prove the statement, "If the shirt costs less than twenty dollars, then it is on sale." Which of the following statements proves this?

    (A) If the shirt costs less than twenty dollars, then it is not on sale.
    (B) If the shirt is on sale, then it costs less than twenty dollars.
    (C) Every shirt costs less than twenty dollars.
    (D) If the shirt is not on sale, then it costs at least twenty dollars.
    (E) None of these choices proves the given statement.

46. A circle with center $(4, -3)$ and radius $3\sqrt{5}$ intersects the x-axis at which of the following points?

    (A) $(0, 5)$
    (B) $(0, 2)$
    (C) $(-2, 0)$
    (D) $(-10, 0)$
    (E) $(8, 0)$

47. Let the graph of $g(x)$ be obtained by translating the graph of $f(x) = 3x^2$ 3 units to the right and 2 units up. What is $g(2.2)$?

    (A) 3.92
    (B) 4.4
    (C) 5.2
    (D) 16.52
    (E) 17.22

GO ON TO THE NEXT PAGE

48. For which of the following is the range of $f(x)$ equal to the set of all positive numbers?

  I. $f(x) = x^2 + 2$
  II. $f(x) = 2^{x+2}$
  III. $f(x) = 1 - \cos(x)$

  (A) I only
  (B) II only
  (C) I and II
  (D) II and III
  (E) I, II, and III

49. What is $\lim\limits_{x \to -2} \dfrac{4x + 10x + 4}{3x + 6}$?

  (A) 0
  (B) 1
  (C) −2
  (D) 4
  (E) The limit does not exist.

50. For $x \neq 2$, $\dfrac{x^3 - 2x - 4}{x - 2} =$

  (A) $x^2 - 2$
  (B) $x^2 + x - 2$
  (C) $x^2 - 2x - 2$
  (D) $x^2 + 2x + 2$
  (E) $x^2 + 2$

S T O P

IF YOU FINISH BEFORE TIME IS CALLED, YOU MAY CHECK YOUR WORK ON THIS TEST ONLY.
DO NOT TURN TO ANY OTHER TEST IN THIS BOOK.

SAT II Math IIC Practice Test II Explanations

Calculating Your Score

Your raw score for the SAT II Math IIC test is calculated from the number of questions you answer correctly and incorrectly. Once you have determined your raw score, use the conversion table on page 17 of this book to calculate your scaled score.

To Calculate Your Raw Score

Count the number of questions you answered correctly: _____
A

Count the number of questions you answered incorrectly, and multiply that number by $\frac{1}{4}$:

$$\underline{\hspace{3cm}} \quad \text{X} \quad \frac{1}{4} \quad = \quad \underline{\hspace{3cm}}$$
B   C

Subtract the value in field C from value in field A: _____
D

Round the number in field D to the nearest whole number. This is your raw score: _____
E

Answers to SAT II Math IIC Practice Test II

Question Number	Correct Answer	Right	Wrong	Question Number	Correct Answer	Right	Wrong
1.	C	—	—	26.	D	—	—
2.	D	—	—	27.	E	—	—
3.	D	—	—	28.	D	—	—
4.	D	—	—	29.	D	—	—
5.	B	—	—	30.	A	—	—
6.	C	—	—	31.	A	—	—
7.	C	—	—	32.	D	—	—
8.	A	—	—	33.	C	—	—
9.	A	—	—	34.	D	—	—
10.	C	—	—	35.	C	—	—
11.	A	—	—	36.	C	—	—
12.	A	—	—	37.	C	—	—
13.	E	—	—	38.	D	—	—
14.	A	—	—	39.	C	—	—
15.	C	—	—	40.	C	—	—
16.	A	—	—	41.	A	—	—
17.	A	—	—	42.	E	—	—
18.	B	—	—	43.	B	—	—
19.	D	—	—	44.	D	—	—
20.	E	—	—	45.	D	—	—
21.	C	—	—	46.	C	—	—
22.	B	—	—	47.	A	—	—
23.	D	—	—	48.	B	—	—
24.	D	—	—	49.	C	—	—
25.	B	—	—	50.	D	—	—

Math IIC Test II Explanations

1. **(C)** Equation Solving

The easiest approach to this problem is first to solve for ab^2c^3 and then square the result. Since the values are given for each variable, simply plug in: $ab^2c^3 = (4)(\frac{1}{2})^2(-1)^3 = (4)(\frac{1}{4})(-1) = -1$. To solve for the final answer, square the last value: $(-1)^2 = 1$.

2. **(D)** Fundamentals

If you punch the expression into your calculator, you'll get the answer in scientific notation, 1.371×10^{12}. This is a 13–digit number, since the 10^{12} represents the digits after the decimal point.

3. **(D)** Graphing in the Entire Coordinate Plane

The function $y = \tan x$ crosses the x–axis when $y = 0$. $\tan x = \frac{\sin x}{\cos x}$, so $\tan x = 0$ when $\sin x = 0$. Therefore, since $\sin x = 0$ at multiples of π, the function $y = \tan x$ crosses the x–axis at $0(\pi) = 0$, $1(\pi) = \pi$, and $2(\pi) = 2\pi$ within the domain $0 \le x \le 2\pi$. You can graph this on your calculator to double–check that it crosses three times.

4. **(D)** Lines and Distance

Because a vertical line in the plane does not have defined slope, it cannot be described in terms of y. However, it can be described it in terms of x by noticing that x is always 3. For every point on the given graph, $x = 3$. And for every point such that $x = 3$, that point is on the given graph. Therefore $x = 3$ describes the graph.

5. **(B)** Equation Solving

To eliminate the radical on the left hand side of the equation, first square both sides. Thus $-6x = 2^2 = 4$. Next, we simply divide both sides by -6, arriving at $x = -0.67$.

6. **(C)** Basic Functions and the Right Triangle

First, solve for θ. Since the value of $\tan \theta$ is given, just take the inverse. $\tan^{-1} 1.73 = 59.97°$. Next, now that θ is known, simply plug it into the sine function, and then square the result to get $\sin^2 \theta$. $\sin 59.97 = 0.866$. Therefore $\sin^2 59.97 = 0.75$.

7. **(C)** Evaluating Functions

Based on the answer choices, it makes sense first to calculate $f(2)$ and $g(2)$:

$$f(2) = 3(2) + 3$$
$$= 6 + 3$$
$$= 9$$
$$g(2) = 2(2)$$
$$= 4$$

Through some simple calculations, you can easily eliminate (B), (D), and (E). Only (A) and (C) remain as possibilities. Evaluate both:

$$f(g(2)) = 3(4) + 3$$
$$= 12 + 3$$
$$= 15$$
$$g(f(2)) = 2(9)$$
$$= 18$$

Clearly, $g(f(2))$ is the right answer.

8. **(A)** Equation Solving

The first step is to take the cube root of both sides of the equation. Therefore, $x + 3 = \sqrt[3]{9} = 2.08$. Next subtract 3 from both sides, giving $x = 2.08 - 3.00 = -0.92$.

9. **(A)** Lines and Distance

The given line is in slope–intercept form, $y = mx + b$. The slope of the given line is b and it crosses the y–axis at $(0, 3)$. Notice that any line drawn through $(0, 3)$ will lie in three quadrants except two specific lines: vertical and horizontal. A vertical line cannot be described in slope–intercept form, so the only possible answer is that the line is horizontal. In fact, a horizontal line through $(0, 3)$ will lie in the first two quadrants. The equation of this line is $y = 0x + 3$, so $b = 0$.

10. **(C)** Trigonometric Identities

Using the double angle formula, $\sin 2x = 2 \sin x \cos x$:

$$\frac{\sin 2x}{\sin x} = \frac{2 \sin x \cos x}{\sin x}$$
$$= 2 \cos x$$
$$= 2\left(\frac{1}{6}\right)$$
$$= \frac{1}{3}$$

So the correct answer is $\frac{1}{3}$. You can confirm this with a calculator, if you like: use $\cos^{-1}$ to find x, then calculate $\frac{\sin 2x}{\sin x} = 0.33333 = \frac{1}{3}$.

11. **(A)** Graphing Functions

The range of a function is the set of all values of $f(x)$. In the answer choice graphs, $y = f(x)$, so to find the range of a function given the graph of that function, only observe which values of y are contained in the graph. If the range of a function is $[-5, 5)$, this means that -5 is included in the range, but 5 is not. (The range is said to be "inclusive" of -5 but exclusive of 5.) The function whose graph shows this trait is the first one.

The other four answer choices all have different ranges. The range of the function graphed in (B) is $(-5, 5)$. The range of the function graphed in (C) is $(-\infty, -5) \cup (5, \infty)$. The range of the function graphed in (D) is $(-\infty, \infty)$. Lastly, the range of the function graphed in (E) is $(-5, 5]$. The domain of the function graphed in (E) is $[-5, 5)$, which may have confused you. If so, just review the definitions of range and domain — remember that the range consists of the values of $f(x)$, whereas the domain consists of the values of x. The first graph is the one with the correct range.

12. **(A)** Polynomials

If $x = -4, 2$, then we know that the quadratic equation includes the factors $x + 4$ and $x - 2$. So we simply find the product of the binomials using FOIL:

$$(x + 4)(x - 2) = x^2 - 2x + 4x - 8$$
$$= x^2 + 2x - 8$$

13. **(E)** Basic Functions and the Right Triangle

The problem can be solved by plugging in for θ. However, the equation can be simplified before plugging in. Recall the definition of the cosecant: $\csc \theta = \frac{1}{\sin \theta}$. Also: $\tan \theta = \frac{\sin \theta}{\cos \theta}$. Substituting these into the original equation gives $\tan \theta \csc \theta = (\frac{\sin \theta}{\cos \theta})(\frac{1}{\sin \theta}) = \frac{1}{\cos \theta}$. Now simply plug in theta, giving $\frac{1}{\cos 76°} = 4.13$.

14. **(A)** Evaluating Functions

This problem is just a matter of performing operations on a function. First, substitute the values into the function. Then carry out the operations.

$$\frac{f(3) + g(4)}{g(5)} = \frac{3 \times 3 + 4^2}{5^2}$$
$$= \frac{9 + 16}{25}$$
$$= 1$$

15. **(C)** Prisms, Solids That Aren't Prisms

Let the height of the pyramid be x and the base area of the pyramid be y. So: volume of the pyramid $= \frac{1}{3} xy$. Then, let the height of the box be p and the base area of the box be q. The volume of the box is thus pq. From the information given, $x = 3p$ and $y = \frac{1}{2} q$, so it's possible to solve for the volume of the box in terms of x and y:

volume of box $= pq$

$$= \frac{x}{3} 2y$$

$$= \frac{2}{3} xy$$

Since $V = \frac{1}{3} xy$, the volume of the box in terms of V is $2V$.

16. **(A)** Graphing Functions

The graph of $y = -f(x)$ will simply be the graph of $y = f(x)$ reflected over the x–axis.

17. **(A)** Statistical Analysis

The total weight of the original group is equal to the total weight of the new group minus 150 (the weight of the new member). Let x represent the number of students in the original group. In the original group, x students average 100 pounds, so their total weight is $100x$. The new group of students, with $(x + 1)$ members, add up to a total weight of $110(x + 1)$. So, set up an equation and solve for x:

$$100x = 110(x + 1) - 150$$
$$100x + 150 = 110x + 110$$
$$40 = 10x$$
$$x = 4$$

The original group had 4 members.

18. **(B)** Basic Functions and the Right Triangle

One approach to this problem is substituting in values for x and y in terms of θ. To do so, remember the definitions of the sine and cosine functions: $\sin\theta = {}^{opposite}\!/_{hypotenuse}$ and $\cos\theta = {}^{adjacent}\!/_{hypotenuse}$.

Using these relationships, it follows that $\sin\theta = {}^{y}\!/_{r}$ and $\cos\theta = {}^{x}\!/_{r}$. Solving for x and y, simply multiply through both equations by r. Doing so produces $x = r\cos\theta$ and $y = r\sin\theta$. Now simply substitute for x and y in the initial equation:

$$\frac{x-y}{r} = \frac{r\cos\theta - r\sin\theta}{r} = \cos\theta - \sin\theta$$

19. **(D)** Equation Solving

After the unknown time t, exactly half the initial amount has decayed. This means that if the initial amount is A_o, and exactly half of that amount remains, then the variable $A = {}^{A_o}\!/_2$.

Plugging this into the equation, $A = {}^{A_o}\!/_2 = A_o e^{-t/300}$. A_o cancels out since it appears on both sides of the equation. Now, $1/2 = e^{-t/300}$. To bring the exponent down and eliminate e, take the natural logarithm of both sides, resulting in $\ln\frac{1}{2} = -{}^{t}\!/_{300} \ln e$. Since $\ln e = 1$, we get $\ln\frac{1}{2} = -{}^{t}\!/_{300}$. Now, to solve for t, multiply both sides by -300, leaving $t = -300\ln\frac{1}{2} = 208$ years.

20. **(E)** Sequences

To answer this question, calculate g_4 and g_2 using the formula given. Since it is given that $g_1 = 2$ and $g_{n+1} = 3g_n$, calculating should be easy: $g_2 = 3 \times 2 = 6$, $g_3 = 18$, and $g_4 = 54$. Thus, $g_4 - g_2 = 54 - 6 = 48$.

21. **(C)** Evaluating Functions

If $f^{-1}(g(3)) = 7$, then $f(f^{-1}(g(3))) = f(7)$. Simplifying, the f and f^{-1} cancel out, giving $g(3) = f(7)$. $f(x)$ is given, so:

$$f(7) = 7(7) + 4$$
$$= 49 + 4$$
$$= 53$$

So $g(3)$ equals 53. To find the correct answer, it is easiest just to try each choice and see which one yields 53. Only $g(x) = 5x^2 + 8$ is correct.

$$g(3) = 5 \times 3^2 + 8$$
$$= 45 + 8$$
$$= 53$$

22. **(B)** Evaluating Functions

To solve this problem, first find $f^{-1}(x)$:

$$f(x) = 2x$$
$$y = 2x$$
$$x = 2y$$
$$\frac{x}{2} = y$$
$$f^{-1}(x) = \frac{x}{2}$$

Now, substitute $3x + 6$ in for x to find $f^{-1}(3x+6)$.

$$f^{-1}(3x + 6) = \frac{3x + 6}{2}$$
$$= \frac{3x}{2} + 3$$

23. **(D)** Basic Functions and the Right Triangle

Choices (A), (B), (E) are incorrect and can be eliminated because the cosine function yields both positive and negative values across all values of θ (e.g., $\cos 0 = 1$ and $\cos \pi = -1$).

The trick to this question is remembering that the cosine function is even. In an even function, $f(-x) = f(x)$ for all values of x in the domain. Thus, if $\cos \theta$ is an even function, then $\cos -\theta = \cos \theta$ for all θ.

24. **(D)** Domain and Range

The graph of the function $f(x) = -3x^2 + 8$ is a parabola opening downward, since the coefficient of x^2 is negative. So, the maximum value of the function will be the y-value of the vertex. To find the vertex of the parabola, set $x = 0$ and solve for $f(x)$. For this function, this gives: $f(0) = -3(0)^2 + 8 = 0 + 8 = 8$. The vertex of the parabola is the point $(0, 8)$, and the maximum value of f is therefore 8.

25. **(B)** Basic Functions and the Right Triangle

The cosine function is even, making choices (A) and (C) incorrect. The square of an odd function is even. This can be seen by using the definition: if $f(-x) = -f(x)$, then $(f(-x))^2 = (-f(x))^2 = (f(x))^2$. Since $(f(-x))^2 = (f(x))^2$, the square of the sine function is even, and so (D) is incorrect. Choice (E) is an even function since both $\sin^2 x$ and $\cos x$ are even functions. Multiplying them together will creates another even function. $f(x) = \sin x \cos x$ is an odd function because $f(-x) = \sin -x \cos -x = -\sin x \cos x = -f(x)$. This satisfies the definition of an odd function.

26. **(D)** Graphing Functions

Let's check each statement individually. Statement I asserts that the range and domain of f are equal. The range and domain of this function can be seen from its graph. The domain (the set of all values of x) is $[-1, 1]$. The range (the set of all values of $f(x)$) is also $[-1, 1]$, so statement I is true.

The second statement is false. Resist temptation to call $y = -1$ an asymptote. An asymptote is a line that a function approaches, gets infinitely close to, but never intersects. Obviously f intersects the line $y = -1$ at the point $(0,1)$. Furthermore, f does not approach the line $y = -1$, as it would if $y = -1$ were an asymptote.

Statement III indicates that $f(x) = f(-x)$, or to rephrase it, that f is symmetrical with respect to the y-axis. This is true. Although this assertion can only be verified at two points, $f(1) = f(-1)$, you can observe visually that the function is indeed symmetrical with respect to the y-axis.

Statements I and III are true.

27. **(E)** Equation Solving

Since both sides of the inequality have the same denominator, it seems that the inequality is true for $0 < a < c$. Don't be fooled, however; this is ONLY true when b is positive. If b is negative, then a must be greater than c and both must be positive (making the quantity $^a/_b$ more negative than, and so "less" than, $^c/_b$). Therefore, the valid condition is $0 < c < a$ and $b < 0$.

28. **(D)** Graphing Functions

Again, don't be misled by a slightly tricky question. It may seem intuitive to think $x = 2$ and $y = \frac{1}{2}$ are two asymptotes of $g(x)$. That answer is incorrect, however.

The visual effect of dividing a function by 2 is to compress the graph, vertically. Each point (x, y) in the graph of $f(x)$ has a matching point, $(x, \frac{1}{2} y)$. Therefore, the vertical asymptote does not change; as x approaches 4, the graph of $g(x)$ must go to infinity or negative infinity, just as the graph of $f(x)$ does. The horizontal asymptote does change, though. The y-component of every point in the graph of $g(x)$ is half of that of $f(x)$, so its asymptote is at $y = -\frac{1}{2}$. Thus, the correct answer is $x = 4$ and $y = -\frac{1}{2}$.

29. **(D)** Domain and Range

Begin by determining for which x–values the function $f(x)$ is equal to 0:

$$3x^3 + 4x^2 + x = 0$$
$$x(3x^2 + 4x + 1) = 0$$
$$x(3x + 1)(x + 1) = 0$$
$$x = 0 \text{ or } x = -\frac{1}{3} \text{ or } x = -1$$

So the graph of $f(x)$ crosses the x–axis three times, at $x = -1, -\frac{1}{3}$, and 0. In other words, at each of these points, and only at these points, the graph of $f(x)$ goes from negative to positive or vice versa. Now, simply test values of x to see where the graph is positive.

For example, for $x \geq 0$, say $x = 1$, $f(1) = 3(1^3) + 4(1^2) + 1 = 8$. So, for this section, $f(x) \geq 0$. Thus, it's safe to eliminate any answer choice that does not include $x \geq 0$, namely, (B) and (E).

So, if the graph of $f(x)$ is positive for $x > 0$, and it crosses the x–axis at 0, $-\frac{1}{3}$, and -1, then the graph is most likely negative for $-\frac{1}{3} < x < 0$, positive for $-1 < x < -\frac{1}{3}$, and negative again for $x < -1$. This can be confirmed by testing a value of x between $-\frac{1}{3}$ and 0, a value between -1 and $-\frac{1}{3}$, and a value less than -1. The correct answer, therefore, is $-1 \leq x \leq -\frac{1}{3}$ or $x \geq 0$.

30. **(A)** Other Important Graphs and Equations

The fastest way to solve this problem is to notice that the point $(2, 3.8)$ has to be exactly 6 away from $(2, b)$. This means b must equal -2.2 or 9.8. Only one of the two possible choices is given, -2.2, and that is correct.

Alternatively, the equation of a circle with center (h, k) and radius r is:

$$(x - h)^2 + (y - k)^2 = r^2$$

So, the equation of this circle is:

$$(x - 2)^2 + (y - b)^2 = 36$$

Since $(-1, 3)$ lies on the circle, simply plug it into this equation and solve for b:

$$(-1 - 2)^2 + (3 - b)^2 = 36$$
$$(-3)^2 + (3 - b)^2 = 36$$
$$9 + (3 - b)^2 = 36$$
$$(3 - b)^2 = 27$$

So $3 - b = \sqrt{27} \approx \pm 5.2$, so $b \approx -2.2$ or 8.2. This means that the equation of the circle is either $(x - 2)^2 + (y + 2.2)^2 = 36$ or $(x - 2)^2 + (y - 8.2)^2 = 36$. Test the second given point, $(2, 3.8)$, in both equations to see which is correct. If $b = -2.2$:

$$(2 - 2)^2 + (3.8 + 2.2)^2 = 36$$

Testing the second equation is unnecessary, since $b = -2.2$ works.

31. **(A)** Domain and Range

Consider each part of the function over its given domain. First, for all $x > -1$, $f(x) = -x^2$. So $f(-1) = -(-1)^2 = -1$. However, because x is greater than, but not equal to, -1 for this function, the graph of the function will end at the point $(-1, -1)$, but will not include this point. The graph of $f(x) = -x^2$ is a parabola that opens downward (since the coefficient of x^2 is negative), so the maximum value of the function will be the y–coordinate of the vertex of the parabola. To find the vertex of the parabola, set $f(x) = 0$ and solve for x. In this case, when $x = 0$, $f(0) = -(0)^2 = 0$, so the vertex of the parabola is the point $(0, 0)$. So, for $x > -1$, the graph looks like this:

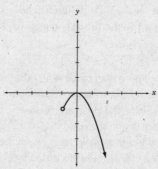

Now consider the second part of the function. $f(x) = 2x + 3$ for all $x \le -1$. So $f(-1) = (2)(-1) + 3 = 1$. Since x is less than or equal to -1, the graph of this function will include the point $(-1, 1)$. The graph of this function is a line with a positive slope, so the function will increase until it reaches the given endpoint of $(-1, 1)$. The graph of the function is:

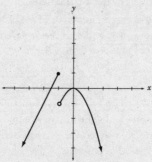

By inspection, it is easy to see that the range of the function is $y \le 1$.

32. **(D)** Equation Solving

First, find t in terms of x by using the definition of logarithm: if $\log_b t = c$ then $t = b^c$. Applying it above, $b = 2$, and $c = x$; therefore, $t = 2^x$. Now, simply plug this into the second equation to get y in terms of x: $y = t^2 = (2^x)^2$. Finally, use the rule for raising exponents to an exponent: $y = (2^x)^2 = 2^{2x}$.

33. **(C)** Equation Solving

Recall the addition rule of logarithms: $\log_b x + \log_b y = \log_b xy$. Adding $\log_3 n$ to both sides gives $\log_3 m + \log_3 n = 1.50$. Using the identity above, $\log_3 mn = 1.50$. Now use the definition of logarithm (if $\log_b a = c$ then $a = b^c$) to solve for mn. In the equation above, if $\log_3 mn = 1.50$, then $mn = 3^{1.50} = 5.20$.

34. **(D)** Sequences

This geometric series has a common ratio $r = {}^3\!/_2$. That is, each term is ${}^3\!/_2$ times the previous term. Whenever the common ratio of a geometric series is greater than one, the sum of the series is infinite.

35. **(C)** Basic Functions and the Right Triangle

The quickest and easiest way to solve this problem is to try each possible answer choice. The third, $\theta = 0$, is correct.

Alternatively, this problem can be solved directly with trig identities. The trick to this is the identity $\tan^2\theta + 1 = \sec^2\theta$. This identity can be derived from the base identity $\sin^2\theta + \cos^2\theta = 1$ by simply dividing through the equation by $\cos^2\theta$, giving $\tan^2\theta + 1 = \sec^2\theta$.

To use this identity, first square both sides of the equality, which gives $\tan^2\theta = \sec\theta - 1$. Next, add 1 to both sides to get $\tan^2\theta + 1 = \sec\theta$. Now use the identity above and plug in $\sec^2\theta$ for $\tan^2\theta + 1$, giving $\sec^2\theta = \sec\theta$. Dividing through, it follows that $\sec\theta = 1$. By definition, however, $\sec\theta = \frac{1}{\cos\theta}$. Substituting yields $\frac{1}{\cos\theta} = 1$. By cross–multiplying, $\cos\theta = 1$. Thus, the only choice for θ that yields a cosine value of 1 is 0.

36. **(C)** Probability

It is given that the coin landed heads up more than twice — in other words, it landed heads up either three times or four times. To find the probability that it landed heads up four times given that it landed heads up more than twice, it is necessary to divide the probability that it landed heads up four times by the probability that it landed heads up more than twice, i.e. $\frac{P(4)}{P(>2)} = \frac{P(4)}{P(3)+P(4)}$.

The probability that the coin landed heads up four times out of four tosses is easy: $(\frac{1}{2})^4 = \frac{1}{16}$. Now the probability that the coin landed heads up three times is a little more complicated; the first toss could have been tails and the rest heads, or the second toss could have been tails and the rest heads, and so on. In all, any of the four tosses could have been the tails toss, with equal probability, $\frac{1}{16}$. So, the probability that the coin lands heads up exactly three times is $4 \times \frac{1}{16} = \frac{4}{16}$. Thus, the answer is $\frac{1}{16} \div (\frac{4}{16} + \frac{1}{16}) = \frac{1}{16} \div \frac{5}{16} = \frac{1}{5}$.

37. **(C)** Other Important Graphs and Equations

To add vectors, just add their respective components. In this case, $\vec{a} = (1,3)$ and $\vec{b} = (-4,1)$, so $\vec{c} = (1 + (-4), 3 + 1) = (-3, 4)$. The magnitude of a vector is equal to the square root of the sum of the squares of its components. The magnitude of $\vec{c} = \sqrt{(-3)^2 + 4^2} = \sqrt{25} = 5$.

38. **(D)** Equation Solving

The key to this question is knowing how to find the inverse function, $f^{-1}(x)$. To find the inverse of a given function, set $f(x) = y$. Then swap variables and solve the new equation: $x = \log_7 3y$. Use the definition of logarithm (if $\log_b a = c$ then $a = b^c$) to isolate y. According to this definition, $3y = 7^x$. Thus, $y = f^{-1}(x) = \frac{7^x}{3}$. Now simply plug in 1.25 for x: $f^{-1}(1.25) = \frac{7^{1.25}}{3} = 3.80$.

39. **(C)** Inverse Trigonometric Functions

Just punch this expression into a calculator. The answer is $\tan^{-1}(\sin 25°) = 22.9°$.

40. **(C)** Sequences

Because this is an arithmetic sequence, the difference between consecutive terms is constant. The first step in answering the question is finding this common difference. By knowing $a_5 = a_{10} - 3$, set up and solve the equation $a_{n+1} - a_n = \frac{3}{10-5} = 0.6$. Now list the terms of the sequence, starting with a_3. $a_3 = -2, a_4 = -1.4, a_5 = -0.8, a_6 = -0.2, a_7 = 0.4$, and so on. The question is answered: 0 lies between the sixth and seventh terms of the sequence.

41. **(A)** Other Important Graphs and Equations

In order for a point to lie inside the sphere, which has a radius of 5, the distance from the point to the origin must be less than 5. Use the distance formula to determine the distance from each answer choice to the origin. Recall that the distance, d, between the point (x_1, y_1, z_1) and the point (x_2, y_2, z_2) is given by $d = \sqrt{(x_2 - x_1)^2 + (y_2 - y_1)^2 + (z_2 - z_1)^2}$. In this case, (x_1, y_1, z_1) is the origin, $(0, 0, 0)$, so the distance from the origin to the point (x, y, z) is simply $d = \sqrt{x^2 + y^2 + z^2}$.

First, find the distance from $(-1, 2, 4)$ to the origin. This is:

$$d = \sqrt{(-1)^2 + 2^2 + 4^2}$$
$$= \sqrt{21}$$
$$\approx 4.58$$

So, the distance from the point $(-1, 2, 4)$ to the origin is less than 5, which means that this point lies inside sphere O, making $(1, -2, 4)$ the answer. The other choices can be eliminated easily, without calculations. Think about it this way: for a point to be inside the sphere, its distance to the origin must be less than 5. However, if one of the point's coordinates is already 5 or greater away from the origin, the distance formula will definitely exceed 5. In each of the other choices given, inspection shows that the points are much further than 5 from the origin. The point within sphere O is clearly $(1, -2, 4)$.

42. **(E)** Basic Functions and the Right Triangle

The figure below depicts the situation described in this problem.

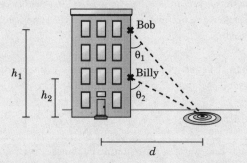

Since Billy and Bob are at different heights, their lines of vision make different angles with respect to the building. Since the horizontal distance of the target from the building is given, as well as the angles of vision, the tangent function will calculate the heights of Billy and Bob. $\tan \theta = {}^{\text{opposite}}/_{\text{adjacent}}$. To find the height of Bob, h_1, use this tangent function definition: $\tan \theta_1 = {}^{d}/_{h_1}$. Solving for $h_1 = {}^{d}/_{\tan \theta_1}$. Next, do the same to calculate the height of Billy, who is lower on the building: $\tan \theta_2 = {}^{d}/_{h_2}$. Again, rearrange the equation to solve for h_2: $h_2 = {}^{d}/_{\tan \theta_2}$. Now it's easy to can calculate the difference (to determine how far apart they are vertically): $h_1 - h_2 = {}^{d}/_{\tan \theta_1} - {}^{d}/_{\tan \theta_2} = d({}^{1}/_{\tan \theta_1} - {}^{1}/_{\tan \theta_2})$.

43. **(B)** Imaginary and Complex Numbers

First, solve this equation. Since it is quadratic, use the quadratic formula to find the solutions.

$$x = \frac{2 \pm \sqrt{2^2 - 4(1)(2)}}{2 \times 1}$$
$$= 1 \pm \frac{\sqrt{-4}}{2}$$
$$= 1 \pm i$$

Now, to find the absolute value of $1 \pm i$, use the distance formula.

$$\sqrt{1^2 + (\pm 1)^2} = \sqrt{2}$$
$$\approx 1.41$$

44. **(D)** Prisms, Solids That Aren't Prisms

The volume of the cube is s^3, where s is the length of a side of the cube. The volume of the pyramid is $\frac{1}{3} Bh$, where B is the area of the pyramid's base, and h is the pyramid's height.

In this case, the base of the pyramid is a square with sides of length s. So $B = s^2$. Also, since A, B, C, and D are midpoints of the edges of the cube, the height of the pyramid is half the height of the cube, so $h = \frac{1}{2}s$. Therefore, the volume can be calculated as follows:

$$\frac{1}{3} Bh = \frac{1}{3} (s^2)(\frac{1}{2} s) = \frac{1}{6} s^3$$

The ratio of the two volumes is:

$$\frac{\text{volume of pyramid}}{\text{volume of cube}} = \frac{\frac{1}{6}s^3}{s^3} = \frac{1}{6}$$

45. **(D)** Logic

The contrapositive (opposite, reverse version) of a logic statement is always true if the logic statement itself is true. That is to say, if the contrapositive of a logic statement is true, this proves that the logic statement is true. Note that choice "If the shirt is not on sale, then it costs at least twenty dollars" is the contrapositive of the statement given. Thus, taken as a premise, it proves the given statement. None of the other choices proves the given statement.

46. **(C)** Other Important Graphs and Equations

The equation of the circle is:

$$(x - 4)^2 + (y + 3)^2 = (3\sqrt{5})^2 = 45$$

When the circle intersects the x–axis, $y = 0$, so the equation becomes $(x - 4)^2 + (0 + 3)^2 = 45$. Solving for x:

$$(x - 4)^2 + (0 + 3)^2 = 45$$
$$x^2 - 8x + 16 + 9 = 45$$
$$x^2 - 8x - 20 = 0$$
$$(x + 2)(x - 10) = 0$$

Therefore, $x = -2$ or $x = 10$.

47. **(A)** Lines and Distance

In order to find $g(x)$ notice what the translation of the graph has done to the function. Translating right 3 units means our new x moved left 3, and translating up 2 units moved $f(x)$ up 2. So, $g(x) = f(x - 3) + 2 = 3(x - 3)^2 + 2$ and therefore $g(2.2) = 3(2.2 - 3)^2 + 2 = 3.92$.

48. (B) Domain and Range

Consider $f(x) = x^2 + 2$ first. The graph of this function is a parabola opening upward, since the coefficient of x^2 is positive. So, the minimum value of the function is the y–coordinate of the vertex. To find the vertex of the parabola, set $x = 0$ and solve for $f(x)$: $f(0) = 0^2 + 2 = 2$. So, the range of this function is $y \geq 2$. This option can be eliminated.

Next, you might wish to consider statement II. However, this is unnecessary because both remaining answers include statement II, so it must be true. Just check the validity of statement III. The function $\cos x$ has a range of -1 to 1, inclusive. Therefore, the range of function $f(x) = 1 - \cos x$ is $0 \leq y \leq 2$. So, the range of this function does not include all positive numbers. The answer is II only.

49. (C) Limits

Since the denominator of this expression is 0 at $x = -2$, the expression is undefined at that value. However, it might still have a limit. Start by factoring the numerator and denominator to see if canceling is possible. Factoring the denominator is easy and leads to $3(x + 2)$. Factoring the numerator gives $(x + 2)(4x + 2)$. Canceling the $(x + 2)$ out gives $\frac{4x+2}{3}$. What this means is that this expression is equivalent to the one given, except that it has the "hole" filled in where $x = -2$ was undefined. The new expression is continuous, and substituting $x = -2$ gives the desired limit.

$$\frac{4(-2) + 2}{3} = \frac{-6}{3} = -2.$$

50. (D) Polynomials

$x - 2$ is probably a factor of $x^3 - 2x - 4$ and it should be checked. It is useful to rewrite the polynomial as $x^3 + 0x^2 - 2x - 4$ and check term by term if $x - 2$ is a factor: the first term, x^3 can only be produced if $x - 2$ is multiplied by x^2. So, this gives $(x - 2)(x^2) = x^3 - 2x^2$. Since the final product has a $0x^2$, a positive $2x^2$ is needed to cancel out the negative $-2x^2$. $x - 2$ multiplied by $2x$ will produce a $2x^2$, so the expression is now $(x - 2)(x^2 + 2x) = x^3 - 2x^2 + 2x^2 - 4x$. The final term of the unknown polynomial has to be a 2, since -2 has to be multiplied by this value to equal -4. So the complete, correct answer is $x^2 + 2x + 2$.

SAT II Math IIC

Practice Test III

MATHEMATICS LEVEL IIC TEST

THE FOLLOWING INFORMATION IS FOR YOUR REFERENCE IN ANSWERING SOME OF THE QUESTIONS IN THIS TEST.

Volume of a right circular cone with radius r and height h: $V = \frac{1}{3}\pi r^2 h$

Lateral area of a right circular cone with circumference of the bace c and slant height ℓ: $S = \frac{1}{2}c\ell$

Volume of a sphere with radius r: $V = \frac{4}{3}\pi^3$

Surface area of a sphere with radius r: $S = 4\pi r^2$

Volume of a pyramid with base area B and height h: $V = \frac{1}{3}Bh$

DO NOT DETACH FROM BOOK.

GO ON TO THE NEXT PAGE →

MATHEMATICS LEVEL IIC TEST

For each of the following problems, decide which is the BEST of the choices given. If the exact numerical value is not one of the choices, select the choice that best approximates this value. Then fill in the corresponding oval on the answer sheet.

<u>Notes:</u> (1) A calculator will be necessary for answering some (but not all) of the questions in this test. For each question you will have to decide whether or not you should use a calcuator. The calculator you use must be at least a scientific calculator; programmable calculators and calculators that can display graphs are permitted.

(2) For some questions in this test you may need to decide whether your calculator should be in radian or degree mode.

(3) Figures that accompany problems in this test are intended to provide information useful in solving the problems. They are drawn as accurately as possible EXCEPT when it is stated in a specific problem that its figure is not drawn to scale. All figures lie in a plane unless otherwise indicated.

(4) Unless otherwise specified, the domain of any function f is assumed to be the set of all real numbers x for which $f(x)$ is a real number.

(5) Reference information that may be useful in answering the questions in this test can be found on the page preceding Question 1.

USE THIS SPACE FOR SCRATCHWORK.

1. If $x + y = 2$ and $\frac{x-y}{2} = 1$, then $xy =$

    (A) –2   (B) –1   (C) 0   (D) 1   (E) 2

2. If a is a positive integer and b is a negative integer, which of the following must be equal to a negative integer?

    (A) $a^2 - b^2$
    (B) $ab - 3b$
    (C) $2ab + b$
    (D) $ab^2 - b^2$
    (E) $b + 2a$

3. In Figure 1, if $\theta = 16°$, what is the area of the triangle?

    (A) 1.19
    (B) 2.36
    (C) 3.36
    (D) 4.72
    (E) 6.71

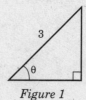

Figure 1

GO ON TO THE NEXT PAGE

4. The region of the xy-plane that satisfies $y > x^2$ or $y > 0$ is

    (A) a circle
    (B) a square
    (C) the region of the plane bounded by a parabola
    (D) a crescent-shaped region in the plane
    (E) the half of the plane above the x-axis

5. If $\sqrt{(x+2)} = 3.52$, then $x =$

    (A) -0.12
    (B) 1.87
    (C) 1.52
    (D) 10.39
    (E) 12.39

6. In Figure 2, $\dfrac{\tan^2 A}{\sin A \cos B} =$

    (A) $\dfrac{b^2}{a^2}$ (B) $\dfrac{a^2}{c^2}$ (C) $\dfrac{c^2}{a^2}$ (D) $\dfrac{b^2}{c^2}$ (E) $\dfrac{c^2}{b^2}$

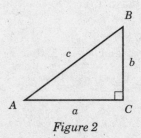

Figure 2

7. If $f(x) = 4x + 2$, what is $f^{-1}(50)$?

    (A) 10 (B) 12 (C) 13 (D) 14 (E) 16

8. $\log_x x =$

    (A) 0 (B) 1 (C) $\sqrt{x}$ (D) x (E) x^2

9. What is the area of the circle with diameter equal to the distance from $(-.5, -.5)$ to $(1.5, 1.5)$?

    (A) 3.14
    (B) 6.29
    (C) 6.79
    (D) 7.79
    (E) 13.31

10. Simplify $\dfrac{\cot \theta \cos \theta}{\csc \theta} + \sin^2\theta$.

    (A) 0
    (B) 1
    (C) $2 \sin^2\theta$
    (D) $\cos \theta + \sin \theta$
    (E) $1 + \sin^2\theta$

GO ON TO THE NEXT PAGE

11. How many asymptotes does the graph of $y = \dfrac{x+3}{x+1}$ contain?

   (A) 0
   (B) 1
   (C) 2
   (D) 3
   (E) Impossible to tell

12. For $x \neq -2$, what is a zero of $\dfrac{2x^3 - 3x^2 - 14x}{x+2}$?

   (A) -7 (B) -5 (C) 1 (D) $\dfrac{5}{2}$ (E) $\dfrac{7}{2}$

13. If $\sin \theta = \dfrac{1}{2}$, $\dfrac{3\cos\theta\sec\theta}{\csc\theta} =$

   (A) -3 (B) 1 (C) $\dfrac{3}{2}$ (D) 3 (E) 6

14. If $f(7x + 5) = 14x + 10$ for all real x, what is $f(x)$?

   (A) $x + 5$
   (B) $7x + 5$
   (C) $2x$
   (D) $2x + 5$
   (E) $2x - 5$

15. If $3x^4 - 22x^2 + 24 > 0$, which of the following is *not* a valid value of x:

   (A) -3.45
   (B) -2.99
   (C) 2.00
   (D) 2.45
   (E) 2.99

16. What is the perimeter of the triangle with vertices $(1, 0)$, $(2, \sqrt{3})$, and $(4, 0)$?

   (A) 0
   (B) 7.65
   (C) 8
   (D) 9.32
   (E) 21.77

GO ON TO THE NEXT PAGE

17. A jar contains two black marbles and one white marble. If a marble is selected from the jar and removed, and then a second marble is selected from the jar, what is the probability that the second marble selected is white?

    (A) $\frac{1}{6}$ (B) $\frac{1}{3}$ (C) $\frac{1}{2}$ (D) $\frac{2}{3}$ (E) $\frac{5}{6}$

18. If $0 < \theta < \pi$ and $\cot\theta = \cos\theta$ then $\theta =$

    (A) 0 (B) $\frac{\pi}{4}$ (C) $\frac{\pi}{2}$ (D) $\frac{3\pi}{4}$ (E) π

19. The value of a certain object increases in value at the unknown rate of $r\%$, annually. If its initial value is \$180, and its value in 15 years will be \$420, what is the rate, r, at which it appreciates?

    (A) 4.4%
    (B) 5.8%
    (C) 9.8%
    (D) 16%
    (E) 233%

20. If $f(x)= \sqrt{x}$ and $g(y) = \dfrac{y^2}{y-1}$, what is the domain of $g(f(x))$?

    (A) $x \geq 0 , x \neq 1$
    (B) $x \geq 0$
    (C) $x > 1$
    (D) $x \geq -1$
    (E) $0 \leq x < 1$

21. In an arithmetic sequence a_n, $a_7 = a_3 + 18 = 4$. Which of the following equations is true?

    (A) $a_n = -5 + 4n$
    (B) $a_n = -27.5 + 4n$
    (C) $a_n = -5 + 4.5n$
    (D) $a_n = -27.5 + 4.5n$
    (E) $a_n = -27.5 + 6n$

GO ON TO THE NEXT PAGE

22. If a polynomial function has six distinct, real roots, what is its maximum degree?

   (A) 3
   (B) 6
   (C) 7
   (D) 8
   (E) Its degree has no maximum

23. For all θ, $e^{4\sin\theta} e^{4\sin(-\theta)} =$

   (A) 1
   (B) e^4
   (C) $e^{4\sin\theta + 4\cos\theta}$
   (D) $e^{8\sin\theta}$
   (E) $e^{16\sin^2\theta}$

24. If $f:(x, y) \rightarrow (x + y, y)$ for every pair (x, y) in the plane, for what points (x, y) is it true that $(x, y) \rightarrow (y, x)$?

   (A) $(0, 0)$ only
   (B) $(1, 1)$ only
   (C) The set of points (x, y) such that $y = 0$
   (D) The set of points (x, y) such that $x = y$
   (E) The set of points (x, y) such that $2x = y$

25. A function f is an even function if, for all values of x in the domain, $f(-x) = f(x)$. Which of the following is an even function?

   (A) $\sin x$
   (B) $-\sin x$
   (C) $\sin x \cos x$
   (D) $\sin^2 x$
   (E) none

GO ON TO THE NEXT PAGE

26. The graph of $y = ax^s - x^2 - 4x + 1$ is shown in Figure 3. Which of the following is a set of solutions for a and s?

(A) $a = 7, s = 2$
(B) $a = 2, s = 3$
(C) $a = 0, s = 5$
(D) $a = -3, s = 5$
(E) $a = 4, s = 4$

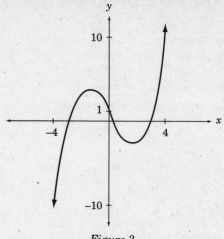

Figure 3

27. If $f(x) = 2^x$, then $f^{-1}(x^2) =$

(A) x^2
(B) x^4
(C) $\log_2 2x$
(D) $\log_{x^2} 2$
(E) $2 \log_2 x$

28. The graph of $y = |f(x)|$ is shown in Figure 4. Which of the following statements must be true?

   I. $f(x)$ is an even function.
  II. $f(x)$ is an odd function.
  III. $|f(x)|$ is an even function.

(A) I only
(B) II only
(C) III only
(D) I and II only
(E) II and III only

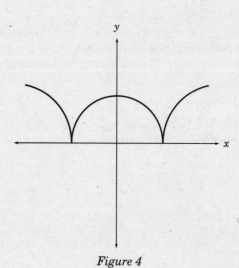

Figure 4

GO ON TO THE NEXT PAGE

29. The expression $\dfrac{2x^2 - 7x + 3}{4x + 10x - 6}$ is undefined for what values of x?

   (A) $\dfrac{1}{2}$ and -3

   (B) -3

   (C) 0

   (D) $\dfrac{1}{2}$ and 3

   (E) $0, \dfrac{1}{2}$, and 3

30. If the line $y = mx + b$ intersects the parabola $y = (x - 5)^2 - 8$ at $x = 0$, what is the y-intercept of the line?

   (A) 16   (B) 17   (C) 23   (D) 26   (E) 32

31. $f(x) = \begin{cases} x^2 - 1 & \text{if} \quad x > 2 \\ -2x + 7 & \text{if} \quad x \le 2 \end{cases}$. What is the range of f?

   (A) $y \le 1$
   (B) $y > 1$
   (C) $y \ge 0$
   (D) $y \ge 3$
   (E) All real numbers

32. If a, b, and c are nonzero real numbers and if $\left| a^{2b} \right| = -c$, which of the following must be **true**:

   (A) $a > 0$
   (B) $b > 0$
   (C) $ab > 0$
   (D) $a^{2b} > 0$
   (E) $c < 0$

GO ON TO THE NEXT PAGE

33. If $x = \dfrac{\sin^2 t}{2}$ and $y = 1 - \cos^2 t$, what is y in terms of x?

(A) 1

(B) $1 - x$

(C) x

(D) $\dfrac{x}{2}$

(E) $2x$

34. In a geometric series, suppose $g_2 = 2$ and $g_6 = 162$. What is $g_n \div g_{n-1}$?

(A) $\dfrac{1}{3}$

(B) 2

(C) 3 or –3

(D) 4

(E) 9

35. If $\sin 2\theta = \tan \theta$, which one of the following is a possible value for θ in radians?

(A) 0.52
(B) 0.79
(C) 0.95
(D) 1.05
(E) 1.58

36. If $2y = x$ and $|6x| = 48$, what are the possible values of y?

(A) –4
(B) 0
(C) –4, 4
(D) 4
(E) 4, 12

GO ON TO THE NEXT PAGE

37. If $\vec{u} = (-4, 1)$ and $\vec{v} = (2, 3)$, what is $2\vec{u} + 3\vec{v}$?

    (A) $(-2, 11)$
    (B) $(-10, 6)$
    (C) $(-2, 4)$
    (D) $(2, -5)$
    (E) $(-14, -7)$

38. If $27^{x+2} = 9^y$, what is y in terms of x ?

    (A) $x + 2$

    (B) $3x + 2$

    (C) $3x + 6$

    (D) $\frac{3}{2}x + 6$

    (E) $\frac{3}{2}x + 3$

39. If $\sin^{-1}(\sin \theta) = \frac{\pi}{2}$ and $0 < \theta < \pi$, then θ could equal

    (A) 0 (B) $\frac{\pi}{4}$ (C) $\frac{\pi}{2}$ (D) $\frac{2\pi}{3}$ (E) $\frac{3\pi}{4}$

40. In a sequence x_n, $x_3 = 4$, $x_4 = 6$, and $x_n = x_{n-2} + 4$. What is $x_n + x_2$?

    (A) $x_n - 4$
    (B) $n - 2$
    (C) $n - 1$
    (D) n
    (E) Not enough information to tell

GO ON TO THE NEXT PAGE

USE THIS SPACE FOR SCRATCHWORK.

41. The distance between points A and B is 7. Which of the following could be A and B?

    (A) $(2, -1, 8)$ and $(5, 3, 5)$
    (B) $(2, 3, -2)$ and $(8, 5, 1)$
    (C) $(1, 3, 3)$ and $(6, 1, 5)$
    (D) $(-2, -1, 5)$ and $(9, 3, 2)$
    (E) $(5, 1, 0)$ and $(5, 7, -6)$

42. A and B are points on circle O, with center at the origin. In rectangular coordinates A is the point $(0,5)$, and B is the point $(\frac{5\sqrt{3}}{2}, \frac{5}{2})$. What is the length of minor arc AB?

    (A) $\dfrac{5\pi}{6}$ (B) $\dfrac{2\pi}{3}$ (C) $\dfrac{5\pi}{3}$ (D) $\dfrac{5\pi}{2}$ (E) $\dfrac{10\pi}{3}$

43. What does $|(7 + 6i)(3 + i)|$ equal?

    (A) 29.15
    (B) 36.80
    (C) 40
    (D) 46.39
    (E) 52

44. Joe is walking along a ridge 40 feet in the air when he accidentally lets go of his balloon. If his balloon rises at a rate of 3 feet per second until it hits a height of 100 feet where the air gets thinner and then rises at a rate of 1 foot per second above 100 feet, how many seconds does it take the balloon to reach a height of 130 feet?

    (A) $\dfrac{130}{3}$

    (B) 30

    (C) 50

    (D) $\dfrac{100}{3} + 30$

    (E) 90

GO ON TO THE NEXT PAGE

45. Suppose the following two statements are true:

   1) All sunny days are dry.
   2) Some, but not all, sunny days are warm.

   Which of the following statements must be *false*?

   (A) All warm days are sunny.
   (B) All warm days are dry.
   (C) Some warm days are sunny.
   (D) Some warm days are dry.
   (E) All dry days are warm.

46. A circle has the equation $(x - 1)^2 + (y + 4)^2 = 25$. Which of the following points lies outside the circle?

   (A) $(1, -7)$
   (B) $(2, 1)$
   (C) $(0, -6)$
   (D) $(-3, -2)$
   (E) $(4, -4)$

47. During March Madness, 64 college basketball teams try to battle their way into the Final Four, or the semifinals of the national tournament. From the original 64 teams, how many different Final Four groupings can there be?

   (A) 64,000
   (B) 256,000
   (C) 542,034
   (D) 635,376
   (E) 834,209

GO ON TO THE NEXT PAGE

48. $f(x) = 3 \sin 3x$ and the domain of $f(x)$ is $-b \leq x \leq b$. If the graph of f crosses the x-axis exactly 7 times, which of the following could be b?

    (A) $\dfrac{\pi}{6}$　(B) $\dfrac{\pi}{3}$　(C) $\dfrac{5\pi}{4}$　(D) $\dfrac{3\pi}{2}$　(E) 2π

49. A hyperbola with equation $(x - \sqrt{5})^2 - (y - 1)^2 = 1$ intersects the y-axis at which one of the following points?

    (A) $(0, -4)$
    (B) $(0, 2)$
    (C) $(0, 5)$
    (D) $(0, -1)$
    (E) $(0, -3)$

50. If $y + 4x = 0$ and $2x^2 - 5 + 5y = 0$, then for $x \geq 0$, $x =$

    (A)　0.86
    (B)　1.12
    (C)　10.24
    (D)　2.55
    (E)　3.23

S T O P

IF YOU FINISH BEFORE TIME IS CALLED, YOU MAY CHECK YOUR WORK ON THIS TEST ONLY.
DO NOT TURN TO ANY OTHER TEST IN THIS BOOK.

SAT II Math IIC Practice Test III Explanations

Calculating Your Score

Your raw score for the SAT II Math IIC test is calculated from the number of questions you answer correctly and incorrectly. Once you have determined your raw score, use the conversion table on page 17 of this book to calculate your scaled score.

To Calculate Your Raw Score

Count the number of questions you answered correctly: _____
A

Count the number of questions you answered incorrectly, and multiply that number by $\frac{1}{4}$:

_____ X $\frac{1}{4}$ = _____
B   C

Subtract the value in field C from value in field A: _____
D

Round the number in field D to the nearest whole number. This is your raw score: _____
E

Answers to SAT II Math IIC Practice Test III

Question Number	Correct Answer	Right	Wrong	Question Number	Correct Answer	Right	Wrong
1.	C	___	___	26.	B	___	___
2.	C	___	___	27.	E	___	___
3.	A	___	___	28.	C	___	___
4.	E	___	___	29.	A	___	___
5.	D	___	___	30.	B	___	___
6.	C	___	___	31.	D	___	___
7.	B	___	___	32.	E	___	___
8.	B	___	___	33.	E	___	___
9.	B	___	___	34.	C	___	___
10.	B	___	___	35.	B	___	___
11.	C	___	___	36.	C	___	___
12.	E	___	___	37.	A	___	___
13.	C	___	___	38.	E	___	___
14.	C	___	___	39.	C	___	___
15.	C	___	___	40.	C	___	___
16.	B	___	___	41.	B	___	___
17.	B	___	___	42.	C	___	___
18.	C	___	___	43.	A	___	___
19.	B	___	___	44.	C	___	___
20.	A	___	___	45.	E	___	___
21.	D	___	___	46.	B	___	___
22.	E	___	___	47.	D	___	___
23.	A	___	___	48.	C	___	___
24.	A	___	___	49.	D	___	___
25.	D	___	___	50.	C	___	___

Math IIC Test III Explanations

1. (C) Equation Solving

By multiplying $\frac{x-y}{2} = 1$ through by 2, it follows that $x - y = 2$. Also, it is given that $x + y = 2$. Adding the two equations together:

$$x + y = 2$$
$$\underline{x - y = 2}$$
$$2x = 4$$

When you combine like terms, y cancels out and leaves $2x = 4$. So, $x = 2$ and plugging the value into in $x - y = 2$, $y = 0$. At this point, the question asks for the quantity xy, which **must** equal 0 since $y = 0$.

2. (C) Fundamentals

The easiest way to answer this problem is to try values for x and y and carry out the expressions. For example, let $a = 2$ and $b = -4$. The only answer choice that produces a negative integer is $2ab + b$.

3. (A) Basic Functions and the Right Triangle

Since θ and the length of the hypotenuse are given, it is possible to solve for the base and the height. Using the definition of cosine, $\cos\theta = \frac{\text{adjacent}}{\text{hypotenuse}}$, solve for the base (the adjacent side):

adjacent side = $3 \cos 16° = 2.883$.

Next, solve for the other leg (the height of the triangle) by using the definition of sine, $\sin\theta = \frac{\text{opposite}}{\text{hypotenuse}}$:

opposite side = $3 \sin 16° = 0.827$

The area of a triangle is $\frac{1}{2}$ base × height = $A = \frac{1}{2}bh = \frac{1}{2}(2.883)(0.827) = 1.19$.

4. (E) Lines and Distance

There is redundancy in the two given inequalities. Notice: if $y > x^2$ then y must be greater than 0. So, the region formed by the inequalities $y > 0$ and $y > x^2$ is the half–plane above the x-axis. Any point with positive y will satisfy the inequalities, and any point with negative or zero y will not.

5. (D) Equation Solving

To solve for x, square both sides and get $x + 2 = 12.39$. Be careful, it's still necessary to subtract 2 from both sides to solve for x: $x = 12.39 - 2 = 10.39$.

6. (C) Basic Functions and the Right Triangle

The trick to this problem is substituting the appropriate ratios for each of the trig functions. Recalling "SOHCAHTOA," $\sin\theta = \frac{\text{opposite}}{\text{hypotenuse}}$, $\cos\theta = \frac{\text{adjacent}}{\text{hypotenuse}}$, and $\tan\theta = \frac{\text{opposite}}{\text{adjacent}}$.

Applying the relationships above, $\tan A = \frac{b}{a}$, $\sin A = \frac{b}{c}$, and $\cos B = \frac{b}{c}$. Substituting these values gives:

$$\frac{\tan^2 A}{\sin A \cos B} = \frac{\left(\frac{b}{a}\right)^2}{\left(\frac{b}{c}\right)\left(\frac{b}{c}\right)}$$

By canceling out variables, this result can be simplified:

$$\frac{\left(\frac{b}{a}\right)^2}{\left(\frac{b}{c}\right)^2} = \frac{\left(\frac{1}{a}\right)^2}{\left(\frac{1}{c}\right)^2} = \frac{c^2}{a^2}$$

7. **(B)** Evaluating Functions

The problem asks you to evaluate the inverse of f at 50. In other words, you need to find the value of x so that $f(x) = 50$. Since this question asks for only one value of the inverse function, the easiest method is just to plug in the possible choices for $f(x)$ and see which one gives 50.

$$f(10) = 4(10) + 2$$
$$= 42$$
$$f(12) = 4(12) + 2$$
$$= 50$$
$$f(13) = 4(13) + 2$$
$$= 54$$
$$f(14) = 4(14) + 2$$
$$= 58$$
$$f(16) = 4(16) + 2$$
$$= 66$$

Only $x = 12$ produces $f(x) = 50$.

Alternatively, you could answer the question by solving for the inverse of the function. Swap the variables in $f(x)$ to get $x = 4y + 2$. Now solve for y: $y = \frac{x-2}{4}$. So $f^{-1}(x) = \frac{x-2}{4}$. Plugging in $x = 50$, $f^{-1}(50) = \frac{50-2}{4} = \frac{48}{4} = 12$.

8. **(B)** Equation Solving

According to the definition of logarithms, $\log_b a = c$ means $a = b^c$. In this question, using the definition of logarithm, $\log_x x = ?$ asks $x^? = x$. Any number raised to the 1st power is always itself. Therefore, $x^1 = x$ and so $\log_x x = 1$.

9. **(B)** Lines and Distance

To find the distance between two points (x_1, y_1) and (x_2, y_2), use formula $d = \sqrt{(x_2 - x_1)^2 + (y_2 - y_1)^2}$:

$$\text{distance} = \sqrt{(1.5 - (-0.5))^2 + (1.5 - (-0.5))^2}$$
$$= \sqrt{2^2 + 2^2}$$
$$= \sqrt{8}$$
$$= 2.83$$

So the area of the circle with diameter 2.83 is $\pi(\frac{2.83}{2})^2 = 6.29$.

10. **(B)** Trigonometric Identities

This question requires knowledge of the Pythagorean identity $\sin^2\theta + \cos^2\theta = 1$ and the definitions $\cot\theta = \frac{1}{\tan\theta} = \frac{\cos\theta}{\sin\theta}$ and $\csc\theta = \frac{1}{\sin\theta}$. Using these, the equation can be simplified:

$$\frac{\cot\theta\,\cos\theta}{\csc\theta} + \sin^2\theta = \frac{\cos\theta}{\sin\theta}(\cos\theta)(\sin\theta) + \sin^2\theta$$
$$= \cos^2\theta + \sin^2\theta$$
$$= 1$$

11. **(C)** Graphing Functions

Graphing the function is the easiest way to answer this question. Hopefully with a graphing calculator, you can simply look to see how many asymptotes there are. Without a graphing calculator, though, the question is still not difficult to answer.

A vertical asymptote occurs in the form $x = a$, at every value of x for which the function is undefined. A horizontal asymptote occurs in the form $y = c$. Most of the horizontal asymptotes you'll see on the SAT II occur in graphs of functions of the form $\frac{ax \pm c_0}{bx \pm c_1}$, where c_0 and c_1 are constants. The horizontal asymptote of the graph of such a function occurs at the line $y = \frac{a}{b}$.

So, using this method of analysis, the graph of $\frac{x+3}{x+1}$ is undefined when $x = -1$ (since its denominator is then equal to zero), and it contains one vertical asymptote, at $x = -1$. Also, the graph has one horizontal asymptote, at $y = 1$. Thus, the correct answer is 2.

12. **(E)** Polynomials

First, you need to try and factor the numerator:

$$2x^3 - 3x^2 - 14x = x(2x^2 - 3x - 14) = x(2x - 7)(x + 2)$$

So the $x + 2$ in the denominator cancels out, leaving $x(2x - 7) = 0$, which means that $x = 0$ or $x = \frac{7}{2}$. The latter, $x = \frac{7}{2}$, is the answer.

13. **(C)** Basic Functions and the Right Triangle

The first step to solving this problem is simplifying the expression $\frac{3 \cos \theta \sec \theta}{\csc \theta}$. Recall the definitions of secant and cosecant: $\sec \theta = \frac{1}{\cos \theta}$ and $\csc \theta = \frac{1}{\sin \theta}$. Substituting back into the original equation gives

$$\frac{3 \cos \theta \dfrac{1}{\cos \theta}}{\dfrac{1}{\sin \theta}}$$

Canceling out the cosine functions, $3 / (\frac{1}{\sin \theta}) = 3 \sin \theta$. $\sin \theta = \frac{1}{2}$, therefore $3 \sin \theta = 3(\frac{1}{2}) = \frac{3}{2}$.

14. **(C)** Evaluating Functions

To discover what $f(x)$ is, look where f maps $7x + 5$. Simply put, f doubles the input; $f(7x + 5) = 2 \times (7x + 5)$. Therefore, $f(x) = 2x$ for all x.

15. **(C)** Equation Solving

The given equation can be factored and solved, but it would take more time than is necessary. Simply plug in the given answer choices to see which is not valid. When $x = 2.00$, the inequality becomes $3(2.00)^4 - 22(4) + 24 > 0$. Simplified: $-16 > 0$. This is clearly false, so 2.00 is the answer.

16. **(B)** Lines and Distance

To find the perimeter of this triangle, calculate the length of each side. The lengths are just the distances between the vertices, so use the distance formula. For (1, 0) and (4, 0):

$$\begin{aligned} \text{distance} &= \sqrt{(4-1)^2 + (0-0)^2} \\ &= \sqrt{9} \\ &= 3 \end{aligned}$$

For (1, 0) and (2, $\sqrt{3}$),

$$\text{distance} = \sqrt{(2-1)^2 + (\sqrt{3}-0)^2}$$
$$= \sqrt{4}$$
$$= 2$$

For (4, 0) and (2, $\sqrt{3}$),

$$\text{distance} = \sqrt{(4-2)^2 + (0-\sqrt{3})^2}$$
$$= \sqrt{7}$$
$$= 2.65$$

The perimeter is the sum of the lengths, $3 + 2 + 2.65 = 7.65$.

17. **(B)** Probability

There are three marbles in the jar and each one has an equal probability of being the second one chosen. Only one of them is white, so the probability is $\frac{1}{3}$.

18. **(C)** Basic Functions and the Right Triangle

Encountering cot θ is a good hint that simplification is the first step. The equality can be cleaned up by substituting in for cot θ. (Remember the identity, $\cot\theta = \frac{\cos\theta}{\sin\theta}$.) Plugging in, $\frac{\cos\theta}{\sin\theta} = \cos\theta$. Divide through by $\cos\theta$, giving $\frac{1}{\sin\theta} = 1$. Rearranging this equation: $\sin\theta = 1$. Since $0 < \theta < \pi$, the only value for which the sine function is 1 is $\theta = \frac{\pi}{2}$.

19. **(B)** Equation Solving

Let P_0 be the object's initial value. After one year, the object will be worth $r\%$ more, and so will be worth $P_0(1+r)$. Now, after a second year, the object will be worth $r\%$ more than its current value of $P_0(1+r)$, and so will be worth $[P_0(1+r)](1+r) = P_0(1+r)^2$. Each additional year, the object will be worth $r\%$ more, and so this quantity will be multiplied by $(1+r)$ for each year. Now, the pattern emerges, and it's possible to write the equation for the value, P, of an object after n years of appreciation at rate r: $P = P_0(1+r)^n$.

Since $P_0 = 180$, $P = 420$, and $n = 15$, r is the only unknown. It can be solved for:

$$P = P_0(1+r)^n$$

$$\frac{P}{P_0} = (1+r)^n$$

$$\sqrt[n]{\frac{P}{P_0}} = 1 + r$$

$$r = \sqrt[n]{\frac{P}{P_0}} - 1$$

Plugging in, $\sqrt[15]{\frac{420}{180}} - 1 = 0.058 = 5.8\%$.

20. **(A)** Domain and Range

In order to find $g(f(x))$, plug $f(x)$ into $g(y)$. That is, $g(f(x)) = x/\sqrt{x} - 1$.

There are two rules that could potentially limit the domain of this function. First, the denominator of a fraction cannot be equal to 0, so find the values of x which produce 0:

$$\sqrt{x} - 1 \neq 0$$
$$\sqrt{x} \neq 1$$
$$x \neq 1$$

Second, the square root of a negative number is undefined, so $x \geq 0$. $x \neq 1$, so the answer must be $x \geq 0$, but $x \neq 1$.

21. **(D)** Sequences

In an arithmetic sequence, the difference between consecutive terms is constant. To find the formula for an arithmetic sequence, two values are needed: 1) the difference between consecutive terms, and 2) the value of a term. The given information easily tells both: the difference between consecutive terms follows from knowing the difference between the third term and the seventh term. If $a_7 = a_3 + 18$, then the difference between a_{n+1} and a_n is $\frac{18}{7-3} = \frac{18}{4} = 4.5$. And the value of a term is given: $a_7 = 4$. Thus, the formula for the sequence must satisfy the following equation: $a_n = 4.5n + x$. Since $a_7 = 4.5(7) + x = 4$, it follows that $x = 4 - 4.5(7) = -27.5$. Therefore, the formula for the series is $a_n = -27.5 + 4.5n$.

22. **(E)** Graphing Functions

All it is possible to tell from the fact that a polynomial function has six distinct, real roots is that its degree is greater or equal to 6. Its degree has only a minimum, not a maximum.

23. **(A)** Basic Functions and the Right Triangle

The trick to this question is remembering that the sine function is odd. In an odd function, $f(-x) = -f(x)$ for all values of x in the domain. Thus, if $\sin\theta$ is an odd function, then $\sin(-\theta) = -\sin\theta$ for all θ.

Knowing this property, substitute $-\sin\theta$ in for $\sin(-\theta)$ above, giving $(e^{4\sin\theta})(e^{-4\sin\theta})$. Now, to simplify, add the exponents to get $e^{4\sin\theta - 4\sin\theta} = e^0 = 1$.

24. **(A)** Domain and Range

In order for $(x, y) \rightarrow (y, x)$, y must equal $x + y$ and x must equal y. These equations can be solved simultaneously:

$$y = x + y$$
$$-y = x$$

$$y - y = x + y - x$$
$$0 = y$$

Then, since $x = y$, x must also equal 0. So the requirement that $(x, y) \rightarrow (y, x)$ is fulfilled for this function only when $x = y = 0$, which is at the point $(0, 0)$.

25. **(D)** Basic Functions and the Right Triangle

The sine function is odd, and so choices (A) and (B) are incorrect (the negative sine does not make an odd function even, or vice versa.). An even function multiplied by an odd function creates an odd function. The sine function is odd and the cosine function is even; consequently, $\sin x \cos x$ is odd. The trick to this question is understanding that the square of an odd function is actually even. This can be seen by using the definition: if $f(-x) = -f(x)$, then $(f(-x))^2 = (-f(x))^2 = (f(x))^2$. Since $(f(-x))^2 = (f(x))^2$, the square of the sine function is even. Therefore, $\sin^2 x$ is even.

26. **(B)** Graphing Functions

The function is a polynomial. This means one can analyze its end behavior and roots to narrow the choices for a and s. The end behavior is as follows: as x decreases, y decreases, and as x increases, y increases. From this it follows that s is odd, and a is positive. Because there are 3 real, distinct roots, we also know that $s \geq 3$. These conditions leave but one choice, $a = 2, s = 3$.

27. **(E)** Equation Solving

The most important part of this question is understanding the inverse function: $f^{-1}(x)$. First, set $f(x) = y = 2^x$. Then swap variables and solve the equation $x = 2^y$ for y. Use the definition of logarithm: if $a = b^c$ then $\log_b a = c$. Applying it above, if $x = 2^y$ then $y = f^{-1}(x) = \log_2 x$. Now substitute in x^2, giving $f^{-1}(x^2) = \log_2 x^2$. However, the correct answer is in a different form. Remember the power rule of logarithms: $\log_b a^n = n \log_b a$. Using this, $f^{-1}(x^2) = 2 \log_2 x$.

28. **(C)** Graphing Functions

Recall than an even function is a function for which $f(x) = f(-x)$, and an odd function is a function for which $f(x) = -f(-x)$. Even functions are symmetrical with respect to the y-axis, and odd functions are symmetrical with respect to the origin.

Figure 4 is the graph of $y = |f(x)|$. This is essentially the graph of $f(x)$ with all negative values made positive (i.e., all negative portions of the graph are reflected over the x-axis). This does not, however, tell us enough information about $f(x)$ to determine whether it is even or odd. To see this, reflect different parts of $y = |f(x)|$ over the x-axis, and all of these graphs are possible graphs of f. Reflecting only part of the $x < 0$ portion of the graph of $|f|$ over the x-axis, like in the figure below,

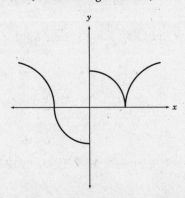

this function is neither odd nor even. This means that neither statement I nor statement II must be true. Statement III is true, however (just by looking at the graph, and seeing that $|f(x)| = |f(-x)|$).

29. **(A)** Domain and Range

A fraction is undefined when its denominator equals 0. So, this function will be undefined when $4x^2 + 10x - 6 = 0$. To find the values of x which produce 0, first factor out the expression:

$$4x^2 + 10x - 6 = 0$$
$$2(2x^2 + 5x - 3) = 0$$
$$2(2x - 1)(x + 3) = 0$$

So, $2x - 1 = 0$ or $x + 3 = 0$. Solving for x, the denominator equals 0 when $x = \frac{1}{2}$ or $x = -3$.

Note that the expression $(2x^2 - 7x + 3)/(4x^2 + 10x - 6)$ may be factored as $(2x - 1)(x - 3)/2(2x - 1)(x + 3)$. To simplify, one may cancel out $2x - 1$ from both the numerator and denominator. However, the function is still undefined at $x = \frac{1}{2}$. Always pay special attention when canceling inside fractions; removing a case where the denominator may be zero actually changes the domain of the expression. The answer is still $x = \frac{1}{2}$ or $x = -3$.

30. **(B)** Other Important Graphs and Equations

The line and parabola intersect when $x = 0$, so plug this value of x into the parabola equation to find the y-coordinate:

$$y = (0 - 5)^2 - 8 = 25 - 8 = 17$$

The line intersects the parabola at $(0, 17)$, and since the y-intercept of a line is the point at which the line crosses the y-axis (at $x = 0$), this point is the y-intercept as well. Thus, 17 is the correct answer.

31. **(D)** Domain and Range

Consider each part of the function over its given domain. First, for all $x > 2$, $f(x) = x^2 - 1$. It is a parabola opening upward, with its vertex at $(0, -1)$. However, only consider this function when $x > 2$. So, for $x = 2$, $f(2) = (2)^2 - 1 = 3$. Because x is greater than, but not equal to 2, for this part of the function, the graph of the function will end at the point $(2, 3)$, but will not include this point. Take a look at the graph of this portion of the function:

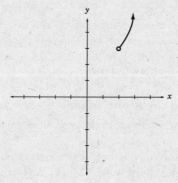

Now consider the second part of the function. $f(x) = -2x + 7$ for all $x \leq 2$. So, for $x = 2$, $f(2) = (-2)(2) + 7 = 3$. So, the graph of this function will include the point $(2, 3)$. The graph of this function is a line with a negative slope and y-intercept of 7, so the function will decrease until it reaches the given endpoint of $(2, 3)$. Here is what the complete function looks like:

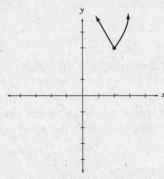

It is easy to see from the graph that the range of the function is $y \geq 3$.

32. (E) Equation Solving

The absolute value of any given quantity is always positive, by definition. When taking the absolute value of the quantity a^{2b}, it becomes positive regardless of whether it itself is positive or negative. (It cannot be zero because of the restrictions on a and b given in the problem.) Therefore, it is not necessary for a, b, or any combination of the two multiplied by each other to be positive. The value of c, however, has to be negative so that $-c$ will in fact be positive; $-c$ must be positive because it is set equal to the absolute value of a quantity (which, by the definition of absolute value, will always be positive). The correct choice is $c < 0$.

33. (E) Equation Solving

$y = 1 - \cos^2 t$, but, based on the identity $\sin^2 t + \cos^2 t = 1$, it follows that $y = \sin^2 t$. $x = \frac{\sin^2 t}{2}$, so $y = 2x$.

34. (C) Sequences

The quotient $g_n \div g_{n-1}$ is simply the common ratio between terms in this geometric sequence. Given two terms of a geometric sequence, find the common ratio between consecutive terms using the following formula: $g_a = g_b \times r^{a-b}$. In this case, $g_6 = g_2 \times r^{6-2}$, or $162 = 2r^4$. Thus, $r^4 = 81$, and $r = 3$ or $r = -3$. Notice that both work; either 2, 6, 18, 54, 162, or 2, –6, 18, –54, 162, is correct.

35. (B) Basic Functions and the Right Triangle

The easiest way to solve this problem is with your calculator. Simply try each answer choice to see which works; 0.79 is correct.

Alternately, this problem can be solved with the trigonometric identity for $\sin 2\theta$: $\sin 2\theta = 2 \sin \theta \cos \theta$. Substituting this back into the original equality gives $2 \sin \theta \cos \theta = \tan \theta$. Since $\tan \theta = \frac{\sin \theta}{\cos \theta}$, you can substitute it:

$$2 \sin \theta \cos \theta = \frac{\sin \theta}{\cos \theta}$$

$$2 \cos^2 \theta = 1$$

$$\cos \theta = \sqrt{\frac{1}{2}}, -\sqrt{\frac{1}{2}}$$

$$\theta = 0.79 \text{ and } \theta = 2.36$$

The correct answer is therefore 0.79.

36. **(C)** Equation Solving

First, plug in $2y = x$ into the absolute value equation to get $|6(2y)| = |12y| = 48$. Then, since the absolute value is the "positive" version of a number, solving this equation has two parts. In the first part, the expression within the absolute value brackets is positive:

$$12y = 48$$
$$y = 4$$

In the second part, the expression within the absolute value brackets is negative:

$$12y = -48$$
$$y = -4$$

Thus, $y = 4$ or $y = -4$.

37. **(A)** Other Important Graphs and Equations

To multiply a vector by a scalar, just multiply each component of the vector by the scalar. So, $2\vec{u} = 2(-4, 1) = (-8, 2)$. Similarly, $3\vec{v} = 3(2, 3) = (6, 9)$.

Then, to add these vectors, just add their respective components. So, $2\vec{u} + 3\vec{v} = (-8, 2) + (6, 9) = (-8 + 6, 2 + 9) = (-2, 11)$.

38. **(E)** Equation Solving

Recall the identity of logarithms that allows bringing down the exponents: $\log_b a^n = n \log_b a$. Applying this above, take the logarithm of both sides (it doesn't matter what base, as long as both logarithms are of the same base; the default base for logarithms on calculators is 10).

However, before doing so, simplify the equation further. Notice that $27 = 3^3$, and that $9 = 3^2$. That means that $27^{x+2} = (3^3)^{x+2}$, and that $9^y = (3^2)^y$. The rule for exponents raised to a power is $(n^a)^b = n^{ab}$. Applying this to the equations above, $27^{x+2} = (3^3)^{x+2} = 3^{3(x+2)}$ and $9^y = (3^2)^y = 3^{2y}$.

Now it's easy to rewrite the given equality in terms of the same base: $3^{3(x+2)} = 3^{2y}$. Then take the logarithm of both sides and solve for y:

$$3(x+2) \log_{10} 3 = 2y \log_{10} 3$$
$$3(x+2) = 2y$$
$$\frac{3(x+2)}{2} = y$$
$$y = \frac{3}{2} x + 3$$

39. **(C)** Inverse Trigonometric Functions

Let $x = \sin \theta$, so that $\sin^{-1} x = \frac{\pi}{2}$. So, by definition of inverse trigonometric functions, $\sin \frac{\pi}{2} = x = 1$. Therefore, $\sin \theta = 1$ and, taking the arcsine of both sides, $\sin^{-1} 1 = \frac{\pi}{2}$. This answer choice can be checked easily with a calculator.

40. **(C)** Sequences

Using the formula $x_n = x_{n-2} + 4$, and the fact that $x_4 = 6$, it follows that $x_2 = 2$. At this point, the answer is still not evident, though. In a problem like this one, it's a good idea to write down a few terms of the sequence, to familiarize yourself with it. In this case, $x_1 = 0$, $x_2 = 2$, $x_3 = 4$, $x_4 = 6$, $x_5 = 8$, and so on. This is just a list of the even numbers, which is also an arithmetic sequence. The formula for the sequence is $x_n = 2n - 2$. Knowing this, it's easy to solve for the expression $x_n \div 2$: $\frac{2n-2}{2} = n - 1$.

41. **(B)** Other Important Graphs and Equations

Plug in each of the answer choices and use the 3–dimensional distance formula to find the pair of points with distance of 7 between them. Recall that the distance, d, between the point (x_1, y_1, z_1) and the point (x_2, y_2, z_2) is given by $d = \sqrt{(x_2 - x_1)^2 + (y_2 - y_1)^2 + (z_2 - z_1)^2}$.

First, find the distance from $(2, -1, 8)$ to $(5, 3, 5)$:

$$
\begin{aligned}
d &= \sqrt{(5-2)^2 + (3-(-1))^2 + (5-8)^2} \\
&= \sqrt{3^2 + 4^2 + (-3)^2} \\
&= \sqrt{34} \\
&\approx 5.83
\end{aligned}
$$

This eliminates (A).

Next, try points $(2, 3, -2)$ and $(8, 5, 1)$:

$$
\begin{aligned}
d &= \sqrt{(8-2)^2 + (5-3)^2 + (1-(-2))^2} \\
&= \sqrt{6^2 + 2^2 + 3^2} \\
&= \sqrt{49} \\
&= 7
\end{aligned}
$$

This is the desired distance, so $(2, 3, -2)$ and $(8, 5, 1)$ are the correct points.

42. **(C)** Other Important Graphs and Equations

First, it's necessary to convert the points from rectangular coordinates to polar. To find the polar coordinates of the point (x, y), use the conversion formulas, $r = \sqrt{x^2 + y^2}$ and $\tan \theta = \frac{y}{x}$. So, for point A, $r = \sqrt{0^2 + 5^2} = \sqrt{25} = 5$, which means that the radius of circle O is 5. And $\tan \theta = \frac{5}{0}$, which is undefined. $\tan \theta$ is undefined when $\theta = 90°$. So, the polar coordinates of A are $(5, 90°)$.

Next, since B is also on the circle O, it will also have an r-coordinate of 5. And, for B, $\tan \theta = \left(\frac{5}{2}\right)/(5\sqrt{3}) = \frac{1}{\sqrt{3}}$. So, $\theta = 30°$, and the polar coordinates of B are $(5, 30°)$.

Now, looking at the figure, one can see that the angle difference between point A and point B is 60°. So, to find the length of minor arc AB, use the relationship $\frac{\text{arc angle}}{\text{total degrees in the circle}} = \frac{\text{arc length}}{\text{total circumference}}$. Recall that circumference is $2\pi r$ and there are 360 degrees in a circle. In this case:

$$
\begin{aligned}
\frac{60°}{360°} &= \frac{AB}{2\pi(5)} \\
\frac{1}{6} &= \frac{AB}{10\pi} \\
AB &= \frac{5\pi}{3}
\end{aligned}
$$

43. **(A)** Imaginary and Complex Numbers

In order to solve this problem, first multiply the two complex numbers together:

$$
\begin{aligned}
(7 + 6i)(3 + i) &= 21 + 7i + 18i - 6 \\
&= 15 + 25i
\end{aligned}
$$

Now, to find the absolute value of $15 + 25i$, use the distance formula on $(15, 25)$:

$$
\begin{aligned}
\sqrt{15^2 + 25^2} &= \sqrt{850} \\
&= 29.15
\end{aligned}
$$

44. (C) Evaluating Functions

Joe must be heartbroken without his balloon. But that doesn't mean he can't solve the problem. In order for the balloon to reach a height of 130 feet, its must travel 90 feet up from the 40 foot high ridge. The balloon travels at 3 feet/second until it reaches 100 feet. From the 40 foot high ridge, the balloon travels for 60 feet at 3 feet/second. This first leg of the balloon's trip should take $^{60}/_3 = 20$ seconds. In the second leg of its trip, the balloon travels 30 feet at 1 foot/second: $^{30}/_1 = 30$ seconds. The total time: 50 miserable seconds.

45. (E) Logic

Notice that the first four answer choices are statements about warm days. However, neither of the two assumed statements says anything conclusive about warm days. This is a good indicator that those statements are impossible to prove or disprove.

However, combining the two given statements, it follows that there are dry days that are not warm. This is because there are sunny days that are not warm, and all sunny days are also dry. Therefore, not all dry days are warm. The last choice, therefore, is false, making it the correct choice.

46. (B) Other Important Graphs and Equations

This circle has center $(1, -4)$ and a radius of 5. Any point outside the circle will have to be farther than 5 from the center. Use the distance formula, $d = \sqrt{(x_2 - x_1)^2 + (y_2 - y_1)^2}$, to find the distance between the center and each answer choice:

(A): $d = \sqrt{(1-1)^2 + ((-4)+7)^2} = \sqrt{0+9} = 3$

(B): $d = \sqrt{(1-2)^2 + ((-4)+1)^2} = \sqrt{1+25} = \sqrt{26}$

(C): $d = \sqrt{(1-0)^2 + ((-4)+6)^2} = \sqrt{1+4} = \sqrt{5}$

(D): $d = \sqrt{(1-3)^2 + ((-4)+2)^2} = \sqrt{16+4} = \sqrt{20}$

(E): $d = \sqrt{(1-4)^2 + ((-4)+4)^2} = \sqrt{9+0} = 3$

The point $(2, 1)$ is the only choice outside the circle.

47. (D) Domain and Range

The number of different unordered subgroups of size r that are selected from a set of size n can be calculated by $\binom{n}{r} = {}_nP_r/_{r!} = {}^{n!}/_{(n-r)!r!}$. So for this problem:

$$\frac{64!}{(64-4)!4!} = \frac{64!}{60!4!} = \frac{64 \times 63 \times 62 \times 61}{4 \times 3 \times 2 \times 1} = 635,376$$

48. (C) Domain and Range

The graph of $f(x) = 3 \sin 3x$ will cross the x–axis when $f(x) = 0$. Since $\sin(x) = 0$ when x is a multiple of π, 3 sin $3x$ will be equal to 0 when $3x$ is a multiple of π. That is, $3x = \pi$, which is $x = {}^{\pi}/_3$. In other words the graph of $f(x)$ will cross the x-axis at every integer multiple of ${}^{\pi}/_3$.

The graph therefore crosses the x-axis at $0, {}^{\pi}/_3, -{}^{\pi}/_3, {}^{2\pi}/_3, -{}^{2\pi}/_3, {}^{3\pi}/_3, -{}^{3\pi}/_3$. So $b > {}^{3\pi}/_3$. If b were less, the graph would not cross exactly 7 times. Finally, note that b must be less than ${}^{4\pi}/_3$, because otherwise the graph would cross in 9 places.

The only answer choice for which ${}^{3\pi}/_3 \le b \le {}^{4\pi}/_3$ is $b = {}^{5\pi}/_4$.

49. **(D)** Other Important Graphs and Equations

When the hyperbola intersects the y-axis, $x = 0$, so the equation becomes $(0 - \sqrt{5})^2 - (y-1)^2 = 1$. Solving for y:

$$(0 - \sqrt{5})^2 - (y - 1)^2 = 1$$
$$(-\sqrt{5})^2 - (y^2 - 2y + 1) = 1$$
$$-y^2 + 2y + 3 = 0$$
$$y^2 - 2y - 3 = 0$$
$$(y - 3)(y + 1) = 0$$

Therefore, $y = 3$ or $y = -1$, and only $(0, -1)$ is an option.

50. **(C)** Polynomials

First, solve both equations for y in terms of x:

$$y + 4x = 0$$
$$y = -4x$$
$$2x^2 - 5 + 5y = 0$$
$$5y = 5 - 2x^2$$
$$y = 1 - \frac{2}{5}x^2$$

Then, set the two equations equal to each other and simplify into a quadratic equation:

$$-4x = 1 - \frac{2}{5}x^2$$
$$-20x = 5 - 2x^2$$
$$2x^2 - 20x - 5 = 0$$

Using the quadratic formula—for an equation of the form $ax^2 + bx + c = 0$, the formula is $x = \dfrac{-b \pm \sqrt{b^2 - 4ac}}{2a}$ —it's possible to solve for x:

$$x = \frac{20 \pm \sqrt{20^2 - 4(2)(-5)}}{2(2)}$$
$$= \frac{20 \pm \sqrt{400 - 40}}{4}$$
$$= \frac{20 \pm \sqrt{440}}{4}$$

The two roots are -0.24 and 10.24. Since $x \geq 0$, $x = 10.24$.